"Many of us consider Tom Sine one of the outstanding futurists of this generation. This book may be his very best. He communicates from both mind and heart his concerns for the church in the Western world. But he does not merely critique. He presents some practical potential solutions which every one of us should prayerfully consider."

— Paul Cedar, chairman, Mission America

"Because Tom Sine thinks carefully about our past and our future, we can take seriously what he says about our present. *Mustard Seed vs. McWorld* is an important book about our present and how, with divine creativity, we might envision our future. An important read that we neglect to our peril."

— Richard J. Foster, author, *Celebration of Discipline* and *Streams of Living Water*

"This book is a must read for any Christian leader who is determined to face tomorrow's challenges equipped for the task. As one who spends a lot of time trying to peer into the future, I cannot commend this book more highly."

— Richard Kew, director, Anglican Forum for the Future

"*Mustard Seed vs. McWorld* provides stimulating and helpful directions for radical changes within the church to effectively meet the future. For the many who greet the future of missions with some trepidation, Sine's book offers hope, if we're willing to make deliberate and innovative changes."

— Dellanna O'Brien, president, Woman's Missionary Union

"An important book about our globalized society and the consumer values which drive it. This is essential reading for all Western Christians committed to shaping their lifestyles according to the teaching of Christ."

— Graham Cray, Ridley College, Cambridge

"*Mustard Seed vs. McWorld* beckons us to choose the seeds of the kingdom and shows us how to plant them. This is essential work if the forces of global materialism are to be uprooted with the power of the gospel. A guidebook for imaginative discipleship, equipping Christians for the third millennium."

— Wesley Granberg-Michaelson, general secretary, Reformed Church in America

"An intriguing book that shows secularism to be a lot deeper than most of us have thought. Sine forces us to confront our hidden accomodations to modernity and invites us to join his conspiracy for nondualistic discipleship."

— Peter C. Moore, president, Trinity Episcopal School for Ministry

"Sine's provocative prose will stimulate you to rethink many of the assumptions which keep us bound to a culture that has little to do with living for the glory of God and everything to do with making a buck."

— Paul E. McKaughan, president and CEO, Evangelical Fellowship of Mission Agencies

"Drawing on wide experience, copious reading, and keen observation, Tom Sine guides us through the maze of a faltering modern world and shows how we can engage the new millennium hopefully. He looks at the world and sees many of the same trends and issues as secular futurists, but rather than reacting as an alarmist, he combines shrewd insight with an evangelical faith perspective to provide a hopeful take on the future."

— Wilbert R. Shenk, Fuller Theological Seminary

"Tom Sine has long been a master of the art of expecting the future. And he has had a keen eye for spotting the kingdom of God that comes in mustard seed ways. Now he puts the two together in a manifesto for Christians living in the age of globalization and change. He makes the vision imaginable and concrete. Bravo!"

—George R. Hunsberger, professor of missiology, Western Theological Seminary

"Tom Sine is more than a futurist. He is a prophet in the New Testament sense—seeing the emerging future and thrusting us into it. It is not always a comfortable ride, but it is essential if we are to be a part of God's purposes and prepared for the missional realities of tomorrow. His latest book, *Mustard Seed vs. McWorld,* is compellingly relevant and positively disturbing."

—General Paul and Commissioner Kay Rader, the Salvation Army

"This book is a must for anyone who wants to be prepared to creatively embrace the challenges that Christianity faces in the third millennium."

—Anthony J. Ciorra, director, Center for Theological and Spiritual Development, College of St. Elizabeth, Morristown, N.J.

"If I had to buy one contemporary book for the third millennium, this would be the one. It is a riveting and life-inspiring read!"

—Clive Calver, president, World Relief Corporation

"This book is enormously informative. I hope that many, many thousands of church, mission agency, and parachurch leaders and followers use it to chart their pilgrimage in the third millennium."

—Rodney Clapp, Evangelicals for Social Action

"*Mustard Seed vs. McWorld* is a comprehensive, remarkably well-informed work. Essential reading for those who want to know where global culture is headed, how it will impact the church, and—most important—how Christians can act creatively, effectively, and with God-given hope and optimism."

—Howard Snyder, Asbury Theological Seminary

"In this book, Tom Sine explores the actual and likely impact of the globalization juggernaut on both the identity and the mission of the church. The book would serve admirably not only as a textbook but as a stimulating and possibly transforming agenda for church, mission, and seminary leadership retreats."

—Jonathan J. Bonk, associate director, Overseas Ministries Study Center

"*Mustard Seed vs. McWorld* must be read by every church leader throughout America. As we career wildly toward a future of massive global change, Tom Sine reminds us that some things never change—God, his own vision for the world, and our renewed passion for the future of God."

—Isaac Canales, director, Hispanic Church Studies Department, Fuller Theological Seminary

"In *Mustard Seed vs. McWorld* Tom Sine creates a trifocal lens of hindsight, foresight, and insight, providing a clear and painful look at the current status of the church in the West."

—William R. O'Brien, director, the Global Center, Samford University

"Tom Sine cuts through corporate one-world propaganda to reveal the dark side of economic globalization and asserts with vigor that the American dream is no substitute for the mission that Jesus gave to the church."

—Stephen A. Hayner, president of InterVarsity Christian Fellowship/USA

"It is refreshing to read a book that not only challenges you with the issues surrounding globalization but also leaves you with an exhilarating sense of innovative approaches to grassroots ministry around the world. The cover of this book should read: seeds of hope enclosed, plant freely."

—Tom F. Balke, Atlantic divisional director, InterVarsity Christian Fellowship of Cananda

"In the postmodern and post-Christian third millennium, the conversation of a Christian missional involvement in tomorrow has been largely limited to the minds of academics and the hands of artists. Sine has now opened the dialogue to include the hearts of a remnant that has deconstructed modern values and is now seeking to uncover a faithful alternative that is local, global, and historical."

—Mark Driscoll, pastor, Mars Hill Fellowship, Seattle, Washington

"Sine's engaging prose quickly draws you into an examination of important issues we face together in the third millennium."

—David Beckman, president, Bread for the World

"Tom Sine has done it again! With keen observation, concern, and insight into the world as it is now and is soon to become, he challenges Christians to lifestyles which incarnate Christ's teachings and are more in tune with God's purposes. You'll be informed, inspired, and challenged by this exciting new publication."

—Linda Fuller, cofounder, Habitat for Humanity

"I urge those who want to make a difference in working with the poor not to pass up this book."

—John Perkins, chairman, Christian Community Development Association

"Tom Sine's message is simple yet extremely important: Christians must rethink basic assumptions of globalism, and then refocus values on community and spirituality over individualism, consumerism, and materialism. Sine invites us to 'use mustard seeds' to make a difference in the world."

—Norm Ewert, associate professor of business and economics, Wheaton College

"Tom Sine's *Mustard Seed Conspiracy* was a prophetic challenge to the international church and deeply affected the course of world mission. This new book had me totally riveted. Here, at last, is a user-friendly analysis of the forces which are shaping our culture, and some clue as to how we can best respond. A book no church leader in the third millennium can ignore."

—Rev. Dr. Rob Frost, National Methodist evangelist

Mustard Seed
vs.
McWorld

Other books by Tom Sine

Cease Fire: Searching for Sanity in America's Culture Wars
Christian Responses to Human Need (editor)
Live It Up: How to Create a Life You Can Love
The Mustard Seed Conspiracy
Taking Discipleship Seriously
Why Settle for More and Miss the Best?
Wild Hope

Mustard Seed

vs. McWorld

Reinventing Life and Faith for the Future

Tom Sine

Foreword by Ravi Zacharias

Baker Books

A Division of Baker Book House Co
Grand Rapids, Michigan 49516

Published by Baker Books
a division of Baker Book House Company
P.O. Box 6287, Grand Rapids, MI 49516-6287

Second printing, November 1999

Printed in the United States of America

Library of Congress Cataloging-in-Publication Data

Sine, Tom.
    Mustard seed vs. McWorld : reinventing life and faith for
the future / Tom Sine.
        p.   cm.
    Includes bibliographical references and index.
    ISBN 0-8010-9088-1 (pbk.)
        1. Christianity—Forecasting.   2. Church and the world.
  I. Title. II. Title: Mustard seed versus McWorld.
    BR121.2.S5548   1999
    261—DC21   99-25951

For current information about all releases from Baker Book House, visit our web site:
http://www.bakerbooks.com

To the new generation of Christian leaders
raised up by God to lead the church
into the new millennium

Contents

Foreword

In a changing world, it is critical for Christians to give a hearing to the voices that have studied and reflected upon the Bible and our culture. Tom Sine is one of those voices, and he contends that the most significant problem facing both the church and society is a crisis of vision: we do not know why we do what we do. *Mustard Seed vs. McWorld* confronts us with a rigorous understanding of our assumptions about ourselves and our culture and challenges us to examine these views through the lens of Scripture.

The phenomenon of globalization has influenced not only society but also the church, says the author. Indeed, the church has often not recognized a wave of change until it has long passed. Not all events are self-interpreting, of course, and with some, readers may have counter-perspectives. But of one thing we can be sure: we know that in our future, as in our past, God is sovereign, and we have a quiet confidence that he is indeed at work in our world. It is thus our task as God's people to bless what he is blessing and to reach our hands where he is reaching. Sine challenges us to do just that.

As you read this book, you will feel you are on a journey of thought toward which you cannot remain neutral. At times you will be daunted by the degree to which our lives have been captured by the speed of change. Quick-fix solutions have trivialized the serious and reduced reality to sound bites. At other times you will be compelled to stand in awe of what changes God has wrought in the most unexpected places. By the time you have finished this journey of thought, you will be grateful for the change this book may bring in you—to be not an apathetic traveler but one who is engaged in a changing world with the changeless message of Christ's gospel.

We are indebted to Sine for giving us this roadmap to show us God's love and care for this world and to guide us through today's shifting cultural addictions.

—Ravi Zacharias

Preface

Over the years, I have tried to pay attention to the lively edge of what God is doing in our world. As a result, Jesus people in the sixties taught me about whole-hearted devotion to Jesus Christ. In the seventies my friends in Haiti taught me a great deal about what it means to trust God in good times and tough times. In the eighties I was repeatedly challenged by the staying power of the black church in our American cities.

In the nineties I believe God raised up a new generation of young people all over the world to lead the church into the new millennium. I discovered these young leaders first in Great Britain. In the early days of this decade, I discovered a remarkable number of young Christians planting churches, starting urban ministries, and reaching out to their contemporaries through creative alternative worship services. In succeeding years, I found them starting performance night clubs in New Zealand and rehabilitating delinquents in Australia.

It got a little later start in North America. But in the last few years hundreds of young people have planted new churches in the United States to reach out to a postmodern generation and developed drama and arts groups in Canada to share the story through new images. I am challenged not only by the commitment of this generation to Jesus Christ but also by the risks they are taking in living their lives and sharing their faith to advance God's kingdom.

Therefore, I have dedicated this book to the new generation of Christian leaders raised up by God to lead the church into the new millennium.

I am deeply grateful for the family, friends, and associates who have been so supportive in this project.

My wife, Christine, has spent countless hours reading and critiquing this manuscript. I sincerely appreciate the support of my sons and their partners, Clint and Jenn and Wes and Emily. I also appreciate Rev. Dorsey and Betsy McConnell and all our many friends at Saint Albans Episcopal Church who have prayed for us. Mark Pierson, Brian Sellers-Petersen, and Stan Thornburg have been very supportive of this project.

I am particularly indebted to those who were kind enough to take the time to read and give me candid feedback on rough copy, including: Norm Ewert, Tom Balke, Richard Kew, Craig Gay, Rodney Clapp, Graham Fawcett, Mike Morris, Mike Crook, Graham Cray, Paul Mc-Kaughan, Bill O'Brien, Mark Driscoll, Linda Fuller, Paul Overland,

Robert Ekblad, Grant Osborne, and Doug Paggitt. I am grateful to David Virtue for encouraging me to return to the promise of the mustard seed.

I appreciate the patient guidance of my two editors, Tony Collins with Monarch UK and Paul Engle with Baker in the United States. Aaron Leighton, a freelance artist, and Robin Black, a graphic designer with Baker, were particularly helpful with the interior visual design of the book. And I am very much aware of the prayers of those who have gone before, including my parents, Tom and Katherine, and that huge family that will welcome us at the Great Homecoming.

Introduction

A Ride on the Wild Side

Hurtling into a Global Future

We hurtled down the mountain freeway in Haiti at ninety-five miles an hour . . . on the wrong side of the road. As the highway took a sharp turn to the right, I could feel the tires begin to lift on the right side. This old Daihatsu truck's very high center of gravity was aggravated by twenty-five Haitians standing in the back, holding on for dear life. Clint, my fifteen-year-old son, and I urged our Haitian driver to slow down. But he continued driving with abandon as though involved in a race to the death with every other vehicle on the road.

Suddenly a huge bus loaded with people careened around the corner at outrageous speed . . . also on the wrong side of the road. The two vehicles rushed toward each other like enraged bulls. Both drivers furiously fought the G-forces to avoid a head-on collision.

Miraculously both vehicles veered back into their respective lanes, barely avoiding disaster. Incredibly, in that three-hour ride to Port-au-Prince, my son and I experienced at least half a dozen near-death expe-

13

riences. It did wonders for our prayer life, but our focus became very immediate and completely excluded the larger world around us. It was a ride on the wild side that focused us totally on the immediacy of survival.

How many of you are taking a ride on the wild side? What kind of pressures are you experiencing in your families and congregations? Are those of you in leadership finding the resources you need to not only make sense of our rapidly changing future but also creatively engage change? You are not alone. As my wife, Christine, and I have the opportunity to work with families, pastors, and those in leadership of Christian organizations in Britain, Australia, New Zealand, Canada, and the United States, we hear an urgent cry for help.

A Cry for Help

As we race into a new millennium, the rate of change seems to be accelerating. We will all have to deal with more change than we are experiencing today. Violent hurricanes, floods, and tornadoes seem to be increasingly shaking our planet. Threats of biological terrorism, nuclear proliferation, and global plagues menace our future. Web-trekking, cyber-freaks, and virtual communities are dramatically changing how we relate to one another.

We are rapidly entering a global society in which Saddam Hussein watches CNN daily, 90 percent of the computers worldwide rely on software from Microsoft, and in Sarajevo they are selling Hard Rock Cafe T-shirts with bullet holes printed on them. Global change is what's happening. It feels as if we've "put the pedal to the metal." Rapid change can be very disquieting, unsettling, and disorienting. And there are virtually no resources available to help parents, pastors, or Christian leaders get ready for the challenges of a new millennium.

Quite honestly, I struggle with change when I travel. Apparently I am one of those born with the "gift" of disorientation, which makes change even more confusing. When I travel without my wife, I frequently get off the tracks and have adventures I never intended. In my wanderings I have become acquainted with some charming cows in the south of France and some very friendly monkeys on a seldom traveled road in Nepal.

I have learned to be philosophical and maintain a sense of humor about my disorientation and the unexpected changes it brings into my life. But growing numbers of individuals, families, and churches are being hammered by change they did not create, and it isn't funny. As we race into a new century, we are going to get ripped apart by change if we don't get ready.

A Cry for Help from Families

As Christine and I work with parents, pastors, and mission executives from Western countries, we hear the same urgent cry for help. Many of these good people tell us they are experiencing a ride on the wild side and feel as if they are losing control. Parents from Pasadena to Liverpool tell us they are working harder and longer just to stay even. They are so busy driving their kids to activities that they have precious little time for family life.

Many of them feel guilty because they are not as involved in the life of their churches as they would like to be, and they report they have little time for prayer or ministry to others. Many parents tell us they are routinely skipping worship service on Sunday morning to take their kids to soccer matches.

But we haven't seen much in the way of practical materials designed to help prepare Christians for a future in which there is likely to be mounting pressure on their lives and families. And people have no idea how to take the message that is preached Sunday morning and make good decisions Monday through Saturday. There are virtually no resources to help Christians put first things first in a rapidly changing world.

A Cry for Help from the Christian Young

Recently, university graduates in both Seattle and London told us a similar story. A surprising number of them are working as temps or at entry-level jobs. Many of them have moved back in with mom and dad. In the book *Thirteenth Gen* there is a cartoon about the young moving back home to the "Boomerang Motel." Signs on the front include: "Mom's Diner," "Pop's Rent-a-Car," "Laundromat: we fold and iron at no extra cost," "Instant Cash," and "Nintendo Video Arcade."[1]

The reason so many of the young are moving back home is the cost of housing. A large number of those under thirty-five in the United States and United Kingdom tell us they are spending over half their income for rent or mortgage. They report that they are frustrated because they have very little time or money to invest in the work of God's kingdom. I have found virtually no Christian ministries that are preparing university-age adults for a future in which many are likely to have less, economically speaking, than their parents' generation. Nor have I seen many stewardship education efforts to enable those of a new generation to find creative ways to reduce their housing costs so they have more time and money to advance God's purposes.

A Cry for Help from Churches

Pastors tell us they are feeling overwhelmed by change, too. They tell us that programs that worked well for decades don't work at all anymore. Groups such as the Alban Institute, which works primarily with mainline churches, and Saddle Back Church, which relates primarily to evangelical churches, are strong advocates of equipping the laity to do the work of the church. This is a position I strongly endorse.

But pastors tell us that even their most active members are getting busier and busier and have less time for the work of the church. In this book we will show why our people are likely to become significantly busier in the future, seriously compromising our ability to find laity who have time to be equipped. Therefore, for those of us who are advocates of equipping the laity to do the work of the church, I believe we will have to reinvent how we equip Christians—that includes serious lifestyle change.

A Cry for Help from Christian Mission Organizations

Christine and I also work with a broad spectrum of mission organizations, helping them create new strategies to address the new challenges of the twenty-first century. From Open Doors Holland, Tearfund England, World Vision Australia, the Baptist Board of Foreign Missions in New Zealand, and World Concern in the United States, we hear the same cry for help. These leaders are struggling to understand how both the fields in which they work and their donor support base are likely to change in the coming decade as we rocket into a very uncertain future.

For example, Open Doors Holland is concerned that persecution of Christians in Muslim countries seems to be mounting. Many new converts in Islamic countries not only lose their families but also are fired from their jobs. Open Doors is seriously looking at reinventing how they help the persecuted church by starting microenterprise projects to provide jobs for the growing number of persecuted believers.

God Hasn't Lost Control!

What all these people have in common is that they all want more for their lives, families, churches, and Christian organizations than simply to survive a ride on the wild side. They are looking for resources, not only so they can make sense of their future but also so they can creatively engage these challenges for God's kingdom.

If you are among those who are experiencing a ride on the wild side, if you are feeling out of control, let me whisper an important word in your ear. All appearances to the contrary, the Creator God is quietly transforming our "future shocked" world. While we may feel out of control, our God isn't. At the very core of our being, we are people of a wild, outrageous hope. We believe that the God who began this entire venture will write the final chapter and make all things new. And Scripture tells us that God invites us to be a part of this venture.

In the early chapters of this book, I will examine some waves of change we are likely to face in the future that can be a little overwhelming. Please remember that for the people of God, all of tomorrow's challenges are opportunities to manifest something of God's compassionate response. Henri Nouwen used to remind us that Jesus Christ is present in every aspect of our world, in both crucifixion and resurrection. Jesus is present in crucifixion in death-squad activity in Honduras and in the persecution of his followers in China.

But Jesus is also present in resurrection in the community in Pasadena that John and Vera May Perkins took back from drug dealers, and in a rundown tenement called Easter House Glasgow, where Christians have helped the poor help themselves by starting a credit union. We all have the opportunity to be a part of God's resurrection response as we discover how God wants us to make a difference.

As we listen to these cries for help, one thing is clear. Business as usual won't even begin to equip us to deal with the new challenges of a new millennium. A number of our tried-and-true methods of being the church won't carry us very far into the future. And I am convinced that a little tinkering and fine-tuning won't be of much help in our lives, churches, or Christian organizations. We will need to find ways to reinvent how we live our lives and act out our faith, if we hope to effectively address the challenges of a new millennium. We will need to learn to think outside of the box.

The place to begin this journey toward creating the new is paying attention to what God is stirring up. We need to pay attention to how God is at work in our world today. Then we need to prayerfully ask the Creator God how we can join the lively edge of what God is doing to make a world new.

Paying Attention to the Lively Edge of the Global Church

Mustard Seed vs. McWorld will take you on a global tour of ways the Holy Spirit is stirring up Christians all over the world to make a difference for God's kingdom. Christine and I have the opportunity to work with churches in Britain, continental Europe, Australia, New Zealand, Canada, and the United States. Plus we both have had the opportunity to work in countries in the Two-Thirds World. Frankly, we often find more creativity per square smile in Britain, Australia, and New Zealand than we do in the States.

I sense that God is giving birth to something altogether new in the church, particularly through a postmodern generation. As we work with twenty- and thirty-year-olds, we are impressed not only by their uncommon commitment to Christ and his mission in the world but by the imaginative ways they give expression to their faith. They are not simply creating younger versions of older models. God is inspiring them to create whole new approaches I believe we can all learn from.

We see the postmodern young relocating to an inner-city community in London to start a food cooperative with the poor, starting performance cafés to reach their peers in New Zealand, designing web pages in Vancouver, British Columbia, to promote missions, and planting postmodern churches all over the United States with the support of the Leadership Network. For example, in Seattle just over a year ago, Mars Hill Fellowship planted a church that has grown to over eight hundred members. And they are planting three new churches.

Unlike many of the successful boomer churches of the nineties, postmodern churches are not interested in highly programmatic, user-friendly models that can be replicated. These young leaders are creating models that are much more relational and that are unique to each situation. Most important, these churches are both reaching the young and discipling them to make a difference.

We need to pay attention not only to what the Spirit of God is stirring up in the church today but also to the new challenges and opportunities likely to come in the third millennium, to which we need to respond.

One World, Ready or Not!

It is no accident that families, our young people, pastors, and those leading our missions organizations are feeling so overwhelmed by change. Not only does the rate of change seem to be accelerating, but in the past decade new driving forces have emerged that are altering the direction and character of change. It is my contention that one of the primary forces driving change as we race into a new century is globalization.

Among some conservative American Christians, there is a growing endtimes fear of a one-world government takeover. Frankly, we seem to be witnessing just the opposite, with more political fragmentation all over the planet. But we are already a part of a one-world technological and economic order.

We are hardwiring our planet electronically into a single global system of satellites, fax machines, and internet communications. Borders are melting. Distance is dying. One and one-half trillion dollars flashes around the planet every day as we witness the rapid creation of a one-world economic order. However, we are belatedly discovering that this new global economic order was not carefully constructed. And as I write, we have no idea how long it might take to overcome recession in Asia and Russia or create a more reliable economic structure for the twenty-first century.

"Economic globalization involves arguably the most fundamental redesign of the planet's political and economic arrangements since at least the industrial revolution," states Jerry Mander, a senior at the Public Media Center, "yet the profound implications of these fundamental changes have barely been exposed to serious public scrutiny or debate. Despite the scale of reordering, neither our elected officials nor our educational institutions nor the mass media have made a credible effort to describe what is being formulated or to explain its root philosophies."[2]

One of the reasons why we are experiencing a ride on the wild side is that this new global economy is fiercely competitive. Sudden decisions half a world away are increasingly having an impact on our lives, regardless of whether we live in London, São Paulo, Chicago, or Sydney.

None of us were ever given an opportunity to vote as to whether we or our respective countries wanted to be part of a one-world economic order. National leaders seem to have reached a worldwide consensus, without our input, that it is the only game in town. And now we are all on board this global race to the top, like it or not. It's like going to sleep in your own bed and waking up jammed into a gigantic global rocket ship with six billion others, all hurtling through space at fantastic speeds with no notion of the destination.

But many of us are already benefiting in a myriad of ways from globalization. We are able to purchase an expanding array of products from all over the world and travel to virtually any place on the planet. We can suddenly be on-line with people half a world away. And coming at us at blinding speed are new technologies that will make our lives more efficient. Nevertheless, there are a growing number of voices from all over the world that argue globalization not only brings many benefits but also raises a number of new concerns.

Mustard Seed versus McWorld: A Global Contest

In every era the church of Jesus Christ has found itself in a deadly contest with the principalities and powers of this world. We are racing into a future in which everything is changing beneath our feet. Throughout this book, I will argue that we will increasingly find ourselves contending not only with escalating global change but also with a system of values that is often fundamentally counter to the values of the gospel of Christ.

Defining the Contest

With the sudden end of the Cold War, for the first time in history virtually all the nations in the world joined in the capitalist race to the top. Not only has capitalism triumphed, but so has McDonald's. It has just passed up Coca-Cola as having the most widely recognized logo in the world. Therefore, we will join others in using the term McWorld as a way to characterize the process of globalization.

But let me be very clear. As I describe this contest between economic globalization and God's agenda for our global future, my battle is not with free-market economics. Centrally planned economies have been abandoned for a good reason—they don't work very well. The free market is more effective at producing goods and services than any system we know. Throughout this book, I will argue not only that we need to grow our respective economies but that we also need to make a massive effort to assist the marginalized to start small businesses and credit unions to help them move out of poverty and achieve a decent way of life for their families.

But the efforts to create a one-world economic order are raising some new challenges that deserve a more thoughtful response by people of faith. I am concerned about some of the consequences of economic globalization, and I am particularly concerned about the values driving it. As I will point out in this book, early evidence suggests that globalization doesn't work as well for the global poor as for those who have resources to take advantage of the liftoff. More troubling is the centralization of economic power, which seems to be one of the consequences of the rapid creation of a global economy.

There are those on both the Right and the Left that talk about globalization in conspiratorial terms. As I will show, I don't believe that there is any conspiracy, but among those who are strong advocates of economic globalization there is a consensus about what the ideal future looks like and how to get there. Therefore when I use the term McWorld, I am simply describing this shared consensus as well as the process of globalization itself.

When I talk about the contest between mustard seed and McWorld, I am primarily talking about the contest between two very different visions for our global future, and two very different systems of values. As I will show, the aspirations and values driving globalization are a product of the Enlightenment and modernity and are in many ways directly counter to the aspirations and values of God's new global order. Therefore we Christians have the challenging task of finding a way to be part of this world, in all of its dimensions, while doing battle with any values that we believe are contrary to God's new global order.

I will show some of the promised benefits of globalization, as well as some of the potential drawbacks. But I will also argue that McWorld is about much more than creating a global system of free enterprise and free trade. The architects of McWorld are not simply trying to increase global free trade and free enterprise; they are, I believe, working to redefine what is important and what is of value in people's lives all over the planet, to sell their wares. This isn't a new phenomenon. The process of international commercial trade has been exporting the values and preferences of modern Western society all over the world for decades. What is new is that as the economy becomes globalized, the rate of export of those secular cultural values is dramatically accelerating.

Pope John Paul, making what was likely to be his last trip to the Americas in 1999, focused on the challenges facing humankind at the threshold of the new millennium. The centerpiece of his concern was economic globalization, of which he identified some of the upsides and downsides. Specifically, Pope John Paul expressed concern regarding "the absolutizing of the economy," the growing distance between rich and poor, and the global media's imposing materialistic values "in the face of which it is difficult to maintain a lively commitment to the values of the Gospel."[3]

I was attending a conference sponsored by World Evangelical Fellowship in Abbottsford, Canada, and two Pentecostal pastors from the Dominican Republic came up to me after I had shared how globalization is already changing the future of their communities and their congregations. They told me, "Five years ago we lost the young people from a number of our Pentecostal churches. It was right after MTV and an invasion of American pop culture came into the Dominican Republic. And to be honest, we haven't been able to find a way yet to win them back from the allure of the values of this new globalized youth culture."

More than any of us in the Western church seem to recognize, the merchants of McWorld are influencing people of faith to buy into the aspirations and values of modern culture. In a fascinating book called *Material World: A Global Family Portrait,* photojournalists persuaded families around the world to move all their worldly possessions into their front yards and then took a picture of each family with their belongings.

Not surprisingly, even a number of the poorest families who had little else found a way to purchase a used TV, and it was always accorded the central place of honor among their meager things. But what I found particularly telling was the portrait of one American family from Texas. Their yard was flooded with a huge range of consumer possessions, including three radios, three stereos, five phones, two TV sets, one VCR, one computer, one car, one truck, one dune buggy, and loads of furniture. And this Texas family, who are believers, stood in front of all their things, holding their big family Bible open, apparently oblivious to the image their portrait communicated.[4]

This American family is not unusual. I think most of us Western Christians would be embarrassed to have our picture taken in front of our possessions, particularly if it were put in a volume with pictures of many of our poorest neighbors. Everywhere we travel, Christine and I see the church losing out big-time to the seductions of modernity and the allures of the American dream. This book is written as a wake-up call to the church to come to terms with the fact that as the values of modernity go global, we Christians everywhere—and our young in particular—will increasingly find ourselves in a contest in which we will have to choose between aspirations and values of the mustard seed and those of McWorld.

An Invitation to Join the Subversive Mustard Seed Movement

In *Jihad vs. McWorld,* Benjamin Barber argues that the two major forces shaping the future of humanity are the forces of globalization (McWorld) and the forces of fragmentation (Jihad). The reader is left with the impression that one must choose between the two.[5] I am arguing that we don't have to choose sides between the forces of globalization and fragmentation. Scripture teaches that there is a third force at work in human society that isn't apparent to those outside the community of faith: the Creator God who passionately loves a people and a world and is working through the subversion of the mustard seed to make all things new.

The power of this new global economic order is awesome, and it has brilliantly demonstrated its ability to market not only its products but its values all over our small world. But I am still betting my life that God's mustard seed agenda, with a very different approach to globalization, will win the day. As I wrote in *The Mustard Seed Conspiracy,* "Jesus let us in on an astonishing secret. God has chosen to change the world through the lowly, the unassuming and the imperceptible. Jesus said 'With whom can we compare the Kingdom of God, or what parable shall we use for it? It is like a grain of mustard seed, which when sown upon the ground is the smallest of all seeds on earth; yet when it is sown it grows up and becomes the greatest of all shrubs and puts forth large branches, so that the birds of the air can make nests in its shade.'"[6]

Economic globalization is being advanced by powerful financiers, influential CEOs of transnational corporations, and international political brokers. The mustard seed agenda for globalization, on the other hand, is led by one who comes on a donkey's back. The architects of McWorld define the ultimate in terms of economic growth and economic efficiency and would have us believe that ultimate satisfaction will come from our increasing consumption of things. The mustard seed movement defines the ultimate in terms of God's kingdom breaking into the world to redeem a new global community from every tongue, tribe, and nation. And Jesus tells us that we will find our ultimate satisfaction not in seeking life but in losing it in service to others.

God's plan has always been to work through the small and insignificant to bring his new global order into being. This book is an invitation to set aside our lesser agendas and join with sisters and brothers all over the world who are finding the enormous satisfaction of having God use their mustard seeds to make a little difference in the world, in anticipation of Christ's return, when God will make all things new.

Recently I was at an urban ministries conference sponsored by the Christian Community Development Association. Half a dozen people came up and told me that the reason why they are in urban ministry today is because a decade ago they read a book called *The Mustard Seed Conspiracy*. Al Tizon and his wife, Janet, were so challenged by the stories of how God used ordinary people to make a difference that he quit his government job and Janet quit her job as a nurse. They left their comfortable way of life in Oregon and moved to the slums of Manila. Al said he was both surprised and gratified to discover that God was able to use their lives to make a difference in the lives of their new friends.

This book is offered to others who are interested in discovering what God can do with their lives if they put first things first. While we will benefit in many ways from globalization, I will show that God's vision for a better future has much more to do with making a difference than with making a dollar. It has more to do with creating a new reconciled global community of justice and celebration than with producing a new global community of consumption (see table). It has more to do with coming home to Jerusalem than with returning to Babylon. It is through the death and resurrection of Jesus Christ that we are all invited to devote

	McWorld	Mustard Seed
Defining the ultimate	Defines the ultimate in terms of economic growth and efficiency	Defines the ultimate in terms of spiritual and societal transformation
Image of the better future	Western progress, the American Dream, and individual economic upscaling	Shalom future of God, redemption of a people, and transformation of a world
Agent of change	Human initiative through technological, economic, and political power	God's initiative through the small, the insignificant, the mustard seed
Primary values	Individualism, consumerism, and materialism	Community, spirituality, and celebration of God's new order
Models of discipleship and stewardship	Dualistic discipleship in which we give our allegiance first to the aspirations and values of modern culture, and then our faith is reduced to personal piety, and we give out of our leftovers	Whole-life discipleship and stewardship in which we reinvent how we use time and money to put God's purposes first in every area of life

	McWorld	Mustard Seed
Models of the church	A culturally accommodated church tends to reflect the values of modern culture in how it operates and defends them as desirable values	A whole-life church attempts to reflect the values of the kingdom in how it operates and becomes a subversive community challenging the values of modern culture.
Consequences for Christian mission	A culturally accommodated church will continue to see a decline in numbers and resources to invest in mission to the mounting challenges of the third millennium.	A whole-life community will not only more authentically reflect the values of the kingdom but dramatically increase its investment in mission to address tomorrow's challenges.

our lives to the subversive cause of the mustard seed that is destined to redeem a people and transform a world.

In Search of a User's Guide to the Third Millennium

Frankly, there aren't many books available to enable Christians and those in leadership to make sense of the rapidly changing landscape of tomorrow's world or to help them find innovative ways to deal with that change. As we cross the threshold into a new millennium, there are, predictably, a growing number of books on various endtimes theories, such as *Left Behind* by Tim LaHaye and Jerry B. Jenkins and *End of the Age* by Pat Robertson.

But these books not only offer little help in making sense of change; they consistently try to fit various global events into a particular endtimes theory. They unintentionally tend to reinforce the fatalistic assumption that we can't make a difference because everything is destined to get worse and nothing can improve.

Let me be clear. I look forward to the return of Christ with great anticipation. But the Bible tells us that the timetable of the last days is God's business, not ours. What is our business? As followers of Jesus Christ, our business is to do what Jesus did and make God's purposes our purposes. In this book I will work from Scripture to outline something of God's purposes for the human future. And then I will show how putting God's purposes first helps us to face the future not only with hope but with a growing realization that God can use our mustard seeds to make a real difference in our rapidly changing world.

There are a growing number of books attempting to help the church change, but most of them don't take the future seriously. They attempt to enable the church to plan as though the future were simply going to be an extension of what is happening now. Even the spate of books on the future and the church written over the past decade tend to focus on the future of the church instead of on the future of the larger society.

There are a few welcome exceptions to this pattern. George Barna, in a recent work, *Generation Next,* does an excellent job of profiling some of the ways our youth culture in the United States is changing. Leonard Sweet provides some vivid impressions of postmodern culture and the church in his new book, *SoulTsunami: Sink or Swim in New Millennium Culture.* Peter Brierley has published a helpful book on the changing demographics of the Western church in Britain, titled *Future Church.*

But I haven't located any books that try to help the reader learn to anticipate change or that attempt to look more broadly at global and national challenges likely to shape our common future. Nor is there much conversation about how we can create new biblical responses to tomorrow's emerging opportunities.

While church leaders show increasing interest in postmodernity, very little has been written about the extent to which the church has caved in to modernity. In fact, many books that are attempting to help the church get its act together are unconsciously promoting values of modern culture that have much more in common with McWorld than with the mustard seed. Rodney Clapp's *A Peculiar People* and Craig Gay's *The Way of the (Modern) World* are two of the few recent publications attempting to challenge the church to become liberated from the seductions of modern culture.

A User's Guide to the Third Millennium: Defining the Direction

Mustard Seed vs. McWorld is written to respond to the cry for help. It is intended to enable Christians, particularly those in leadership, to more fully anticipate, and more creatively respond to, the challenges of our global future in a way that advances the purposes of God's new order. It is a book designed to help you find creative ways to put God's purposes first so you can live, thrive, and serve God in a rapidly changing future. It is designed to help you think and create outside the box.

This book is written to address three serious crises that threaten the ability of the church to carry out its mission in the twenty-first century and that receive virtually no attention in the literature:

1. a crisis of foresight—a failure to take the future seriously;
2. a crisis of vision—a failure to take the future of God seriously; and
3. a crisis of creativity—a failure to take our God-given imagination seriously.

Essentially the book will be broken into three sections.

1. *A crisis of foresight.* In chapter 1 I will explain why it is essential that all Christians, particularly those in leadership, learn to take the future seriously. Then I will outline specific practical ways in which those in leadership can anticipate how their churches and the communities in which they minister are likely to change. In chapters 2 through 6 I will explore how globalization is likely to have an impact on our lives, families, churches, and larger world. I will explain how, for people of faith, all of tomorrow's challenges are really opportunities for creative biblical response.

2. *A crisis of vision.* In chapter 7 I will argue that many of us Western Christians have unwittingly allowed modern culture, rather than Scripture, to define much of the direction of our lives and the direction of Christian organizations because we haven't thought enough about why we do what we do. As you will see, one of the reasons many of us are out of control in our personal lives is that the aspirations and values of modernity have set the primary agendas of our lives and shaped much of the character of our churches and Christian organizations. In chapter 8 I will go back to the Bible and present an alternative vision to the American dream, a vision that can help us find new meaning for our lives and a new sense of purpose for our churches. I will show that God can help us live our lives and steward our churches with a greater sense of intentionality for the advancement of God's new order.

3. *A crisis of creativity.* In chapter 9 I will outline how we Christians can put God's purposes at the center of life and then find innovative ways to reinvent our lives and reorder our priorities to put first things first. I will describe how we, as "whole life" disciples, can create a way of life that is more festive and less stressful than the rat race, a way of life in which God can use our mustard seeds to make a difference in our rapidly changing world. In chapter 10 I will explore how to reinvent our churches and Christian organizations to more creatively and effectively advance God's mission purposes in response to the challenges of tomorrow's world. Finally, in the epilogue I will invite you to join Christians all over the world on our web page in creating new possibilities for life and mission for a new millennium.

I will define the future in three ways.

1. The future as anticipation is the likely future, the new challenges that are coming at us whether we like it or not.
2. The future as vision is the ideal or preferred future, God's new order, the future we want to see come into being.
3. The future as creativity is God's Spirit working through our imagination to enable us to create means to advance God's vision in ways which address the anticipated challenges of the future.

Since people are very busy, particularly those in leadership, I want to make this book as reader friendly as possible. I have attempted to open it up a bit with graphics and provide icons to help you find your way through the book as easily as possible and to use the book for group discussion. If you find a section a little hard going, feel free to skip ahead. The most important thing is to prayerfully pay attention to what God is saying to you and act on it. Throughout the book, you will find the following icons to make your journey as easy as possible.

Finding the focus icons point you to the intent of the chapter.

Key points icons highlight the key points of the chapter.

Planting a seed icons indicate descriptions of creative ways people are making a difference.

Opportunities for Christian leaders icons mark lists of specific ways those in leadership can both respond to new challenges and create new possibilities.

Questions for discussion and action icons indicate questions at the end of each chapter.

This book is designed to be used as a textbook in colleges and seminaries as well as for adult study in churches. Questions are included at the end of each chapter to encourage this use.

One last word. I am not an economist but a historian and a futurist trying to make sense of very complex areas of economic change. As a layperson, I have made my best effort at trying to share with other noneconomists what I have been learning from a broad array of literature about globalization with help from a friend and economist from Wheaton College, Norm Ewert. I recognize that on our best day we all

"see through a glass darkly." The intent of this book is not to offer defin-
itive answers but to raise important questions about the future and the
church as we charge into a globalized new millennium. I pray that this
book will be a valuable resource in preparing you to effectively serve
God and to lead the church into a rapidly changing future.

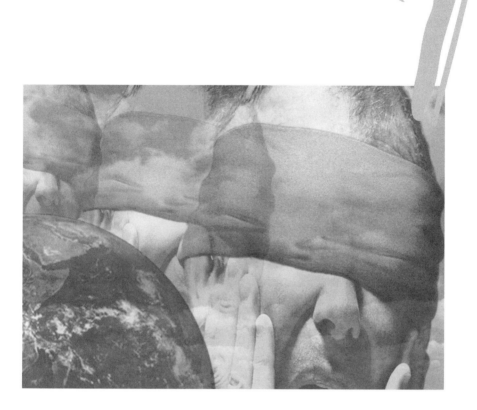

Part 1

A Crisis
of Foresight

Learning to Take the Future Seriously

WHILE WORKING WITH A GROUP of Aboriginal Christian leaders in Sydney, Australia, my wife's hometown, we were introduced to a more relaxed form of conferencing. When these Christians get together, they don't conference day and night. They have their formal meetings in the daytime, then party and tell stories at night. An Aboriginal pastor came up to me the first night of enjoying each other and caught me a bit off guard.

The pastor said, "We wouldn't have this mess we have in the world today if we Aboriginals had been the ones in the Garden of Eden instead of you guys."

I said, "What are you talking about?"

He replied, "If we had been the ones in the Garden of Eden instead of you guys, we would have thrown away the fruit, eaten the snake, and we wouldn't have any of these problems we are dealing with today!"

To get ready for the third millennium, we are all going to need a new perspective. We need to take the future seriously.

Speaking to sixty Christian businessmen in Christchurch, New Zealand, I asked, "How many of you forecast before you plan in your business?" Every hand in the room went up. "Now," I asked, "how many of you, as leaders in your churches, forecast before you plan?" Not a single hand went up. While leaders of corporations routinely make an effort to determine, before they plan, how the future is likely to change, leaders of churches and Christian organizations rarely do. We plan as though we are frozen in a time warp.

Why It Is Essential to Take the Future Seriously

I have been serving denominations, Christian colleges, and mission organizations as a consultant for twenty years. In that time, I have discovered that it is rare to find Christian organizations or churches that, before they plan, make any effort to systematically research how both the context in which they operate and their donor support base are likely to change in the future. We do so-called long-range or strategic planning as though the future were simply going to be an extension of the past. Anyone who has lived through the last three decades knows this assumption is false.

We are living in a world changing at blinding speed, yet in our homes, churches, and Christian colleges we unconsciously prepare our young to live and serve God in the world in which we grew up instead of in the world of the third millennium. Don't we have a responsibility to prepare our young to live in tomorrow's world?

As a consequence of leaders' failing to lead with foresight, churches and Christian organizations have in recent years not only been repeatedly hammered by change; we have missed a lot of opportunities to advance the gospel of Christ in a changing world. Instead of driving into the future with our eyes firmly fixed on our rearview mirrors, we need leaders who learn to lead with foresight.

Leading with Foresight

We can no longer make plans in the church, raise our young, or order our lives as though the future were simply going to be static. We need to anticipate not only the change that is rushing toward us but also how globalization is likely to alter our common future. Globalization will offer us a huge range of benefits in the future, some of which may come with a high price tag.

To the extent that we leaders can anticipate possible areas of change in our lives, churches, and communities, we have lead time to create new biblical responses. We have lead time to be proactive instead of reactive.

In the first chapter in this section, I will ask, What tools are available to help those of us in leadership anticipate areas of change that are likely to confront our lives, churches, and the larger world? Then, in chapters 2 through 5, I will ask, What new needs, challenges, and opportunities are likely to face us in our lives, churches, and mission organizations as we race into an increasingly global future? Finally, in chapter 6 I will ask, How effectively will the church be able to respond to these challenges, given changes that are also taking place in the church? Enjoy your trip back to the future!

A Ride on the Wet Side

Learning to Surf with Shakespeare

I DUG HARD INTO THE CHOPPY WAVES with both arms. My huge surfboard breached the final wave, and I joined the small cluster of surfers, waiting for my first ride back to shore. It had taken me fifteen minutes to paddle out from the beach near Lahaina, Maui, and I was winded. It was a hot April day on this Hawaiian island, and I decided to lie on my board and watch the other surfers while I caught my breath. One after another, they positioned themselves to an inbound wave. Then they paddled like fury and suddenly were lifted to the crest of the wave like a feather on the wind. The surfers catapulted toward the beach with tremendous speed. I watched one Filipino lad turn into the curl and ride down the pipeline with all the grace of an Olympic figure skater.

How hard could it be? Ten years before, I had mastered skiing the first time I hit the slopes. By the end of the day, I was thoroughly enjoying myself. My friends were amazed that I got up the first time I went water-skiing on Strawberry Lake in California. I did a complete circuit of the lake. No problem.

I took a deep breath and did exactly what I saw the others do. I turned my board toward the shore and paddled with all my strength. A huge wave hit me and the board and sent us both to the bottom with brutal force. As I swam back to the surface, I looked up, and there was my nine-foot board hurtling down toward my head. I dove and barely escaped decapitation. When I finally swam back to shore, there was my board lying innocently on the beach. Instead of catching the wave, I'd had a ride on the wet side.

Amazingly, over the next three hours I was able to repeat this exercise over a dozen times with the same conclusion: getting dumped into the deep. Sometimes the waves passed me by entirely and I found myself sitting in the doldrums. I simply didn't have a clue as to how to anticipate which waves would give me a ride or how to catch them. Exhausted, after one final ride on the wet side I called it a day and dragged my board ashore, watched by the bemused surfers. Do you know what it's like to either get hammered by waves or have them pass you by?

Believe it or not, William Shakespeare had some important insights on surfing. In his play *Julius Caesar,* Brutus addresses Cassius after the slaying of Caesar, attempting to refocus the political life of that community. "There is a tide in the affairs of men which taken at the flood leads on to fortune; amid it all the voyage of their life is bound in the shallows and in miseries. On such a full sea are we now afloat, and we must take the current when it serves us or lose our ventures."[1]

I am persuaded that Shakespeare's counsel is spot on. In a world changing as rapidly as ours, we must either learn to surf with Shakespeare or experience repeated rides on the wet side. Wayne Burkan, a corporate futurist, puts it a little differently: "To survive in an ever changing world, it is vital to anticipate the future."[2]

Looking Forward to Surfing with Shakespeare

One has only to look back on the waves of change that have battered the church in the last three decades, and see the waves we have missed, to realize there must be a better way. For example, we failed to anticipate the impact of MTV and video games on the young in the eighties and nineties. And the church has been decades late in waking up to the growing need for racial reconciliation in America. Promise Keepers belatedly discovered that this is a serious issue evangelical Christians need to address.

Too often in the past the church has either been jolted by waves of change or allowed them to pass it by altogether, because it has made virtually no effort to anticipate them. And as a consequence, we have missed repeated opportunities to make a difference.

As I complete this book, millennial fever is growing. The most exotic destinations in the world, from the Sphinx in Egypt to the Space Needle in Seattle, have been booked years ahead as sites for lavish celebrations to welcome a new millennium. Tony Blair is building a huge millennium dome as a center to help people in Britain focus on the new opportunities for the United Kingdom in a new millennium.

For others, the journey into a new millennium is whipping up an apocalyptic frenzy. New Agers are flocking to Brazilia in the thousands to await the dawn of a new era. Some survivalists are certain that the millennium bug is going to usher in the end of the world and are building camps in the mountains. And, reportedly, militia groups in the United States are arming themselves to the teeth because they believe that crossing the threshold into the year 2000 will ignite Armageddon.

Regardless of whether you view entering the new millennium with apprehension or anticipation, it is causing us all to give much more thought to the future. The intent of this book is to persuade those in leadership to wake up to the changes that are likely to confront us in the new millennium and to take seriously the responsibility to prepare the church to find creative ways to address those changes, with full confidence that we can trust God to guide us.

Eventually I learned the secret to catching the waves instead of getting hammered by them. All it required was to anticipate the wave's arrival. The first time I finally caught a wave, it was like getting shot out of a cannon. Riding the power of the crest is much more exhilarating than getting dunked in the deep. I strongly recommend it!

Finding the Focus

The purpose of this chapter is to provide specific practical ways for you to learn to lead with foresight. It is designed to provide you with a tool kit to enable you, as a Christian leader, to not only anticipate but creatively respond to the waves of change rushing toward us. I am sure you too will find that riding the crest is a lot more satisfying than dredging the bottom.

First, it is essential to remind you that we have an unprecedented tsunami racing toward us: globalization. You can be certain that this McWorld tsunami will repeatedly swamp all our boats if we don't make an effort to take the future seriously. As we rush into a new millennium, we need to anticipate both the opportunities and the challenges that globalization will present us, our families, our churches, and the world God has called us to care for.

Back to the Future: Identifying the Fingerprints of God

The first way that people of faith seek to make sense of change is beyond the scope of secular futurists. We believe that our God is not only alive and well but active in history. Therefore, the first way we need to make sense of change is to pay attention to how the Creator God seems to be at work within history, based upon what the Bible teaches us about God and the growth of God's subversive mustard seed.

In *Wild Hope* I wrote that some of the important changes of the past decade seemed to reflect something of the work of God. I wrote that I believed that the dance on the Berlin Wall was the dance of God. The joyous songs sung by children at the release of Nelson Mandella, and now the reunification of South Africa for all its people, are the songs of God. And the prayers increasingly raised all over the world for the peace of Jerusalem are certainly the prayers of God.[3]

In other words, the first way to lead with foresight is to discern how God seems to be at work through the in-breaking of God's mustard seed in human history, so we can seek to collaborate with a God intent on subverting human arrogance and transforming the world through the small and the insignificant.

Back to the Future: Is Forecasting Possible?

People often ask me, "How do futurists try to predict the future?" I usually respond, "I prefer using sheep entrails; I don't find tea leaves terribly reliable." Seriously, Christians often ask if it is even possible to make sense of the future. Let's be clear: only the Lord Almighty knows fully what the future holds. We need to remember that we live in a complex world with an incredible number of variables, a world in which both natural and supernatural forces are at work and over which we have little understanding or control.

In spite of that, I am convinced we can use the intelligence the good Lord gave us and a little discernment to read some of "the signs of the times." I believe we can anticipate some of the change coming at us and find ways to creatively respond before the waves reach us. While the planning and forecasting methods I am discussing in this chapter are certainly a product of modernity and to some extent postmodernity, I believe these tools can enable people of faith to become more creative stewards of their lives and churches.

Forecasting Is a Messy Art

Let me say up front that trying to make sense of the future is not a science. It's a messy art. And futurists often get it wrong. Herman Kahn was one of the leading corporate futurists who in the seventies predicted a future of ever increasing prosperity for everyone on the planet, with no mention of any possible dislocations. Both Richard Naisbitt's optimistic projections for the future and Faith Popcorn's consumer snapshots have sometimes proved to be dead wrong.[4]

In *The Mustard Seed Conspiracy,* published in 1981, I accurately predicted a widening gap between rich and poor in America in the eighties and nineties, and a period of growing political conservatism in the United States. But I missed a major change when I wrote *Wild Hope,* published in 1991. I correctly projected the creation of three major economic coalitions in the Americas, Europe, and Asia. But I didn't anticipate the decline in the Japanese economy, even though I had a colleague—a businessman—who accurately predicted what has happened.

In spite of the fact that we sometimes get it wrong in this business of attempting to make sense of the future, we have only two options. Either we can ignore change entirely and live our lives, raise our young, and run our organizations as though the future were simply going to be more of what's happening now—and enjoy repeated rides on the wet side—or we can make our best effort to anticipate some of the change racing toward us, so we have lead time to respond to it. I, for one, think Shakespeare is right. It makes more sense to "take the current when it serves."

Forecasting: The Possible and the Impossible

"Merely to survive, churches must learn not simply to ride each wave of change. . . . We should be finding out how to anticipate, as far as possible, what the future holds in store for us," urge Richard Kew and Roger White in their helpful book *Toward 2015.*[5] Of course, there is no way we can accurately predict even a relative representation of what the landscape of tomorrow's world will look like. There are, however, some areas of change that we can predict with a fairly high level of confidence. Other forms of forecasting are highly speculative. And it is essential that those in leadership learn to distinguish between solid and speculative forecasting.

To illustrate the point, demographic projections ten to fifteen years into the future are usually very reliable. For example, one can predict with a fairly high degree of certainty how many Americans will reach retirement age in 2010, when the boomers start to retire.

We can, with a fairly high degree of certainty, predict some of the new technologies that are likely to invade our homes, lives, and churches in the next ten years. Virtual reality will certainly be one of those new technologies. Armed with the forecast that various forms of virtual reality will be available in our stores within ten years, a Christian organization could test a process called consequence forecasting. I am confident that if we conducted solid research on virtual reality, we could successfully predict some of the positive and negative applications of this new technology in our homes, schools, and churches. And then we would have time to develop ways to steward this new technology before it arrives.

Other forms of forecasting are much less reliable. Personally, I have little confidence in those who predict how the stock market will be performing in two years. And I don't believe anyone can predict with any degree of confidence what the youth culture will look like five years from now. These kinds of forecasting border on pure speculation. Christian leaders can learn reliable ways to make sense of some of the changing landscape of tomorrow's world, by learning from those who have the most experience.

Back to the Future: Learning from the Horizon Watchers

Those who have the best record in attempting to make sense of the future are those in the corporate world. I have yet to find a major corporation that doesn't do some form of forecasting before planning. And there are over three dozen major consulting firms, from the Center for Alternative Futures to Coates and Jarratt to Brain Trust, that offer sophisticated forecasts at high prices to their corporate clients. It is obvious that corporations wouldn't spend money for these forecasting services if they didn't have real value.

We at Mustard Seed Associates work with Christian organizations and churches to help them anticipate new challenges and opportunities. But there are few other groups who work with Christian organizations to help them make sense of change.

Of course, the reason corporate leaders are so keen to try to anticipate change is because they have learned from bitter experience that repeated rides on the wet side can be very expensive. Christian leaders need to anticipate change not to make a profit but to gain lead time to create new ministry responses to make a difference.

Even the book *The Fortune Sellers,* which is very critical of all types of forecasting, from weather forecasting to speculating on the stock market, still recognizes the value of taking the future seriously. Author William Sherden states that we dare not ignore the future. "We must continue to plan for the future by considering scenarios of what might happen and adapting our plans accordingly. To do otherwise would be foolhardy. We cannot blind ourselves to all predictions, because some contain vital information about our environment—not necessarily what *will* happen but what *could* happen."[6]

User's Guide for Surfing with Shakespeare

Over the last four decades, the corporate world has pioneered most of the methods, and developed most of the tools, designed to make sense of how the future is likely to change. I will briefly overview these tools, then recommend which specific tools those in Christian leadership might use.

1. *Trend extrapolation.* Economists and demographers use trend extrapolation as one of their basic tools. They use recent birth rates, for example, to project how many people are likely to be available to join the workforce in the next five years in Canada or the United States.

2. *Issues analysis.* Issues analysis is one of the newest tools in the kit. Essentially, business or government leaders search the horizon to identify and monitor ten to fifteen key issues that could either send them to the bottom or enable them to catch the crest of change.

3. *Delphi polling.* Delphi polling is a method of forecasting by sampling expert opinions about how the future is likely to change. (Typically, you poll them three times, so experts can read their colleagues' responses and then change their own responses without losing face.) For example, one might survey one hundred of the top leaders in cancer research to predict the likelihood of a cure for the various forms of cancer by the year 2010.

4. *Intuitive insight.* Intuitive insight relies on subjective hunches about how the future is likely to change. Faith Popcorn's predictions about the future are based on substantial research. But she takes intuitive leaps to interpret this data to her clients. She creates terms to reflect these subjective leaps, such as "cocooning," "mom-food," and "down-aging."

   Bill O'Brien, director of the Global Center at Beeson Divinity School, has worked with John Andersen of NASA to develop a nonlinear forecasting method they call horizon mission methodology. Essentially, in this more intuitive method, they project on the screen of tomorrow's world a possible future. For example, at a recent workshop they projected the emergence of Africa as a global power by the year 2050. Then participants were invited to identify the conditions, enterprises, and relationships that would have to be formed to bring this possible future into being.[7]

5. *Prophetic insight.* One has only to read the prophets of the Old Testament to realize that at times God gifted some with prophetic insight about the future. I believe this gift is still operational in the church today, and I think I have seen some examples. But quite honestly, the majority of cases I have heard of have often missed the mark. Having said that, I believe prophetic insights need to be taken seriously, but I think churches need to develop guidelines, in community, as to how they might be incorporated.

6. *Contextual forecasting.* Leaders of large corporations often attempt to broadly scan how the context in which they do busi-

ness is likely to change. Typically, they scan economic, demographic, technological, political, and cultural trends. From this they paint a picture of how they believe their context is likely to change in the next five to ten years. One of the few Christian organizations I have found that uses this method is the American Bible Society.

7. *Scenario forecasting.* All of the tools we have briefly reviewed in this kit have merit. But I firmly believe the most valuable tool for large organizations, which have the resources to do a good job, is scenario forecasting. Essentially, scenario forecasting draws heavily on good contextual forecasting. It always incorporates intuitive leaps in the writing of the scenarios. Typically, what you do is write three to four possible stories about the future, all based on good data. Then you ask your staff to play through each scenario as though it were the future. Unlike contextual forecasting, you don't bet the farm on a single scenario. You train your staff to deal with change in each of the scenarios, so they learn to think and plan contingently. When I was working at the Weyerhaeuser Corporation New Business Research Division a few years ago, I hired science fiction author Frank Herbert to write three scenarios occurring ten years in the future. The New Business staff found it helpful to explore how they would start new businesses in each of those possible futures.[8]

One of the colleagues I consulted with in futures research when I worked with Weyerhaeuser was Peter Schwartz, who was employed at the Stanford Research Institute at the time. In his recent book, *The Art of the Long View,* Schwartz makes a compelling case for using scenario forecasting as an important tool for catching waves of change instead of getting battered by them.

Working with Royal Dutch–Shell in 1983, Schwartz developed a possible but improbable scenario for the implosion of the Soviet Union and its economy. In this scenario Schwartz concluded, "To continue to keep any semblance of a standard of living, the Soviet Union had only two alternatives: Either to muddle through or open up."[9]

Schwartz reported that with his help in thinking through this scenario, the leaders of Shell were able to catch the huge wave that swept through the Soviet Union and profit by change that swamped the boats of many of their competitors, who never seriously considered that the implausible would become reality.[10]

Given the available tools for anticipating change, which should Christian leaders consider using? How can we learn to catch the waves instead of getting pounded by them?

Opportunities for Christian Leaders: Preparing a New Generation to Surf with Shakespeare

Those of us who are parents, grandparents, pastors, educators, and youth workers have a special responsibility to equip the young for life in a demanding future. But most of us are unwittingly preparing the young to live in the world in which we grew up instead of the world of the third millennium. As a direct consequence of this lack of foresight, I believe many of our approaches to parenting, youth ministries, and education are the wrong stuff. I believe we are often doing the opposite of what we should be doing to equip our young people to live, thrive, and serve God in a new millennium.

As I will discuss in the next four chapters, tomorrow's McWorld global society is likely to be a more complex, demanding environment than the one in which we grew up. To live, thrive, and serve God in that world, I am convinced our young people will need to have high initiative. They will need to be self-starters and problem-solvers. And to survive in tomorrow's globalized economy, many of them will probably become entrepreneurs.[11]

Now, stop and think about how many well-intended parents are raising their kids today. Many, out of love, are waiting hand and foot on their young and raising them in a highly indulgent environment. This is not solely an American phenomenon. In Australia they call it overparenting. The worst thing we can do for young people is to rob them of initiative. I believe that young people raised on the farm fifty years ago, who had serious responsibility at an early age, would be better equipped for life in the third millennium than most of today's young people.

How do we typically conduct youth ministry in our middle-class congregations? Hire a guy with a sports car to run activity-driven programs to entertain the young people and keep them busy, distracted, and out of trouble. Doing for the young again. High school students are perfectly capable of planning and running their own programs.

Planting a Seed of Leadership Empowerment in the Young

Andy Hickford, when he was a youth pastor at Stopsley Baptist Church in Britain, took the risk of reinventing the entire youth program, to enable young people to run their own program and develop their sense of initiative. One new thrust was to send three secondary students to the church's mission project in Ethiopia. He didn't send them to get stretched by a global experience, as many congregations do. He sent them to Ethiopia with a major adult assignment. Their assignment was to film a professional video documentary of the mission project. In preparation these three students learned to storyboard, write a script, and use the video equipment.

When they arrived in the village, they developed for their documentary a story around the life of one child. They videotaped the documentary, edited it, and put music behind it. When they returned to Luton, England, they weren't just three high school kids waiting for adults at church to tell them what to do. They began traveling to churches all over the region, showing their video and challenging older adults to get involved in ministry to those in need in Ethiopia.

Planting a Seed of Futures Education

Few schools, colleges, or seminaries intentionally prepare students for life in a world that will be different from the one their parents graduated into. One of the few exceptions are MBA programs in some of America's more progressive business schools. According to Mary Lord, "Long accused of training managers to fight the last business war, America's B-schools are now consciously preparing students for the challenges that lie ahead."[12] Attending these schools is reportedly like playing Nintendo on speed.

One of the courses offered at MIT Sloan School of Business is "Inventing the Organizations for the Twenty-first Century." In this course, students are invited not only to study what has been done in the past, and what is being done today, in the world of business but to create new models for the future. This is a model I would highly recommend for adaptation in Christian colleges and seminaries.[13]

Creating a Futures Watch Process for a New Generation

Steve Hayner, president of InterVarsity Christian Fellowship in the United States, has asked Mustard Seed Associates to develop within three regions of IVCF a futures watch process that will provide the basis for creating a nationwide futures watch process for InterVarsity. The purpose of this process is to enable campus ministry leaders to help students identify some of the new opportunities and challenges likely to be waiting for them in the third millennium. Then before they graduate, they can begin exploring how, as Christians, they will creatively respond to these new challenges.

Opportunities for Christian Leaders: Preparing Churches to Surf with Shakespeare

I recommend that before church leaders begin planning, local congregations develop a simple futures watch process using trend extrapolation. In this process, they seek to answer two very straightforward questions:

1. How is the community in which your church is planted likely to change in the next ten years?
2. How is your congregation and your funding base likely to change in the next ten years?

How Is Your Community Likely to Change?

To help church leaders answer the first question, I simply ask them to draw a circle around a map of the community in which they are ministering, and then I ask, How is the population in this community likely to change in the next ten years? Who is moving out? Who is moving in? How is your community likely to change by age, race, and economic level in the next ten years? What are the needs of the people in your community likely to be, and how will you have to change your approach to evangelism and ministry to address those needs? In other words, I invite them to do a futures need assessment.

For instance, while working with leaders of a Presbyterian church in southern California, I asked them to identify one population that was likely to move into their community in growing numbers in the next ten years. One of the leaders responded, "We are going to have a huge increase in the number of single-parent moms." So I asked, "What are the special needs of single parents?" A leader responded, "Child care, emotional and economic support systems." Before the day was over, they were beginning to proactively create a new course for single parents, to help address the needs of this population as it became a growing presence in their community.

How Is Your Congregation Likely to Change?

In preparation for conducting a Millennium III Creativity Workshop with a Baptist church in Vancouver, British Columbia, we at Mustard Seed Associates asked the pastor to provide us with a demographic profile of the congregation. The profile revealed that fully a third of the church was over age sixty-five and that there were virtually no forty- and fifty-year-olds. The rest of the congregation consisted of a transitional group of young people who were attending the University of British Columbia and Regent College. In our research we discovered why so many of the young would move away. Housing prices in the community started at five hundred thousand dollars.

I asked the pastor to research how much apartments cost. To his surprise, eight-unit apartment houses were selling for only eight hundred thousand dollars, or one hundred thousand dollars a unit. So during our creativity workshop, leaders came up with the idea of purchasing three or four apartment blocks and transforming them into condos and selling units to younger members so there will be someone to lead the church into a new millennium.

One of the greatest benefits of learning to surf with Shakespeare is that it gives us time to be creative. Through Mustard Seed Associates, Christine and I have had the opportunity to be part of a team, led by Steve Gaukroger, that was given the task of designing curriculum for Spring Harvest 1999, a training course for some eighty thousand British Christians. Peter Meadows had the job of taking all the input and drafting curriculum to help prepare British churches and believers to create a new response to the challenges of tomorrow's world.

Opportunities for Christian Leaders: Preparing Mission Organizations to Surf with Shakespeare

I realize that most Christian organizations typically have little money to spend on research, particularly research on future trends. Therefore, I recommend that leaders find among their constituents those who are already tracking information about the future on the internet. Ask four to eight of these supporters to become an ad hoc on-line futures watch group. I suggest that this group use contextual forecasting and scenario forecasting to anticipate some of tomorrow's challenges.

Contextual Forecasting

Have your futures watch group collect a broad spectrum of information on demographic, economic, technological, political, and religious trends. Then have them combine their information into a contextual forecast for the next ten years. It is essential that the major trends identified are based on responsible sources and don't rely on speculative predictions about the future.

For example, Doug Balfour, the CEO of Tearfund England, initiated a process called the Jordan Project. One aspect of the project was to conduct a contextual forecasting process in which two questions were asked.

1. How is the context in which we work with the poor in Africa, Asia, and Latin America likely to change in the next ten years? And what are likely to be the emerging needs?
2. How is the church in the United Kingdom, and our donor support base, likely to change in the next ten years?

In answering the second question, leaders found that their donor base was aging—an issue for many Christian agencies. In response, Tearfund added a new program to find ways to reach those under thirty in order to have a donor base to support their mission into the twenty-first century.

Scenario Forecasting

One of the limitations of contextual forecasting is that you tend to place all your fortunes on one possible projection for the future, which may not always be accurate. The advantage of scenario forecasting is that it enables the members of your leadership team to think contingently about several possible futures before they embark on strategic planning. In conducting scenario forecasting, I recommend that you use the information gathered in the contextual forecasting phase by your futures watch group to write two to four possible scenarios about the future.

Open Doors asked my wife and me to help them with scenario forecasting. One of the scenario exercises involved their work with the underground church in China. We invited the Open Doors leadership team to think through two different scenarios for China's economic future. First, using some material from a World Bank book titled *China 2020,* we presented an optimistic scenario in which China's economy continues to grow at 8 to 9 percent for the next ten years.

We asked Open Doors leaders to identify the possible impact of a high-growth economy on those in the underground church. On the positive side, they stated that greater economic growth would probably encourage a greater openness to the outside world. But they pointed out that growing prosperity could be as corrupting for vital Christianity in China as it has been for Christians in Eastern Europe since the Berlin Wall came down. Therefore, Open Doors leaders responded by proposing to design training materials to prepare members of the underground church to deal with the possibility of growing materialism.

The second scenario focused on a future in which the Chinese economy experiences an economic meltdown. In this case, the leaders predicted that Chinese society would become more repressive toward the church. Christians would be the first ones fired and would endure more severe hunger and deprivation. The leaders' response was to explore how to create microenterprise projects to enable members of the hidden church to support themselves.

Preview of Coming Attractions

The church desperately needs leaders who lead with foresight rather than simply trying to survive a ride on the wild side or recover from a ride on the wet side. We need leaders who learn both to anticipate and creatively respond to waves of change, to be proactive instead of reactive.

In the next four chapters I am going to take you on some trips back to the future. I will offer you my attempt at a contextual forecast that describes different ways in which globalization could have an impact on your life, family, congregation, and those with whom we share this planet. Remember, we can approach the future with confidence because we know the end from the beginning: the mustard seed wins the day.

Questions for Discussion and Action

1. Why is it important for Christian leaders to learn to take the future seriously?

2. How can we discern God's activity in the change that fills our world?

3. What are some specific ways you could use the seven forecasting tools given in this chapter to anticipate how change is likely to have an impact on your life, family, church, and community?

4. Anticipate one likely area of change in the community in which you minister, and create one way to respond. What are the potential benefits of forecasting?

McWorld: A Race to the Top

"IN QUEENSLAND'S FAR NORTH the sky, the water, the reef and the clouds mingle the blues in a dazzling cocktail. From a boat it is one of the wonders of the world—the black-blue of the distant deep and the azure blue of the shallows. There's cobalt in the sky, and below the water's staggeringly beautiful world of coral and fish."[1]

After three years of Peace Corps service in Fiji, Thomas and Eileen Lonergan were on holiday, enjoying the incredible coral and fish of Australia's Great Barrier Reef. They had decided to treat themselves to one last holiday before they returned home to Baton Rouge, Louisiana, and started their family. Since they were experienced scuba divers, they signed on with the party on the dive boat *Outer Edge* one warm, sunny morning in late January. Their fellow divers reported that Tom and Eileen were thoroughly enjoying the unique beauty of the reef as the day wore on.

"But take away the boat, the Lonergans would have been utterly alone; beauty would have melted to fear. Maybe they saw the M.V. Outer Edge motoring back to port. The crew was serving savories, the bar was busy and in the jumble on the decks no one noticed the Americans' unattended bags."[2] Incredibly, it was fifty hours before anyone noticed that the young

American couple had not returned with the dive boat. Belatedly, an intensive search began for Thomas and Eileen. But they were never found.

My wife and I were visiting her family in Australia when this tragic story unfolded. On January 29 I listened to the radio while the search for the young couple continued. One reporter interviewed a representative from the local tourist authority. In a very cool, detached voice the representative stated, "This incident may have a short-term impact on the dive business and a few tourists might ask questions, but it certainly will not detrimentally impact the local tourist economy. There is absolutely no reason for anyone to be concerned about the economic impact of this isolated incident."

It's the Economy, Stupid!

During this entire interview there was no mention of the tragic human loss or the pain to the families who were waiting for word regarding their loved ones. The focus of the interview was singularly on the economic impact on the local tourist industry. Let me hasten to add there were other interviews that did focus on the human dimension. And this interview could have taken place anywhere in the world, because economic impacts are increasingly seen as our most important concern.

In Woody Allen's nostalgic film *Radio Days,* we are witnesses to the re-creation of another human tragedy that took place in the forties. I was in elementary school at the time and can still vividly remember listening to this drama on the radio. A little girl in Texas fell down a deep well. Over a number of hours, emergency crews were repeatedly frustrated in attempting to rescue her. I was impressed at how the whole nation seemed to come to a complete halt, transfixed by this harrowing crisis.

We became like one large extended family with our ears glued to the radio, praying and waiting until we finally heard the word. After many long hours, the emergency crews dug a parallel tunnel and successfully rescued the child. Upon receiving that good news, the whole nation joined in a collective sigh of relief. It is difficult for me to imagine that scene taking place in America today.

The point is that over the last fifty years society has changed dramatically in terms of its understanding of what's important and what's of value. Increasingly the overwhelming message from modern culture about what's important couldn't be clearer: "It's the economy, stupid!" Like the representative from the tourist industry Down Under, many of us in Western societies tend to see economic concerns as the ultimate concerns. As I will show in this chapter, this is no accident. Many of us, including people of keen biblical faith, have been influenced by modern culture to define what is important and what is of value largely in economic terms, too.

👉 *Finding the Focus*

The intent of this chapter is to ask, How is economic globalization likely to change our common future and particularly our view of what is important and of value? In this contextual forecast I will begin identifying some of the possible upsides and downsides of economic globalization. Together we will try to understand the future to which the architects of McWorld promise to take us, and the vehicle they will use to transport us there. Finally, I will ask, What impact is economic globalization likely to have on our lives and communities of faith as we race into a new millennium, and how should we prepare to serve God in that world?

A Race to the Top: Looking Backward

I remember when San Francisco went through two huge convulsions of celebration at the end of World War II. Mayhem reigned on Market Street at the end of both our war with Germany and that with Japan. The sense of hope for our common future as the wars ended was almost palpable. As a sixth grader, I was invited in 1946 to enter a citywide poster contest to help promote the economic development of our former enemy, Japan. My poster read, "Help Japan to Help Herself." To my astonishment, my poster took first place, and in the ensuing years the United States did indeed help Japan and Germany, as well as our allies, to help themselves.

Before the First World War there had been an attempt to create a global economic order. But the great depression of the 1920s and 1930s brought this move toward globalization to an abrupt halt. On December 8, 1941, when the United States entered World War II, the United States and Great Britain were essentially the only capitalist countries in our world.

As a direct result of America's helping its former enemies to help themselves, Japan and Germany not only became economic dynamos; they became partners in a burgeoning free-market alliance. With the unexpected end of the Cold War, all the centrally planned economies wound up in the trash bin of history, and for the first time ever, virtually every nation chose to join the global capitalist race to the top.

Globalization: Determining the Shape of the World to Come

It is my contention that the number one force that will shape the future of our lives, families, congregations, and the larger world is globalization. Someone has written, "For better or worse we have girded our planet in a global electronic nervous system of satellites and fax machines from which there is no exit." It is through that global electronic system that we have witnessed the creation of a new one-world economic order.

Kenichi Ohmae, a leading Japanese economist, offers a description of this borderless economy. "With the emergence of 'electronic highways' all corporate players can 'plug' into the global marketplace freed of government interference to participate in a new open transnational economy."[3]

The strongest advocates for a new global economic order, like Ohmae, are well-intended economic and political leaders who want what is best for our planetary community. They have been schooled in a worldview that defines what is best largely in terms of economic growth and efficiency. And they have concluded that the best way to achieve those outcomes is through the creation of a borderless economic order.

There is no question that for those of the middle class to sustain life and help the poor achieve a decent way of life, we need to grow our economies. I am not as sure as the architects of McWorld are that the best way to achieve that goal is to create a one-world economic order. Where I have a particular problem with their advocacy is that from a Christian perspective, I will never be able to define what's best or what's ultimate in terms of economic growth and efficiency. And I believe we need to create forums in which Christian economists, theologians, and historians discuss not only where the globalization of the economy is likely to take us but what values drive it.

To understand this crusade to create a global economy, it is important to realize that not all the national economies joining this race are working from the same economic models. The economies of Europe and Japan are essentially "stakeholder" economies, which have a sense of responsibility not only to those who buy stock but to the workers, the communities in which the firms are based, the larger society, and even their suppliers.

The United States and Britain, on the other hand, operate as "shareholder" economies, in which the concern is almost entirely focused on meeting the expectations of the corporation's shareholders. In this very competitive race to the top, the shareholder model is setting the pace, because the stakeholder model is considerably more expensive.

Those economists, like Ohmae, who are strong advocates for economic globalization promise that this rocket ship will transport us to a new future of unbelievable affluence for all peoples. And the advocates of the shareholder model are arguing that their model is the most efficient way to get there. In any case, virtually all of the world's nations have joined in this brutally competitive economic race because economic growth and efficiency are seen as the ultimate good. Leaders of most nations seem to be convinced that high economic growth increases stability at home and political power abroad. So like it or not, we are all along for the ride. The creation of the European Union and the Euro is an obvious example of this trend.

All that is required from us is to trust our lives and futures to the twin rockets of global free enterprise and global free trade. We are told that if we allow the market to have complete freedom and if we support completely free trade in which everyone is able to fish in everyone else's pond, the global economy will enter a long boom, a rising tide that will lift all boats. But as I write, we are in the midst of a global economic crisis that for some is raising serious questions as to whether the benefits of creating a global economy outweigh the perils. However, short of a total meltdown, I don't think we are likely to get off this course.

Conspiracy or Consensus?

Not everyone is excited about the creation of a borderless world economy. Pat Buchanan sees the creation of a global economy in the most sinister terms. In his book *The Great Betrayal,* he seeks to rally those on the Right to oppose free trade, to protect American economic power, American jobs, and American nationalism. Some on the extreme Right believe that globalization is being engineered by a conspiratorial elite of Zionist bankers.

There are those on the Left who talk in the darkest tones about a global conspiracy directed by wealthy corporations, and they aggressively oppose the North American Free Trade Agreement, free trade, and the work of the World Trade Organization. But contrary to the inflamed opinions of both the Right and Left, I haven't found any evidence of a global conspiracy orchestrated by a small elite of corporate CEOs or European financiers.

In fact, everything I have seen convinces me that no one seems to be in the driver's seat of this runaway global economy. And I find the prospect of a ride on the wild side with no one at the wheel even more terrifying than that of a small sinister elite calling the shots, because no one—including the most ardent advocates of economic globalization—has any idea where this ride will take us.

William Greider characterized this powerful movement toward economic globalization as a race and a revolution. "The present economic revolution, like revolutions of the past, is fueled by invention and human ingenuity and a universal aspiration to build and accumulate. But it is also driven by a palpable sense of insecurity. No one can be said to control the energies of unfettered capital, not important governments or financiers, nor dictators or democrats. And, in the race to the future, no one dares fall a step behind, not nations or major corporations. Even the most effective leaders of business and finance share in this uncertainty, knowing as they do that the uncompromising dynamics can someday turn on the revolutionaries themselves."[4]

While I believe there is certainly no conspiracy, there is among the advocates of globalization a growing consensus about what is important and what is of value. Not surprisingly, these values come directly from the aspirations and the values of modern culture. And in many ways, I believe, those aspirations and values are in direct conflict with those undergirding a biblical faith.

While a number of economists see globalization as simply the creation of an unregulated transnational economy for the free exchange of goods and services, others are convinced that there is more to it than that. For instance, in *Jihad vs. McWorld* Benjamin Barber contends that the fabricators of McWorld are also intent on creating a new global culture that reflects its core values.

McDonaldization of Our Planetary Community

"McWorld is a product of popular culture driven by expansionist commerce," Barber writes. "Its template is American, its form style. . . . It is about culture as a commodity, apparel as ideology. Its symbols are Harley-Davidson motorcycles and Cadillac motorcars hoisted from the roadways, where they once represented a mode of transportation, to the marquees of global market cafes like Harley-Davidson's and the Hard Rock, where they become icons of a lifestyle. . . . Music, videos, theater, books, and theme parks—the new churches of a commercial civilization in which the malls and public squares . . . are all constructed around image exports creating a common world taste around common logos, advertising slogans, stars, songs, brand names, jingles and trademarks."[5]

In other words, Barber is arguing that our creation of a global free exchange of goods and services is not a values-free or culturally neutral activity. Quite the contrary. McWorld is driven by the aspirations and values of modernity and is aggressively at work creating a one-world consumer culture in which the shopping mall is replacing the church as the center of religious devotion, and all of life is reduced to a commodity.

The Best of Times

As my wife and I left a wharf-side restaurant in Seattle, we were greeted with a huge display of luxury yachts open for inspection. And at a recent home show here in the Northwest, it seemed that every second display was composed of lavish hot tubs large enough to test a kayak in. If you drive in the hills above Microsoft, you will see gigantic, multi-million-dollar minicastles with bathrooms that would rival the baths of ancient

Rome. The amazing thing to me is that these luxury items have been selling like red-tag specials at Kmart. Bingeing has become a way of life.

Here in Seattle, hundreds of middle-class people boarded the Microsoft rocket in the eighties and have joined the ranks of the Microsoft millionaires in the nineties. I have met those in the financial districts of London who have also benefited handsomely from the recent McWorld liftoff. And millions of us in the middle class have seen our consumer choices expand dramatically in the past ten years with the globalization of trade. Even those in poorer countries have benefited from economic globalization.

For example, in the last ten years Martha Fûnes and nine of her relatives have risen from a hand-to-mouth existence in a rundown border town to the American middle class. Her new car, new suburban home, and more affluent lifestyle have all come because Martha and her relatives are employed by Dell to box computers for an exploding global market.[6] Martha and her family are representative of numbers of people who are celebrating their move into a new "glocal" neighborhood and directly benefiting economically from this race to the top.

We are all being rocketed at breathtaking speed into a new "glocal" neighborhood of megamergers, digital entertainment, and consumer cornucopia. Borders are melting and distance is dying as five billion of us now shop at the same macromall and stare transfixed at the same electronic images. The *New York Times* heralded this extraordinary period of global economic growth as the "best of times."[7] The advocates for a McWorld future insist we haven't seen anything yet.

Futurist Peter Schwartz paints a vivid scenario of the better future to which the long economic boom brought about by globalization promises to transport us. "We are watching the beginnings of a global economic boom on a scale never experienced before. We have entered a period of sustained growth that could eventually double the world's economy every dozen years and bring prosperity for—quite literally—billions of people on the planet. We are riding the early waves of a 25-year run of a greatly expanding economy that will do much to solve seemingly intractable problems like poverty and to ease tensions throughout the world. And we will do it without blowing the lid off the environment. . . . These two metatrends—fundamental technological change and a new ethos of openness—will transform our world into the beginnings of a global civilization . . . that will blossom through the coming century."[8]

Opportunities for Christian Leaders

How can those in leadership prepare their people to deal with both the opportunities and the challenges of a long-boom scenario?

1. Some of the people who are in the middle class might begin to ride the same escalator used by the Microsoft millionaires. They would become more economically secure, send their young to the finest universities, and purchase goods that were out of reach before. And they would have more money to give to the church. But a number of Microsoft millionaires will tell you that one of the costs of that ride to the top was that they weren't around to see their kids grow up. Pastors working with those who have joined the ranks of the very affluent report that these wealthy individuals have often become more preoccupied with issues of status, materialism, and influence than with issues of faith and have dropped out. Therefore, to get people ready for a long-boom scenario, those in leadership will need to develop educational materials to enable Christians to deal with the seductions of the consumer culture and learn to steward their lives to put first things first.

2. If church members earned better incomes, they would have more financial resources to give to the church and worthy causes. During the boom from 1991 to 1999 in the United States, giving did increase but not as rapidly as the salaries of church members rose. Congregational leaders, in the long-boom scenario, will need to offer instructional courses to enable members to become responsible stewards of their increased affluence.

3. One of the most promising aspects of the long-boom scenario is that increased economic growth could mean that more of those on the margins in our country and abroad will have an opportunity to provide the essentials of life for their families. It won't happen automatically, however. Therefore, in the long-boom scenario, affluent churches need to partner with poorer congregations in this country and overseas to create small-scale businesses and credit unions so the poor don't miss this opportunity to create a decent way of life for their families.

4. One of the most troubling consequences of a long-boom scenario is that it will dramatically increase the rate at which we use and degrade environmental resources. Therefore, Christian leaders will need to place much more emphasis on caring for creation, in partnership with organizations such as the Evangelical Environmental Network.[9]

The Worst of Times

"The global capitalist system, which has been responsible for the remarkable prosperity of this country in the last decade, is coming apart at the seams," declares global financier George Soros.[10] In his new book, *The Crisis of Global Capitalism,* Soros warns of a possible global meltdown if steps aren't taken to manage this new global economic order.

As I edited this manuscript, an editorial in the *Economist* questioned the optimism that is lifting the American economy after the nation overcame a recession scare. "The most striking evidence of why this [economic boom] cannot last is that total household savings turned negative in September for the first time in 60 years. Companies have also been borrowing heavily to finance capital investment. As a result, the combined private savings rate [the gap between total private income and spending] has fallen to levels below anything ever seen in America before."[11]

Report from the Trenches

Tim Dearborn, at World Vision U.S., explained to me that economic meltdown is having a devastating impact on the lives and families of many of our poorest neighbors. In a number of cities in the poorer countries of Asia—Thailand, Indonesia, and Malaysia—unemployment is soaring and families are having difficulty keeping their children fed. As a consequence, more and more children are being forced into the international child prostitution trade, and more people are accepting sweatshop jobs with very low pay and brutal working conditions.

Dearborn said that the only people who are somewhat better off in this depression are the rural poor who use their land to grow food for their families now instead of using it to grow cash crops for global trade.

The Slow Meltdown

Working on this manuscript before anyone else caught the "Asian flu," I wrote, "One of my concerns is that as we all become more tightly hardwired together in a one-world economy, we also become more vulnerable. If Russia, China, or Brazil experience a major depression, none of us will be spared the pain." Since I penned those words, the Soviet economy has imploded, but with outside help, China's and Brazil's have avoided meltdown. Now it appears that troubled Asian economies are slowly turning around.

But that doesn't mean this new global economy is out of trouble. Deep down, many realize that what goes up must come down. A number of authors feel this new one-world economic order is more volatile than the old. They argue that this volatility is a direct result of our many national economies becoming more highly connected and that these connections have often been made without an agreed-upon set of rules.

Michael Mandel, writing for *Business Week,* stated, "Today, it's clear that both globalization and technological change are creating new risks. The increased interconnectedness of the global economy means that economic or financial disturbances in Asia or Russia can be transmitted much faster and more powerfully to the rest of the world."[12]

John Heilemann, an editor for *Wired* and an enthusiastic booster for economic globalization, shares the same concern about economies becoming more tightly wired together. "The invention of superhighways made transportation better and safer overall. But it also increased the risks of spectacular smashups. I think the development of modern financial markets and greater interconnectedness is very much like the development of the superhighway."[13] A global meltdown could give us all a firsthand experience of what it would be like to be in a "spectacular smashup" and discover just how vulnerable we are in a new, more volatile, global economic order.

"There is no international body able to play the role of global regulator, and an inability by the United States and other powers to impose changes on the often-reluctant governments and banks in nations at risk"[14] was the diagnosis of the *New York Times.* Global financial leaders are working feverishly to construct a new global architecture. But it is still years away, and a number of people doubt that we will ever develop the universal ground rules essential to avoid a smashup. It is as though we have signed up for a joint checking account with six billion other people and everybody makes up their own rules.

We are rapidly moving into a more uncertain economic future in which many of us are likely to be more vulnerable and most of us aren't prepared for a serious downturn. Leaders need to help people prepare for two scenarios: the bingeing of the long boom and the crashing of the slow meltdown.

Getting Ready for the Millennium Bug

One of our first experiences of the risks of being wired together in a new global order is the coming of the millennium bug. As we cross the threshold into the year 2000, we will discover how serious the breakdown is going to be as a result of a failure to make all computers Y2K compliant. There are some religious extremists who are linking the Y2K bug to their pet endtimes theories, selling their homes and stockpiling food and guns in mountain hideaways. Frankly, this hysteria isn't terribly helpful, and the survivalist movement causes people to become self-involved in times of crisis instead of concerned for the needs of others. This fear-mongering might cause more of a crisis than the bug itself. As followers of Christ we aren't called to be survivors but servants to the most vulnerable.

Having said that, I believe we should take the Y2K bug seriously. If you know when an earthquake is coming, common sense dictates you get ready. I have encouraged a number of Christian organizations to develop a broad range of contingency plans so they are prepared to deal with worst-case scenarios.

A number of Third World countries will not be ready and are likely to face major infrastructure breakdowns which could take a high toll on the urban poor. And the poor in America are also among those that are likely to be hit hardest by the Y2K bug. Some of the most helpful sources I have found on the subject are:

www.josephproject2000.org

www.y2kprepare.com

www.year2000.com

I was among those who urged InterVarsity Christian Fellowship to postpone Urbana for a year, since it was slated to take place as we entered the year 2000. I was concerned about the risk of transporting some twenty thousand college students from all over North America at a time when it isn't clear how many airlines will be Y2K compliant.

In any case, as we enter the new millennium, we will all discover together how bad the Y2K crisis is going to be. It is likely to have an impact on the global economy. The fear of Y2K could cause more disruption than the bug itself.

Opportunities for Christian Leaders

Christian leaders have a responsibility to prepare their members not only for the possibility of the long boom but also for the possibility of the slow meltdown scenario. Those of us in North America and Europe will sooner or later experience an economic recession. So we need to get people ready, even as Joseph prepared Egypt for seven bad years, while increasing our trust in God. Leaders have the opportunity

1. to prepare individuals and families to get ready for a more volatile economic future in which we will all be more vulnerable. I suggest we encourage people to reduce their exposure by reducing their debt as much as possible, increasing their savings, and planting gardens (where possible) to increase both interdependence and self-reliance. It is essential that Christians in hard times be encouraged to put their faith in God and learn to work together in the body of Christ to help others.

2. to enable local churches to design programs of mutual care and cooperation (like starting food co-ops) in advance of hard times,

so Christians are able to help not only one another but particularly those in need in their communities.

3. to enable those who work with the poor to develop a buffer of emergency food and medical supplies against hard times because the poor are always hit hardest by recessions or natural disasters. Urban ministries also should encourage the poor to use their back-yards and rooftops to grow food and thereby increase their self-reliance. And we should create a range of partnerships between middle-class and urban churches to work together to address the needs of our poorest neighbors during a time of economic crisis.

4. to get our people and Christian organizations ready for the com-ing of the Y2K crisis and future breakdowns. I believe it is always prudent to, like those of the Mormon faith, have some food, water, blankets, medical supplies, and batteries set aside for any disas-ter. This could help us, in a time of crisis, to focus beyond our own survival and help others in need. I urge all Christian organ-izations to develop carefully thought-out contingency plans to deal with a crisis.

Welcome to the Great McWorld Auction

Regardless of whether we experience a slow meltdown or a long-boom future, we are going to see continued rapid globalization of every aspect of God's world and our lives. We are racing into a McWorld future in which everything from jobs to small businesses to our own bodies are up for auction. Economists assure us that it is just good common business sense to assign everything a price.

British author Charles Handy explores where this business of assign-ing a price to everything might take us. "If people want to sell their kid-neys, or their bodies for sex, why shouldn't they, as long as there are willing buyers? In this rhetoric the value of anything is in its price. It gets tempting, this commodification of everything. It reduces everything to a convenient common denominator. One can even, technically, demonstrate that the marginal productivity of some members of society is too low to allow them to purchase the cost of living. Should they then perish?" Handy concludes, "A society which was a grand auction block would not be a society worth having. It might even be far less economi-cally successful than its proponents imagine. We should not be over-impressed by the early energies released by deregulation. Not everything can be for sale."[15]

But as we will see, the architects of McWorld are intent on creating a new global economy of free enterprise and free trade, in which everything is up for auction and everything is for sale. Let's look at where this great global auction could take us.

The Great Job Auction

An exhibit by impoverished photographers living in the ramshackle Mexican border town of Juarez conveys a different picture of life for those employed in the new global factories than did the story of Martha Fūnes, which I related earlier. Multinational corporations have located here in Juarez for the same reason they are locating in Vietnam and Thailand: cheap labor. The multinationals operating in Juarez pay their workers a bit more than do Mexican factories in the area, but many of the people don't make enough to pay for child care, let alone to afford to move out of the squalor in which they are trapped. The photographic exhibit, on display in the United States, shows pictures of cardboard shantytowns with no electricity, heat, or water.[16]

One of the essential conditions of economic globalization is that all businesses have unlimited access to the global labor pool to produce goods as efficiently as possible. This viewpoint insists that the employer has no responsibility either to the worker who loses his job in a car plant in Flint or to the worker who replaces him in Juarez. The employer's singular responsibility is to show shareholders a profit. It is up to the free market to sort out the future for those in Flint whose jobs went south. And it is up to the free market to set the wages of workers in Juarez, even if the going wage is not enough to provide a decent way of life for their families.

Even the North American middle class is being impacted by the great job auction. Computer programmers in Bangalore, India, are willing to work for a tenth to a fifth of what their counterparts in San Jose are paid. And their work arrives via the internet twenty-four hours a day.[17]

Pat Buchanan, on the Right, and Richard Gephart, on the Left, are both challenging the contentions of prominent free-trade economists that this global job auction will have little impact on workers in major industrialized nations such as the United States. Both men tilt in the direction of protectionist policies.[18]

I find it difficult to imagine an alternative to this global free-trade rocket ship on which we are all riding. Protectionism does seem to be fraught with difficulties. However, a member of the European Parliament proposes one alternative I find intriguing. He urges that we "reject the concept of global free trade and replace it with regional free trade. That does not mean closing off regions of the world from trading with the rest of the world. It means allowing each region to decide whether and when they want to enter into bilateral agreements with other regions for mutual economic benefit. We must not simply open our markets to any and every product regardless of whether it benefits our economy, destroys our employment, or destabilizes our society."[19]

Planting a Seed in Juarez

There are a number of firms, such as the Body Shop, the Gap, and Levis, that have taken the initiative to pay their workers a living wage even if it is more than the prevailing market wage. *Forbes* magazine grudgingly acknowledged the successful work of Roman Catholic Sister Susan Mika in her advocacy for the working poor in Juarez, many of whom are employed in this McWorld industrial park. Sister Susan, working through a shareholder's group, persuaded General Motors to construct seven thousand basic homes for its workers who had been living in wooden or cardboard shacks with no plumbing.[20] There are thousands of others who, like Sister Susan, are working as a part of God's mustard seed movement to challenge those in positions of power to act justly.

The Great Small Business Auction

We are rapidly moving into a future in which the family farm, the small retailer, and the mom-and-pop restaurant are rapidly becoming artifacts of a bygone past. They are all on the auction block because small is inefficient. Economists assure us that we have all benefited from their gradual disappearance.

Undeniably, Wal-Mart's huge purchasing power often allows it to offer the consumer a lower price than the neighborhood shop. But as the neighborhood stores disappear, many people are belatedly discovering that they provided our communities with much more than consumer goods. They offered our communities services and a presence that the huge superstores will never replace. As neighborhood shops disappear, we are finding that our communities are disappearing, too. And the new shopping options appearing on the internet may even gobble up the superstores.

Destruction of Local Communities and Families

Wendell Berry, a Christian ecologist, decries the destruction of local communities and families in the name of economic efficiency and centralization of economic power. "The danger of the ideal of competition is that it neither proposes nor implies any limits. It proposes simply to lower costs at any cost, and to raise profits at any cost. It doesn't hesitate at the destruction of the life of a family or the life of a community."[21]

We are witnessing for the first time in history the fashioning of a highly centralized global economy in which a handful of economic Godzillas will increasingly establish their domination. As these monoliths mate, they create even larger offspring. And while this will mean high dividends for shareholders, I believe it will often come at a high price to families and local communities.

"Did Somebody Say McDonald's?"

Ronald McDonald has accomplished what neither Napoleon nor Hitler was able to achieve. Ronald and the invading armies of McDonald's have made it all the way to Moscow and become a visible bastion of this new economic order. "The scale of the global Mac Attack is impressive," reports the *Economist.* In 1996 McDonald's planned to open at least thirty-two hundred new outlets a year until the year 2000. Michael Quinlan, chairman of McDonald's board of directors, declared, "I am open to any course that helps McDonald's dominate every market."[22] In the McWorld business auction, domination is the name of the game as huge corporations all over McWorld seek to establish their supremacy in this new one-world market.

In many regions all over the world, the fare once served at mom-and-pop eating spots is being replaced with a globally standardized diet of Big Macs, KFC chicken strips, and Pizza Hut's latest hit. Sylvester Stalone's film *Demolition Man,* set in the year 2032, parodies pop culture today, celebrating the fact that only one restaurant survived the franchise wars and established global domination. In the film, everyone dines exclusively at Taco Bell. Now there is a better future we can all get excited about!

Dominating the Global Food Supply

There are a handful of corporations that are just as intent on dominating global food distribution as McDonald's is to dominate the fast-food market. One of the leaders in this race is Conagra, an agribusiness colossus, based in the United States, that aspires to dominate the global food business within the next ten years. While most people have never heard of Conagra, many Americans consume its products seven days a week. The company produces everything from Armour and Butterball meat products to Wesson Oil and Peter Pan peanut butter. It controls a huge share of U.S. fertilizer, grain, and frozen food production.[23]

While Conagra is committed to dominating the global food distribution network, Monsanto is committed to dominating the genetic seed stock for the world food supply. This company and others are busy creating new genetically engineered plants that increase their own built-in pesticides. Monsanto's goal is to persuade farmers to switch to these genetically engineered seeds to increase their profits. Companies like Monsanto are genetically altering the seeds with a terminator gene so seeds from one year's crop can't be planted the following year.

Europeans are adamantly opposed to what they call "frankenplants." But in the United States the food industry has passed a law making it illegal to inform people that they are eating genetically engineered potatoes and corn or drinking genetically engineered milk.[24]

This all began with a Supreme Court decision. "In 1980, in a historic five-to-four decision, the Supreme Court ruled that new life forms created in the laboratory could be patented. That decision was the harbinger of a whole new age," I wrote in *The Mustard Seed Conspiracy*.[25] Since that historic vote not only have corporations been involved in a genetic gold rush to patent new life-forms created in the lab; they have been patenting plant, animal, and even human genetic material from all over the planet for their private economic gain. Some people have labeled this multi-billion-dollar-a-year business "biopiracy" because the people from whose regions this genetic material is "prospected" often derive little of the economic benefit.[26] Even human DNA has been reduced to a commodity.

Will we all feel more secure when a handful of corporations control the global seed stock and the food distribution networks? Is this an inevitable future, or are there ways in which individuals can find access to alternatives? The concern is not only about the control of our food supply but also about its safety in a McWorld future.

Food Efficiency versus Food Safety

Globalizing the food supply has brought us an extravagant selection of foods from all over the world. Raspberries in the winter from Guatemala, grapes from Chile, prawns from Thailand, mangos from Mexico. But even this has a downside. Thousands of Americans became ill last year from a parasite that was imported with the raspberries.[27] As we are dramatically increasing the amount of food we import in the United States, we are cutting back funding for inspectors, to reduce the drag on the U.S. economy in this global race to the top.

One of the benefits to allowing the food giants to take over greater control of food production is that it has reduced costs. But unfortunately we are discovering that cost reduction in the efficient production of our food sometimes comes at a high price in food safety. Mad cow disease was one of the outcomes of cutting feed costs in Britain by putting animal waste into the feed. The recent outbreak of a particularly virulent strain of E. coli bacteria that killed 250 Americans and made thousands of others seriously ill wasn't an accident. It was a direct consequence of ranchers trying to produce beef more efficiently. The World Health Report tells us that in recent years ranchers wanting to protect the quality of their cattle routinely gave them subtherapeutic doses of human antibiotics. This inadvertently created a strain of E. coli bacteria that has become dangerous to humans because it is extremely resistant to antibiotics.[28] This is only one of a growing list of concerns about the efficiently produced food supply.

Planting a Seed in Community-Supported Agriculture

A movement called Community-Supported Agriculture is giving small family farms some hope for the future while providing safer and better-quality food for members. There are roughly six hundred CSA farms all over the United States. Essentially, members in these food cooperatives pay farmers to grow a year-round selection of fruits and vegetables for their families. Michael Docter started a CSA farm in Hadley, Massachusetts. Shares in the farm cost $350 to $450 per year. "We serve nearly 600 families," he explained. "The size of the share is so large that two or three households often buy them together."[29]

Families know their food is safe. The farms yearly grow over two hundred thousand pounds of produce on sixty acres, at or below supermarket prices. "The farm annually gives away half of what they grow to emergency food pantries, shelters and programs for the elderly in their community."[30]

Christine and I are, as a Christian stewardship goal, attempting to grow the majority of our fruits and vegetables on one urban lot. We presently grow 60 percent of our vegetables, but our fruit trees have a lot of growing to do. Based on this research, we are beginning to purchase more organically grown food as well. And we support legislation to set a very high standard for what can be labeled as organic.

The Great Creation Auction

Since the leaders of McWorld view economic growth and efficiency as the greatest good, creation is viewed as simply a resource to be used in the cause of accelerating economic growth. This has fostered a reductionistic view of God's creation and has placed major areas of the environment in peril.

The Long Boom: The Environmental Price Tag

Our expansive and growing appetites are already responsible for overharvesting many of the earth's forests and fish stocks, as well as seriously eroding some of our best agricultural land. In the future, we are likely to see growing conflicts due to competition for shrinking freshwater resources. And some people even predict a new oil crisis in the future because of the tremendous amount of fossil fuels required to power this race to the top.

Few nations have adequate resources to clean up the toxic, chemical, and nuclear waste that is a by-product of a half century of rapid growth and development, let alone to clean up the pollution that will be generated by the next half century of growth.

The summer of 1998 was the hottest on record, and this plus dramatic changes in global weather has heightened public concern about pollution and climate change. Ironically, the insurance companies are the ones who are raising the greatest concern about global warming. The reason for their sudden fit of conscience is that they are getting hammered by huge losses due to an unprecedented number of weather-related claims in the last eight years.

If the long-boom scenario continues, it will dramatically escalate the rate at which we auction off our planetary resources and pollute our environment. Rarely do economists factor the cost of environmental degradation into their equations. Short-term decisions often have long-term costs. Do we really believe that if we continue to use dwindling resources to produce a short-term gain, there won't be long-term costs to our children and grandchildren? Do we really believe that somehow the magic of the marketplace will resolve this mounting crisis?

Considering Growing the Economy on Purpose

Not only are the next generation and God's creation imperiled by our short-term and often shortsighted economic policies, but so are the world's poor. Reportedly, it takes 12.2 acres of land to supply the needs of an average American. In the Netherlands the basic needs are met with the resources of eight acres, and in India only a single acre is required. If the implicit promise of McWorld were realized and all the world's people were to achieve an American lifestyle, it would take three planets the size of ours to support the present world's population.

Stuart Hart, who writes for the *Harvard Business Review,* wants to persuade corporate leaders to develop a sustainable approach to economic growth, in which the goal is to enable all the world's people to achieve a decent way of life for themselves and their kids so they don't lose out in this devil-take-the-hindmost race to the top. Hart points out that our poorest neighbors simply aren't able to compete with us in this great earth auction. "Owing in part to the rapid expansion of the market economy, existence in the survival economy is becoming increasingly precarious. Extractive industries and infrastructure development have, in many cases, degraded the ecosystems upon which their survival economy depends.

"Rural populations are driven further into poverty as they compete for scarce natural resources. Women and children now on average spend four to six hours per day searching for fuel wood and four to six hours a week drawing and carrying water. . . . Worldwide, the number of such 'environmental refugees' from the survival economy may be as high as 500 million today and the figure is growing."[31]

Planting a Seed in BMWs

Hart cites how a German "take back" law required auto manufacturers to take back their cars at the end of their useful life. Innovators like BMW now design cars for easy disassembly and profitable recycling. Hart concludes, "In the coming decade, companies will be challenged to develop clean technologies and implement strategies that drastically reduce the environmental burden in the developing world while simultaneously increasing its wealth and standard of living."[32] And they will discover that such policies aren't just good for the environment, they are good for business too.

Planting a Seed in Furniture "Upcycling"

Ciba-Geigy, a European company, accepted the challenge of developing fabrics for chairs that could be "upcycled." That is, when the chairs eventually wind up in a landfill, the decomposing fabric not only doesn't add toxic chemicals to the soil, it puts in nutrients that enrich the soil. Not only did the company succeed in creating this "upcycled" fabric, but the water running out of the production plant was found to be as clean as the water going in.[33]

Planting a Seed in Belize

While the Christian Environmental Association was in Belize, negotiating for a small property it planned to use as an environmental study center, it learned that Coca Cola was also there, bidding on eight thousand acres of rain forest. Apparently, in the great earth auction it is cheaper for Coke to produce Minute Maid orange juice by clear-cutting the rain forest in Belize than by growing oranges in Florida. Obviously, this provides short-term benefits for its shareholders but comes at a very high price in terms of the long-term impact on the rain forest and future generations. The young Christians who head the Christian Environmental Association decided to challenge Coke in a bidding war. To their own amazement, they outbid Coke for this eight-thousand-acre parcel. They have set up the Eden Conservancy to preserve this huge section of rain forest in perpetuity. They did this because they believe that the Bible teaches that this huge section of rain forest was more than a commodity to be auctioned off like so many used cars.

As we have seen, the values implicit in McWorld are often in conflict with the values implicit in a biblical faith. I am deeply concerned that the growing commodification of everything could usher in a new dark age of the human spirit.

Opportunities for Christian Leaders

Christian leaders have the opportunity not only to get ready for the long-boom or slow-meltdown scenarios but also to enable people to contend with the great earth auction that increasingly is going to be a major part of our McWorld future.

1. We need to create an international Christian forum to talk about the future of economic globalization in terms of the values that are driving it and of the consequences of economic centralization and the commodification of virtually everything on our families, local communities, and the environment.
2. We need to expand our sense of Christian responsibility to include not only efforts to care for individuals and families who are poor or middle class but also, in the face of globalization, efforts to strengthen local businesses and the local communities of which they are a part.
3. We need to enable people, where possible, to grow more of their own food or join agricultural cooperatives to have a more reliable food supply.
4. We need to encourage economic growth that seeks to promote a decent way of life for our poorest neighbors while caring for God's good creation.

Redefining the Ultimate

As we rush into a new millennium, we are entering a future changing at blinding speed. Certainly, one of the primary forces directing the course of that change is globalization. In many ways most of us have benefited from globalization. McWorld promises us that if we can successfully navigate through this time of troubles, we can look forward to a long economic boom. Others are warning of a global meltdown. We need leaders with foresight who will help the church prepare for times of both economic crisis and economic bounty.

But we also need leaders skilled at making sense not only of change but also of the values that are driving change. Many people, including

Christians, treat our current form of free enterprise and economic globalization as though it were values neutral or values free. As we have seen,
the architects of McWorld are intent on not only changing the course of
international trade and economics but redefining what is ultimate and
what is of value.

In the opening story about the young couple who perished in the Great
Barrier Reef, the tourist representative seemed singularly concerned
about the economic impact of this tragedy, as if the ultimate concern is
always economic. The clear message from many well-intended advocates of economic globalization regarding what is ultimate: "It's the economy, stupid!"

When the Cold War abruptly ended, Francis Fukuyama wrote in his celebrated article "The End of History" that we're witnessing the end of history as the nations of the world join in the capitalist race to the top. Fukuyma
asserts, "The laws of economic efficiency and growth have replaced the
divine plan."[34] Have they? Lester Thurow, an MIT economist, states, "To
flourish, human societies need a vision of something better."[35] Is the ultimate vision of "something better" to be defined primarily in terms of economic growth, centralization, and efficiency, or is there something more?

Our present form of free enterprise not only isn't values free; it has
implicit within it a set of assumptions as to how the world works that is
a product of the Enlightenment and modernity. Many of the advocates of
this new global order define the ultimate primarily in economic terms. It
appears that we are traveling into a future in which virtually everything
in God's good creation, including human beings, will be reduced to a commodity and assigned a price.

Jane Collier, a British economist, calls this set of assumptions undergirding the modern economic enterprise "economism." According to the
Oxford English Dictionary, "Economism imposes the primacy of economic causes or factors as the main source of cultural meanings and values." As an economist and a Catholic, Collier is concerned about the way
in which the values of the marketplace increasingly seem to be shaping
the values of human culture.[36] Deep down I think most of us are not keen
to see our lives and God's creation reduced to an economic value.
Economism is not the source of ultimate value, and McWorld is not our
real home. As followers of Jesus Christ, aren't we sojourners in search of
a better homeland?

Questions for Discussion and Action

1. What has brought about the rapid economic globalization
of our planet, and what are the twin rockets of globalization that
promise to transport us to a more affluent future?

2. Describe both the upsides and downsides of the long-boom scenario, and how our families, churches, and communities need to get ready.

3. Describe both the upsides and downsides of the slow-meltdown scenario, and how our families, churches, and communities need to get ready.

4. How is the great auction likely to impact our lives, our communities, our congregations, the poor we work with, and the creation we care for, and what can we Christians do to make a difference?

A Trek Into a Cyber-Future

*Rewiring Our Communities and Politics
for the Third Millennium*

A SMALL BLACK BOX strapped to Stewart's head covered the left lens on his glasses. With this microtechnology, he was videotaping Morley Safer, who was interviewing him on *Sixty Minutes*. While *Sixty Minutes* was being broadcast on network television, this MIT student was broadcasting the interview on his own web page and storing it in his own data bank. The unit strapped to his head also contains a small computer screen that he constantly monitors with his left eye while viewing his immediate surroundings with his right eye. In other words, he lives constantly on-line, regardless of whether he is in class or at a party. He also has a state-of-the-art five-key entry pad strapped to his left hand so he is able to access data every waking moment.

Morley Safer asked the obvious question, "Why do you want to be constantly on-line?" The student responded, "Because I am immediately in contact with the entire world, and I have unlimited access to information. Ask me any question." Safer asked him what the lifetime statistics for Mickey Mantle were. Immediately Stewart's left hand went to work, and he reported that he was receiving a number of hits on his screen. Within moments he was sharing in detail the lifetime statistics for Mickey Mantle. But as he parroted the stats, it became immediately evident he had no idea that Mickey Mantle was a baseball star.

This unusual interview gives us a glimpse into cyber-future, where many of our kids and grandkids will be wearing computers as part of their wardrobe. We are racing into a future in which we are going to be much more tightly wired into a global electronic community than we ever imagined.

In the last chapter we awakened to discover that we are all part of a one-world economic race to the top, in which we are increasingly being influenced to define what is important and of value in terms of economic efficiency and growth. As we saw, what has made the globalization of the economy possible is the creation of a global electronic nervous system. Even as I write, the final satellites are being placed in orbit so all peoples are permanently linked in a single interactive system in which information is rapidly becoming the most prized commodity.

Finding the Focus

This new electronic nervous system is more than simply a conduit for planetary commerce. Being connected into a single economic order and a single electronic grid is radically changing how we relate to one another in community and how we govern ourselves politically. The intent of this chapter is to anticipate some of the new challenges and opportunities that McWorld and this cyber-connection are likely to raise for the ways in which we relate to one another and conduct our politics. We will particularly identify the implications of these challenges for people of faith and those in leadership.

Welcome to Cyber-Future

Net.goddesses, newbies, cyber-surfers, cyber-punks, MUDders, stalkers, flamers, zippy wavers, web trekkers, internet geeks, intranet techheads, and virtual freaks are residents in the new cyber-future to which we are being transported via cyber-space. Frankly, as one who is "predigital," I feel a bit apprehensive about the internet, community in cyberspace, and some of my new neighbors. But I am also fascinated by some of the new opportunities it affords, as well as by the challenges it raises.

In London you purchase your morning cappuccino at the Cyberia Cafe for $2.35 and for an additional fifty cents purchase a half hour's access to the internet on one of ten computers. By 2010 every Japanese home will be connected to the new sophisticated interactive fiber-optic system. While there are still a few bare spots in central Africa and Mongolia that are not hardwired into this global network of satellites, fiber optics, and personal computers, it is only a question of time.[1]

A remarkable number of people are actually "homesteading" in cyber-space, starting a broad range of cyber-cities. You can travel to virtual Vienna and enjoy classical music, or go to any one of twenty-nine cyber-cities where you can live, love, and put down roots.[2] While traveling in Britain, I learned of a new cyber-community being planted on an imaginary island in the Hebrides, where "residents" from Johannesburg to New York City cooperate in land-use planning for their community, as well as in creating a culture and activities on their imaginary island in keeping with local customs and tastes.

While few of us will ever homestead in cyber-space, the net affords a wonderful opportunity for all of us to get to know our neighbors all over the world. The internet could be a tool to help us all get to know people from other cultural, religious, and political backgrounds to foster mutual understanding and respect.

The net also provides a tremendous new educational resource to mission organizations working with the world's poor. Within five years many remote areas that today have no access to books, schools, or libraries could be hooked up to the net. In other words, it would be possible to start schools where none exist, fully recognizing that there are also some risks to getting wired in.[3] Nicholas Negroponte of the Media Lab predicts that people in the Two-Thirds World might use the capacity of the net to leapfrog into the twenty-first century.[4] How is our getting connected to one another through this cyber-technology likely to impact our lives and alter how we relate to one another?

Cyber-Community and McWorld: The Good, the Bad, and the Predatory

Belinda made her daily mile-long trek to her campus minister's office at the University of Alabama in Birmingham. The campus minister told me she showed up like clockwork every day during lunch hour to use his computer. When I asked what this unusual ritual was all about, he suggested I ask Belinda. I caught her racing back out the door. She immediately responded, "Oh, there's no mystery. I need to pick up my daily email, mostly from women on my dorm floor back on campus." I said, "You walk a mile every day to the campus ministry office to use the computer to communicate with your friends back on campus on your dorm floor?" She replied, "Absolutely! Don't you think it's important to keep up with friends?" She completely misunderstood my mystification. When I was a college student, light-years before the advent of computers or email, we simply wandered down the hall and talked to our friends. It seemed so simple.

I Have Seen the Future and It Looks Like Finland

How could this remarkable new technology alter our lives, and particularly the lives of our children, as we race into a cyber-space future together? One way to answer this question is to watch what is happening in Finland. Finland leads all other nations in hooking into the global network. Almost a third of all Finns have cellular phones. There are sixty-two internet host computers for every one thousand Finns—twice the numbers in the United States. Some people speculate that the reason for this high level of Finnish connection is the long, cold nights. Whatever the reason, if we want to observe where this wave might take us in the future, we should watch the impact that life on the net is having on the lives and communities on the front edge of this wave in Finland.[5]

Computer Wearables for a New Generation

Another way to anticipate where this wave might take us is to pay attention to the emergence of new technologies and explore where these waves of change might go. One of the ongoing developments in technological innovation is miniaturization of various computer and communications technology. This has led to the introduction of "wearable technology," like Stewart was using in the opening story, and the earliest manifestation of a new community of cyborgs or technologically augmented humans.

These first crude models consist of an assortment of computers, sensors, video cameras, and headgear. Some of the wearables are nothing more than a geek fashion statement. But most enable the wearer to be constantly hardwired into cyber-space. One laser device projects onto the back of a person's retina a transparent computer screen that seems to appear three feet in front of the subject.

Within a few years we will be able to purchase a wardrobe with built-in technological devices. It is only a question of time until those interested in serious human augmentation create ways to implant these devices. What are the long-term consequences of a generation permanently hardwired and constantly on-line?[6]

Opportunities and Perils

With many of our young people already heavily involved with TV, MTV, video games, and now the net, how do we prepare them for both the opportunities and risks of life in cyber-space, particularly in light of growing concern about violent video games and media?

One of the major waves of the future is that a number of people are turning to the net and cyber-space to find community. "Relationships can be complicated in cyber-space because the very technology that draws people together also keeps them apart. Over time, the safe sense of distance that initially seems so liberating to newcomers on the net can become an obstacle to deepening bonds of friendship, romance and community," David Hughes of the Old Colorado City Electronic Cottage declares. "You can't lead a total life on-line."[7]

But some people seem to be satisfied not only with a "vicarious community" but also in a real sense with a vicarious way of life, living on-line through the lives of others. Some are "lurkers" who, like voyeurs, simply watch and don't enter. Some are "stalkers" who fixate on certain people on the net and habitually harass them. "Flamers" are those who come on-line enraged, drunk, or stoned and are simply abusive and hostile. Too often people who don't have much of a social life become addicted to the virtual community of the net, even sneaking on-line during work.

Glenn Cartwright at McGill University in Canada raises questions about the impact of these new technologies on the development of human identity and personal relationships. He voices concern that some people will, through the net, develop their own parallel reality in which they appropriate a new identity, perhaps change genders, or live through a more attractive virtual body. Of course, their parallel identity might become preferable to their real identity.

Cartwright not only discusses the obvious dangers of living out a virtual identity but also suggests that the tendency of some people to do so could create a host of "de-centered" persons who could become dangerously self-destructive. It is possible that individuals could also develop "distributed," or multiple, identities that could impair their ability to function in reality. He concludes, "The twenty-first century may well be the century of technologically induced disaffection, characterized by an increased sense of loneliness, alienation, powerlessness, and disembodiment."[8]

I have had a number of church youth workers tell me that one of the most addictive aspects of cyber-space is on-line sex. One worker told me how, as a fifth grader, he had made a copy of the key to his dad's computer room and, unbeknownst to his parents, spent several impressionable years satisfying childhood curiosity by taking in the swill available on the net. Douglas Groothius's book *The Soul in Cyber-Space* does an excellent job of highlighting these dangers.[9]

Perhaps even more concerning are the growing numbers of pedophiles who deliberately stalk the young on the net, sometimes posing as children to develop trusting friendships. In 1996 sixteen men from the United States, Finland, Canada, and Australia who were a part of an on-line pedophile group called the Orchid Club were indicted in the United States for their illicit activities. "Its members shared homemade pictures, recounted sexual experiences with children and even chatted electronically as two of the men molested a 10-year-old girl."[10]

The 1996 Telecommunications Act was passed in the United States to help protect children from these on-line predators. But since there is such a huge and expanding worldwide market for all kinds of violent and pornographic material, I am not convinced that this is going to reduce the flow or protect the young. We need some new, creative approaches to prepare the young to live in a highly connected, seductive, and violent cyber-future.

Coming Soon: The Brave New World of Virtual Reality

We are not far away from creating virtual reality chambers in our labs, offices, schools, and homes. These may not fully achieve the "touchy-feely" environments of Brave New World, but they will create stunningly lifelike three-dimensional worlds that will be very convincing.

Imagine the educational applications of such virtual reality chambers. Students will never go to sleep in history class again. You will be able to transport them back in time to the landing at Normandy at the climax of World War II, where they will be surrounded by the violent conflict, as in the film Saving Private Ryan. You will be able to take them out into space three-dimensionally and lead them on a tour of Mars. And in a science class, you will be able to transport them three-dimensionally down into molecular structures. Imagine the possibility for the arts of creating richly textured environments that have never existed before.

We are already seeing the creation of virtual reality entertainment centers all over the United States. But you can be sure that the same folks bringing hard-core sex and violence to the internet, stage, and screen have plans to bring us virtual sex and virtual violence. And our young will have to contend with forms of addiction that have never existed before. We are rapidly entering a new one-world cyber-age.

Neil Postman expresses concern that this new cyber-age is lacking a transcendent narrative to provide moral underpinnings for our technological innovation, or strong social institutions to steer it. Even more concerning he predicts, "Symbols that draw their meaning from traditional religious or concerning national contexts must therefore be made impotent as quickly as possible—that is, drained of sacred or even serious connotations. The elevation of one god requires the demotion of another. 'Thou shalt have no other gods before me' applies as well to technological divinity as any other."[11] This process will directly challenge the authority of biblical faith in the twenty-first century. Our technological systems are no more values free than our economic systems.

Typically, the young watch at least twenty hours of TV a week plus spend a huge amount of time with CDs, video games, and the internet. It is a joke to believe that one hour of Sunday school a week will have much influence against this McWorld onslaught. We will need to create much more serious approaches to Christian nurture that involve families and communities.

Planting a Seed in Bible Gateway

However, there are many positive ways Christians can use this technology. Gospel Communications has created a web site called Bible Gateway that not only offers a broad spectrum of translations of the Bible but has been designed so users can search topically for material. The organization also provides on-line devotionals and a selection of Christian magazines.

Planting a Seed in a Wired Center for Global Mission

Bill O'Brien, foreseeing the potential of the internet for world mission, has created a new global center for strategic mission planning at Beeson Divinity School at Samford University. Essentially, O'Brien has created a sophisticated computer database linked into World Bank and United Nations databases to enable mission strategists from all over the world to monitor information regarding global trends (wrobrien@samford.edu).

Opportunities for Christian Leaders

Christian leaders have an opportunity not only to use the emerging new technologies but to enable local churches to develop guidelines for the stewardship of these new technologies before they arrive. Christian leaders have the opportunity:

1. to establish forums in which Christians can strategize how to deal with the growing range of new ethical and theological issues that these technologies are creating, particularly regarding the changing character of human community and the character of transcendent faith.
2. to create new ways in which the new cyber-technology, including virtual reality, can be used to advance the cause of God's kingdom.

3. to design church guidelines for the stewardship of existing and emerging technologies in our homes and communities to reduce exposure of our young to violent and prurient materials in cyberspace plus create more intensive ways to nurture the young in a vital faith.

4. to create innovative ways to use the new technologies to empower the poor in our own communities and abroad.

Politics of McWorld: The Good, the Bad, and the Conspiratorial

Not only is the globalization of communications dramatically changing the ways in which we relate to one another, but it is also decisively changing how we conduct politics. One of the immediate benefits of using the net to create a global economic order is that world leaders have been motivated to work for political stability, because conflict and war are expensive and get in the way of doing business. The architects of McWorld are a major force, therefore, for peace and stability in our world.

Satellite communications, cellular phones, and photocopy and fax machines are creating de facto open societies, and totalitarian states can no longer control access to information. This, of course, helps further the cause of democratization and the movement toward the rule of law.

There are a number of people who are advocating using the internet to create a direct form of representative government. There is no question that the internet can be used to create a more participatory civil society in which citizens have more input not only within their own communities and countries but even in the shaping of global political policy making.

Planting a Seed through Internet Activism

A Nobel Peace Prize was awarded in 1997 to the international campaign to ban land mines. Jody Williams, who directed the effort, rose as early as 3:30 A.M. to answer e-mail messages from all over the world. As a direct result of this small group's lobbying on the internet, an overwhelming number of world leaders voted to ban the production and use of land mines.[12]

Eclipse of the Nation-State

The twentieth century has been called the century of the state. In the twenty-first century we will witness the declining influence of state: first, because economic globalization is rapidly eclipsing the influence of individual nations; second, because many Western nations are undergoing a process of devolution, in which power is being shifted back to more responsive local governments. The widespread movement toward privatization is one expression of this movement.

In the past five years the United States has experienced a revolution of devolution, shifting programs and controls from the federal government back to state and local governments. In Britain, Tony Blair has been a keen advocate of a devolution of power to Scotland, Wales, Northern Ireland, and throughout England as well.

An article in the *Economist* states, "Devolution is occurring in some new ways, too. Regional co-operation across old national borders [some of them are evaporating as the European Union integrates] may in time engender a new set of economics-driven loyalties that weaken the pull of old nation states . . . but without necessarily breaking them up."[13] In many nations power is indeed shifting back to the grass roots, eroding the influence of central governments everywhere.

Those on the political left and right both favor the development of strong local communities in which people have much greater control of their own destinies. These community associations have the potential to stand up not only to the totalitarian inclinations of the state but also to the growing centralizing tendencies of McWorld. And through the internet, communities with a common cause are beginning to have important influence beyond their national borders, on global policies such as human rights, religious liberty, and concern for the care of creation.

Another expression of the movement toward the decentralization of power is a worldwide movement of indigenous peoples, who have often been denied a voice in determining their own future. From the Maori in New Zealand to the Aboriginals in Australia to Native peoples in Canada and the United States, indigenous peoples are calling for just treatment in the lands of their ancestors.

Planting a Seed for Reconciliation

Ray Minniecon is an Aboriginal Christian leader who has been one of the leaders of a movement for reconciliation in Australia. Groups of Aboriginal and European [Australian] Christians visit and pray over massacre sights together, asking for God's forgiveness, reconciliation, and healing. Aboriginal Christian leaders have also found a sincere welcome among indigenous leaders in Canada and Hawaii, who are also struggling with land-claim issues. The internet has become a vital link between these leaders in their common struggle for justice.

There has been little similar effort by Christians in America to deal with the history of our crimes against Native Americans or to recognize that much of our prosperity today is a direct by-product of our appropriation of native lands. I pray that someday we can see this same widespread quest for reconciliation with Native Americans become part of the church in America. Regrettably, not all the concerns for national and ethnic self-determination in our world today are positive.

Jihad versus McWorld–Unleashing the Furies

We are witnessing a rapid rise of alienated ethnic, nationalist, and extremist groups all over the world. The most destructive expressions of this fragmentation can be seen in ethnic cleansing in Kosovo, terrorist activities in Europe, and militia movements in the United States.

Benjamin Barber states that one of the major causes in the rise of extremist groups is an almost visceral reaction to the homogenizing, modernizing, and colonizing inclinations of McWorld, which threatens to take away people's sense of identity and self-determinism.[14] I believe that these alienated groups often create for themselves distorted conspiratorial views of what has gone wrong. They then convince themselves that these challenges, real and imagined, can only be addressed by adopting extreme measures.

For instance, right-wing hate groups are becoming more visible and vocal in Germany, France, and America. "This is a global phenomenon with its strongest influence now in Europe, from the Balkans to Russia," says James Hooper, editor of *Fascism Watch*. "They are much better organized than in the U.S., and unlike the U.S., they have a formal expression through the parties of [Jean-Marie] Le Pen in France, [Gianfranco] Fini in Italy, and especially [Jörge] Haider in Austria."[15] These groups are successfully using the internet and web pages to market their message. They also produce CDs featuring their own brand of racist rock.

Five years ago white supremacist, Nazi, or militia groups in the United States might have been able to get thirty people together in a garage to ventilate their conspiratorial fears and show off their firepower. Today a small hate group can reach millions of potential new disciples on the internet. Recently, extremist groups in America have enjoyed a 20 percent increase by going on-line and targeting a broader audience.

What is particularly concerning in America is that leaders of many of these right-wing militia and white supremacist groups have bought into endtimes conspiracy theories espoused by some leaders on the religious right. And these groups are reportedly stockpiling weapons so they are ready to go to war in the year 2000 against the American government, which they are convinced is in league with European socialists to collectivize us for a one-world antichrist takeover.[16] I predict that if terrorism does increase, those who are intent on protecting the emerging global economy will take decisive, repressive action to try to quell the threat.

McWorld versus the Nation-State

McWorld's sole interest is in creating a borderless market for free trade. There is growing evidence that McWorld is, in a number of ways, eclipsing the influence of the state while showing little concern for the common good. "McWorld forges global markets rooted in consumption and profits, leaving to an untrustworthy, if not altogether fictitious, invisible hand issues of public interest and common good once nurtured by democratic citizeneries and their watchful governments," charges Benjamin Barber.[17] The traditional conservators of freedom, constitutions, and bills of rights, will be replaced, he claims, by "new temples of liberty": McDonald's and Kentucky Fried Chicken.[18]

Instead of constitutional principles guiding our political course, I believe we will see market efficiency becoming the new arbiter of justice. And I am concerned that growing numbers of citizens will seriously confuse the expanding consumer choice ushered in by McWorld with political liberty and constitutional freedom. There are different levels at which the globalization of the economy is already beginning to seriously erode national sovereignty and undermine popular consensus, from a fire in a toy factory in Bangkok to decisions made regarding the rules of international trade in Belgium.

The worst industrial fire in the history of Thailand took place in the Kader Toy Factory on the outskirts of Bangkok in 1993. It left 188 dead and 469 injured. Young workers were trapped on upper floors with no fire escapes, and their fate was sealed. Scattered among the dead in this macabre scene were soot-covered dolls: Bugs Bunny, Bart Simpson, and Big Bird.

The government in Thailand sought to force the Kader Toy Company to install minimum safety equipment, including fire escapes and a sprinkler system, when it rebuilt its factory. Corporate leaders stated that in a globalized economy, they had no intention of building safer factories in Thailand when they could open new factories in Burma or China without that concern. The government of Thailand backed off from enforcing its worker safety legislation since this tragic accident, and the number of work-related accidents in Thailand has tripled.[19]

Citizens versus the World Trade Organization

Even more concerning is the reality that we citizens are losing our ability to determine through legislation the quality of life in our own communities. Increasingly, as we pass legislation in our respective countries to protect workers and food supplies or care for the environment, these laws can be set aside by those who direct global trade.[20]

Through a series of international agreements, the World Trade Organization has been given sweeping powers over the domestic politics of nations such as Britain, Canada, and the United States. Ralph Nader charges that "under the new system, many decisions that affect billions of people are no longer to be made by local and national governments but instead, if challenged by any WTO member nation, would be deferred to a group of unelected bureaucrats. . . ." The bureaucrats can decide whether or not people in California can prevent the destruction of their last virgin forests or determine if carcinogenic pesticides can be banned from their food; or whether European countries have the right to ban the use of biotech hormones in their meat.

"Moreover, once the secret tribunals issue their edicts, no external appeals are possible; worldwide conformity is required. A country must make its laws conform or else face perpetual trade sanctions. At risk is the very basis of democracy and accountable decision making that is necessary for undergirding of any citizen struggle for sustainable, adequate living standards and health safety, and environmental protections."[21]

McWorld: The Best Government Money Can Buy

In the last chapter we witnessed the creation of huge economic behemoths that have announced that they are intent on global domination of the international marketplace. We need to realize that this growing economic domination inevitably means growing political clout. Because of their singular concern for their shareholders' investments, these corporations are under the gun not only to expand their economic influence but to politically protect their huge global investments as well.

It is important to remember that of the one hundred largest economies in the world today, fifty-one are corporations. General Motors is bigger than Denmark, Ford is bigger than South Africa, and Toyota is bigger than Norway. Wal-Mart by itself is larger than 161 countries.[22] We are likely to see a continuation of megamergers between corporations, banks, and other financial institutions, which makes shareholders happy but will also mean that these humongous corporations will seek to expand their political influence in all our societies.

Not only do the wealthy elite of these corporations have inordinate influence in all our nations; William Domhoff, in his book *Who Rules America Now?* persuasively argues that a relatively small, affluent elite is significantly overrepresented on interlocking boards and foundations and exert a high level of influence over government policy.[23] One person, one vote is largely becoming fiction in the era of big-money politics.

The cost of being elected to political office in America has soared in the last five years. It costs between $10 million to $20 million to successfully run for a seat in the U.S. Senate. In 1995 both Bill Clinton and Bob Dole set a new record, raising roughly $25 million each. In that same year, all the major presidential candidates also set a new record, raising over $110 million in private money.[24] Scarcely a week goes by that we don't hear new allegations about the illegal ways in which both Democrats and Republicans have sought to raise these huge amounts to insure their grip on power. Charles Lewis, in his important book *The Buying of the President,* documents how we have increasingly become a people whose government is run by wealthy special interests.[25] American humorist Will Rogers once observed, "We have the best government that money can buy."

McMedia Shaping Political Opinion

Those who are running McWorld have a big stake in using every facet of the new international order not only to move their products but also to shape our political views and our personal preferences. Small groups of powerful corporate interests control virtually all of the news and entertainment industry. They are also rapidly becoming the gatekeepers on the internet, so they will even control the information that private citizens are able to access.

An article in the winter 1999 issue of *Adbusters* states, "The flow of information worldwide is controlled by an ever-shrinking number of transnational media corporations led by seven giants: Time-Warner, Disney, Telecommunications, Inc. (TCI), Bertelsmann, General Electric, Viacom and Rupert Murdoch's news corporation. . . . Between them these media giants . . . have pretty well taken over the whole global mindscape and 'developed' it into a theme park—a jolly terrifyingly homogenized Las Vegas of the mind. What does freedom of speech mean in this kind of mental environment?"[26]

These "opinion makers" have become skilled at manipulating public opinion. Particularly troubling is the enormous amount of information about us that corporate interests are constantly collecting. There are serious discussions as to how to use this information to create "narrowcast" commercials targeted at people with specific profiles, not only to change their consumer preferences but also to alter their political opinions.

Robert Kaplan notes that "material possessions not only focus people toward private and away from communal life but also encourage docility. The more possessions one has, the more compromises one will make to protect them."[27]

Steven Miller raises yet another concern regarding that larger world of McMedia and the future of humanity: "As advertising and marketing become increasingly integrated into every aspect of our media-mediated culture, we will be fed an endless diet of advertorials, infomercials, and advernews—all carefully purged of anything that might annoy potential sponsors, anger important market segments, provoke public controversy, or lead us to question the overall process into which we have been drawn."[28]

Perhaps one of the reasons why there seems to be so little concern about the growing influence of the economic sector over our lives and politics is that our attitude toward the state and the free market is changing. Many Americans have an enormous and growing distrust of the state, and a swelling confidence in the free market. In fact, there are those who would turn our schools, social-service institutions, and prisons over to free-market solutions. Considering the track record of for-profit HMOs, some of us aren't that enthusiastic.

And other westerners, while not sharing this high distrust of the state, seem to share some of the optimism toward the free market. It might be helpful to put this discussion of trust in the state versus trust in the free market in a historical frame for a moment.

Utopian State versus Utopian Free Market

At the threshold of the last century there were competing notions regarding the nature of the better future to which we should aspire and the vehicle on which we should rely to transport us there, the state or the free market. These discussions bore remarkable similarity to some of our conversations today. And intriguingly, both of these views found their expression in two very different streams of nineteenth-century literature.

Looking Back on the Potential of the State

In 1887 Edward Bellamy, a Christian and a journalist, was so deeply moved by the inequities and suffering he witnessed every day in Boston that he had chronic problems sleeping at night. His distress motivated him to write a book, *Looking Backward,* that caused something of a social revolution throughout America.

Bellamy's hero, Julian West, goes to sleep in 1877, oversleeps a bit, and wakes up in the year 2000 to a Boston transformed. No longer is the city filled with entrenched poverty and suffering. No longer are families living under bridges, and no longer are children being orphaned and running in the streets. He wakes to an egalitarian modern society in which all work has dignity, everyone has opportunity, and all people are treated with respect.[29]

In response to this compelling utopian vision, people all over America started hundreds of "Bellamy groups," in which they set to work attempting to transform their own communities. The instrument that Bellamy chose to transport society to this humane new future was the state, the government. Bellamy was not only a Christian with a sensitive social conscience but a nationalist and a patriot. He truly believed that the government was capable of fashioning a more egalitarian, just, and compassionate society. This view is one expression of a stream of social

Darwinism that has been shaped by the ideas of democratic liberalism, which in turn has impacted many Western countries.

As we reach the end of the twentieth century, political conservatives, the religious right, and particularly libertarians have become hostile toward the government in the United States, in a way that is incomprehensible in Europe or Down Under. These groups are convinced that the government has no capacity to achieve anything positive in terms of promoting social change. They are particularly hostile to the utopianism and so-called social engineering of those on the Left and would have little sympathy for Edward Bellamy's vision of society transformed through the humane efforts of the state.

Looking Back on the Potential of the Free Market

Horatio Alger, a graduate of Harvard Divinity School, was also aware of the plight of the young and vulnerable in our urban communities at the end of the nineteenth century. In 1867 he wrote a book called *Ragged Dick.* In this book and in a series of others, including *Mark the Matchboy,* we are shown a different hopeful vision for the future. Alger's was an individualistic, not a corporate, vision. It certainly wasn't the vision of a new egalitarian order in which everyone had opportunity and dignity. In his utopian novel, Alger tells how a little urchin named Ragged Dick overcomes poverty and scorn to become successful and prosperous "through a little luck and a little pluck." And then because of his mythic success, Ragged Dick is able to become a protector and mentor for Mark the Matchboy and start him on the upwardly mobile quest for a life of prosperity and for the upscaling not only of his income but also of his social status.

While Bellamy's vision emphasizes a form of social Darwinism in which the state was seen as the agent that could enable society to achieve the common good, Horatio Alger was an advocate of something much more akin to economic Darwinism. He believed that the market was a more certain agent to deliver us to a better future and that we could trust the marketplace to determine winners and losers. He espoused a belief which in our globalized economy has almost been elevated by some to the state of religious dogma. He believed that if we all pursued our own economic self-interest, not only would our lives improve economically, but the condition of those around us would automatically improve as well.[30]

Those who are devoted to this viewpoint don't seem to recognize that their vision is no less utopian than that of those on the other end of the political spectrum. Nor are they able to explain the rationale behind their optimistic belief that if we create a completely free market, all boats will be raised and a future of unbelievable affluence and prosperity will be created for all peoples.

Political Centralization versus Economic Centralization

The reason for looking back to the discussion of the nineteenth century is to reflect on where this debate could take us in the twenty-first century. Frankly, I am very concerned. I share the skepticism of those who doubt that the state is capable of creating a utopia on earth. But I am equally skeptical that the free market can fashion the utopia that the apostles of McWorld promise us. Since the rise of the nation-state, we have repeatedly seen the disastrous results of the centralization of political power. We are at the threshold of witnessing the unprecedented centralization of economic power. Do we have less to fear from the centralization of economic power than from the centralization of political power?

In his book *The Spirit of Democratic Capitalism* Michael Novak states that the free market is designed "to defend efficiency, productivity, inventiveness and prosperity. It is also a defense of the free conscience—free not only in the realm of the spirit, and not only in politics, but also in the economic decisions of every day life. It is a defense of the pluralist order of democratic capitalism against the unitary and commanded order of socialism."[31] While democracy does indeed create an environment that encourages free-market capitalism, there is growing evidence that the reverse is not true.

Rob van Drimmelen points out that the Oxford Declaration on Christianity and Economics advocates that all people should have adequate decision-making opportunities for the issues that affect their lives. As we have seen, the United States, Great Britain, and a number of other nations are experiencing a devolution of political power, in which more and more decision making is moving from the central government to local municipalities and therefore into the hands of average people.

But as we have also seen, the momentum of McWorld is rapidly moving in the opposite direction. More and more political influence is moving away from local and even national centers of decision making to global economic centers in which the average person has no input at all. Donald Hay states that the "internationalization of the world economy tends to shift political and economic decision-making centers away from local levels."[32]

Free-market advocates have no trouble vividly describing the totalitarian character of centrally planned political and economic systems. But it seems to be difficult for them to realize that the creation of a global capitalist economic system could have some of the same tendencies. In his book *After 1989: Morals Revolution and Civil Society,* Ralf Dahrendorf warns, "Liberty is often at risk. The new economism of capitalists is no less illiberal than the old one of the Marxists."[33]

I don't know whether Dahrendorf is right. But I believe we need to create an international forum in which Christians from many nations can come together and have a thoughtful discussion about the future of economic globalization and the way in which it could shape our common future.

Opportunities for Christian Leaders

In light of this conversation on the changing character of politics, leaders have the opportunity

1. to create an international Christian forum to discuss how economic globalization and the centralizing of economic power could impact political systems as well as our lives and communities in the future.
2. to create ways to encourage Christians on the internet to join transnational groups of believers committed to unmasking all powers political and economic that threaten people's lives and freedoms.
3. to participate in creating civil societies where none have existed before, to give people more influence over their lives and families.
4. to become advocates for the free flow of information and to reduce the influence of powerful elites in the political forum in all countries.

Questions for Discussion and Action

1. What are creative ways in which we can use new technologies to advance the purposes of God?

2. What are some guidelines that might be helpful in enabling Christians to more responsibly steward existing technologies as well as emerging ones? How should we nurture our young in a vital faith?

3. To what extent should we trust our common future to the state? The free market? Or something else?

4. How is economic globalization likely to change the character of politics, and how should Christians respond?

A Race to the Bottom
for the Western Middle

BRYAN APPROACHED ME immediately after the Sunday morning service in a Baptist church in Wellington, New Zealand. He was obviously distressed. I had just asked, "How many people are feeling overbooked and overcommitted?" Virtually every hand in the room went up, including Bryan's. Christine and I find we get the same response whether we ask this question in a house church in London or a Presbyterian church in Philadelphia. People in all Western countries seem to be feeling mounting pressures on their lives and families.

Bryan, a forty-two-year-old engineer with a wife and three kids, told us his story. He explained that two months earlier his employer had offered him a promotion. Since it provided an opportunity for advancement and a small increase in pay, Bryan took it. The condition for the promotion was that he work not only harder but longer. His new position required him to increase his work hours from fifty to seventy hours a week. He suddenly woke up to the fact that he has little time left to spend with his wife and kids. He also belatedly realized that he needed to resign his responsibility on the church council and counts himself fortunate when he can make it to church once in a while.

Bryan also shared that in order to increase productivity, he is under pressure from management to persuade his new staff to ratchet up their hours at work from fifty to seventy hours a week, without an increase in pay. Bryan said, "I am feeling very guilty both for the impossible situation I have created for myself and my family and for the pressure I am supposed to put on my staff."

Do you know what Bryan and his family are going through? Are you among those who never seem to have enough hours in the day, or enough coins in the cookie jar to make ends meet, as we race into a McWorld future?

Finding the Focus

In the last chapter we saw how our global society is being wired together into a new cyber-community in which our political influence is both growing and diminishing at the same time. In this chapter I will identify some of the hidden costs of economic globalization for those of us on the middle rungs of the economic ladder, and particularly for our young. The intent of this chapter is to enable those in leadership to help their members and their members' children to get ready for the new opportunities and challenges that are likely to confront them in a new millennium.

Welcome to the McWorld Macromall

According to the United Nations' *Human Development Report,* "World consumption has expanded at an unprecedented pace over the 20th century, with private and public consumption . . . reaching $24 trillion in 1998, twice the level of 1975 and six times that of 1950."[1] One of the most remarkable achievements is the rate at which McWorld has created a global macromall in which the wealthy and those of us on the middle rungs have been presented with an incredible and exploding array of consumer choice.

Without leaving home, we can shop on-line, purchasing digital TVs from Korea, Parma hams from Italy, or elegant jewelry from Tiffany's in New York. Those on the middle rungs are consuming as never before. For example, home sales in the United States reached a thirty-five-year high.[2]

McWorld Wants More of Your Life and Money

Expanding Our Appetite for More

We have experienced a decade of incredible economic growth in the United States, Canada, and Britain. Not only the wealthy but also many of us in the middle class have benefited from this long boom. What will be required to enable the entire global economic order to experience the level of growth that shareholders all over the world have come to expect? There simply won't be enough growth in developing markets to make it happen. What it will require is for all of us, and particularly our kids and grandkids, to dramatically increase our appetite for more.

In his provocative book *The End of Work,* Jeremy Rifkin recalls how in the 1920s corporations began designing a strategy to motivate us all to want more. They invented a market strategy to create a permanent class of "dissatisfied consumers." Until then most people were quite content if they were able to meet their essential human needs. Once people reached that point, their rate of consumption leveled off.

Consumers being satisfied with enough has always been a serious problem to those who want to promote a high level of economic growth. Economist John Kenneth Gailbraith stated that the new mission of business, therefore, was to "create the wants it seeks to satisfy."[3] And the only way in which it is possible to create new wants is to persuade people to change their values. Over the past seventy years the corporate world has succeeded brilliantly in persuading us to change our values and our wants, and the church has hardly seemed to notice.

In recent years marketers have discovered an effective way to persuade us to increase our appetite for more. They have sought to convince us that in addition to the basic human needs of air, water, food, and shelter, we all have a fifth human need: the need for novelty, "the need throughout our life for a continuous variety in external stimulation of our eyes, ears, sense or organs and all our nervous network."[4] And by far the majority of us, including people of faith, seem to have bought this propaganda. In this constant quest for novelty, we have accepted McWorld's claim that yesterday's luxuries are today's necessities.

It isn't surprising that we succumb. Over any twenty-four-hour period we are assaulted with an average of three thousand messages that seek to persuade us that we are inadequate if we don't purchase the newest novelty.[5] Before children enter first grade, they will be exposed to over thirty thousand advertisements not only to give them an appetite for novelty but also to decisively shape their worldview. The message of the McWorld "consumer church" couldn't be clearer: "The ultimate meaning of human existence is getting all this stuff."[6]

Spending More in the McWorld Macromall

It isn't enough to persuade us to expand our appetite for more. The pied pipers of McWorld are constantly fashioning novel ways to convince people to spend more, too. Coming soon to a megamall near you: "shoppertainment." Listen to this testimony of a satisfied shopper: "I've just survived 12 straight hours of . . . 'shoppertainment.' . . . I rescued comrades from deep space via virtual reality . . . stood eyeball to eyeball with live bobcats, lizards, and badgers . . . got jostled into pulp in a flight simulator . . . participated in a movie rather than merely watching one . . . destroyed fake temples . . . rode fake jet skis, and a skate board on a fake obstacle course."[7]

The news from the new Ontario Mills Mall in southern California couldn't be better for the corporations who bring us McWorld and for their shareholders. The typical visitor to Ontario Mills Mall spends three hours and $167 per trip. Reportedly, that is a $100 more per head than a visitor would currently spend at an old-fashioned mall.[8] I don't know about you, but I can hardly wait until they build one of these new malls in our neighborhood.

McWorld has even found a way to move their macromalls into cyberspace. Their new on-line free-for-all auction welcomes the grasping and the brutal. "Not so fast, TR, you overweight lardo." That not very polite message appeared recently on On Sale, an internet web site that auctions everything from computer gear to Omaha steaks. Civility takes a backseat to acquisitiveness as net surfers wrangle over everything. "People are bidding on nose hair trimmers," says a bewildered Kirk Loevner, president and chief executive of Internet Shopping Network. "It's just bizarre."[9] Increasingly, McWorld is drawing in our lives so it can auction off everything in sight, and there is evidence that this is already changing our notion of what is important and of value.

Flash: More Doesn't Happiness Make

There is growing evidence that even though we are consuming much more from all over our shrinking global village, it isn't making us happier. Just the contrary. Sixty percent of successful professionals report that they are suffering from chronic stress and depression. Forty-eight percent of top corporate executives report that their lives are empty and meaningless. For the past twenty-five years the American Index of Social Health has tracked the well-being of Americans. While the gross domestic product has risen continually for the past twenty-five years, the social health index is fully 52 percent lower than it was in 1973.[10] Is the long-boom future to which McWorld promises to transport us really going to satisfy our deepest human longings?

The High Cost of More on Family Life

Australian commentator Bob Santamaria insists it isn't an accident that families are feeling more pressured. He contends the global economy has declared war on the family. He points out that the take-home salary of the average production worker in the United States is lower than it was twenty-five years ago. "At first, American families, believing this was only a temporary phenomenon, adapted. High consumption levels were maintained. This was possible because family income was 'stretched' on the one hand by the depletion of savings, by the increase in borrowing—particularly through the growth of consumer credit—and partly by the de facto conscription of married women into the work force. Marriages were postponed. Birth rates were lower. Household savings declined. Families went into debt."[11] Let's look at how much this race to the top is costing average families.

The High Cost of Buying More Than You Can Afford

One of the immediate consequences of persuading those on the middle rungs to continually ratchet up their level of consumption in the global macromall is that we aren't saving for a rainy day nearly as much as we used to. In the United States, savings have fallen from 8 percent to an all-time low of .02 percent. Total household debt in America has soared to $5.4 trillion. The share of disposable income that households must pay simply to service debt has risen by 18 percent.[12]

The average consumer debt load per household was $38,734 in 1990. It rose to $50,529 in 1995 and is projected to reach over $65,000 by the year 2000.[13] In 1996 1.1 million Americans declared personal bankruptcy. That was a 29 percent jump from 1995, and new records are still being set.[14] On the one hand, financial institutions want to continue making it easy for people, including those who aren't good risks, to secure credit and receive bankcards, and on the other hand, they want to make it tougher for people to file for bankruptcy protection.[15] These financial corporations refuse to take any responsibility for their heavy-handed marketing techniques. And the young, who are most vulnerable, are being swamped with credit cards, as are many who are in continual economic crisis.

McWorld Wants More of Our Time

In this increasingly competitive global economy, McWorld wants not only more of our money but also more of our time. We find that employers from Liverpool to Los Angeles expect their employees, like Bryan, to work longer and harder. In 1977 less than half of all families in the United States relied on dual incomes. Today the proportion of dual-income families has dramatically increased to two-thirds and is still climbing. Some women are working simply to help pay the bills and keep their families afloat. Some are working to be able to buy extras.[16]

For a number of years not only the American poor but also the American middle class have been losing ground economically. The level of income has not kept pace with the rate of inflation. But in 1997, for the first time in years, American income for a typical household rose by 1.2 percent. "After years of salary stagnation in the early 1990's the American household was better off for the second straight year in a row—though admittedly, it was still 3% worse off than it had been in 1989," according to the *Economist*.[17] What isn't clear is whether the recent upturn is an indication that middle-class incomes are finally leaving a long period of chronic stagnation or whether it can be explained by the fact that people are taking on additional part-time work.

Juliet Schor, in her book *The Overworked American,* tells us that middle-income, dual-earner families with two children were spending 6,500 hours at work in 1995, up from 5,000 hours in 1969.[18] One of the reasons these spouses are spending more hours at work is because employers are pressuring their employees to spend more time on the job.

According to *Money* magazine, we now also have a new phenomenon: the four-income family. "Just about every American knows that the one-earner Ozzie and Harriet family doesn't live here anymore. Today, however, a growing rank of the middle class is realizing that the two-career couple of the '70s and '80s is giving way to the four-income household of the '90s.

"Simply put, it can now take four—or more—jobs to provide the level of comfort and financial security that one income delivered only a few decades ago. As a result many Americans are working 55 or more hours a week. Since 1980, the number of Americans who hold more than one job has grown by 54% to more than 7 million, or almost 6% of the labor force according to the U.S. Bureau of Labor Statistics."[19]

"'The economy is creating tens of thousands of new jobs, that's the good news,' says a man looking up from his newspaper. 'So what's the bad news?' he is asked. 'To support a family you'll need three.'"[20] The poor and the young are the ones who are having particular difficulty making it economically on only one McJob.

Bottom line, people in Western countries are spending more time at work, so they have significantly less time left for other things, including things of faith. The Harris Poll reports that the average American spent forty-one hours per week at work in 1973. In 1997 that had increased ten hours to fifty-one hours per week.[21] That represents a loss of ten hours of discretionary time. As we gallop into a new millennium, McWorld will insist that we spend even more of our waking hours at work. That means we will have less time for family and friends, less time to pray and study Scripture, and less time to volunteer to address the mounting needs of the poor in our societies.[22]

McWorld Wants More of the Life and Money of the Young

Branding the Young

"You must get kids branded by age 5 if you want to have them as faithful consumers of your product," admonished a marketing executive in a corporate training session. The footage of this training session was included in a compelling documentary on consumerism called *Affluenza*, which aired on PBS.[23]

"What I wanna, wanna, really wanna be," sings Cyndy, a four-year-old, as she is getting ready for Sunday school in her home in Birmingham, England. The Spice Girls seem to be the first popular music group to sell four-, five-, and six-year-olds on "girl power" and brand them with their label.[24] A primary-schoolteacher in the north of England told me that students ridicule classmates who aren't wearing acceptable corporate logos on their clothing.

In North America, corporations have created a fund-raising gimmick to get into the schools and brand kids with their logos. The program, which started several years ago, is called "Tattoo You Too!" Appealing to the current tattoo craze, corporations offer schools a certain amount of money for each child they can brand with a temporary tattoo, such as the Nike "swoosh" or a grinning Joe Camel, on his or her arm. "The companies . . . are pleased with the response. Brad Randolph, industry insider, said, 'This is wonderful. It delights me to see that so many people's lives are enriched by such an innovative program.'"[25]

Generation Y Programmed to Want More

Generation Y is the front edge of what demographers call the baby boomlets. The baby boomers—seventy-seven million strong, born from 1946 to 1964—have been busy having kids. While the generation that followed them, the baby busters—born from 1964 to 1983—contains only fifty-five million people, the baby boomlets comprise seventy-two million very active young people.[26]

Madison Avenue has dubbed the twenty-seven million thirteen- to nineteen-year-olds who are the front edge of this population generation Y. Marketers describe them as "America's most free-spending, jobless and unskilled laborers who finance their role of arbiters of cool with ever greater amounts of disposable cash." Robert Williams, executive director at the Rand Youth Poll, stated, "They have a higher incremental allowance from their parents, and with growth in the service economy, they're able to secure jobs easily and at rising minimum wages. They're exposed to so many different products on TV, in the mall and through their friends. It's a generation who grew up with excess as a norm."[27] Recent research indicates that of the 5.5 million pathological gamblers in America, 1.1 million are adolescents twelve to seventeen years of age, and tragically, their numbers are growing.[28]

In addition to marketing their wares to this generation through the media, the internet, and the mall, corporations are also gaining a firm foothold in our schools. For example, tobacco companies are providing schools with educational materials on smoking. Many educators justify the slow McDonaldization of the school on the grounds that it saves money.

Since 1969 Dr. Alexander Astin has been taking a survey snapshot of freshman students. In the early seventies about 70 percent of young people went to college to develop a meaningful philosophy of life. Today 75 percent of freshmen in McWorld go to college to be very well off financially, and the ratio of students who go to college to develop a meaningful philosophy of life has dropped to 40 percent. While working with a Baptist campus ministry in Tennessee, I asked a junior what his major was, and he told me he was a "pre-wealth major." More and more of our young people, including Christian young people, believe that the ultimate goal of life is to get ahead economically.[29] While some are doing smashingly well in this boom economy, many others are not.

Western Young and the Race to the Bottom

While unemployment among young adults in parts of Europe is as high as 40 percent, there is little shortage of work for young people in Britain and the United States. But much of it is McJobs or temporary positions. And the temp agencies not only do not offer benefits or health care; you can't even get sick. If you get sick, you get canned.

However, it is a different story for young people with degrees in business and computer science. They are in high demand. Norm Ewert, a professor of economics at Wheaton College, said he has never seen such a demand for college graduates in those fields. And as they are starting out, these young people are as economically comfortable as some of their poorer cousins are economically insecure. But many of our young people are hitting the economy at a difficult time. And there is virtually no one in our churches, Christian colleges, or campus ministries who is preparing them for the economic realities they are likely to face in a new millennium.

Recently when I spoke at Biola University, I ran into a disturbing number of students graduating with debts ranging from $20,000 to $60,000. For those who want to get involved in mission work, it will be out of the question for at least a decade. We are running into more and more young people from Britain and New Zealand who are beginning to graduate with school debt, too.

The relationship between what young people earn and what they can buy has changed drastically since I graduated from a Christian college in 1958. The annual cost then for tuition, fees, books, and room and board was seven hundred dollars a year. I had no problem paying that amount by working as a janitor during the summer. In the intervening forty years, educational costs have soared to more than twenty times what I paid. But summer jobs today pay roughly only double the amount what I earned in the late fifties. As a consequence, it is impossible for the young today to earn enough from a summer job to pay their annual schooling costs.

The relationship between what the young earn and what they are able to afford in housing has also dramatically changed since I was a young man. The first house I bought in 1961 was a fully restored four-bedroom home in Portland, Oregon, with two and a half baths, a huge front porch, and a full basement. An older couple had added a modern kitchen and bath, put in new wiring and plumbing, and painted this beautiful old bungalow inside and out. The price was $14,500. My monthly payment was only $100 a month. I had no trouble making that payment on a welfare-level salary of $4,800 a year, working for Cascade College, where I had graduated.

Today the same house would probably sell for over $400,000—more than twenty times what I paid. But two young people today with good incomes would have difficulty even qualifying for a loan on a mortgage of that size. As my wife and I work with young couples in Great Britain, New Zealand, Australia, Canada, and the United States, we find that more and more of them are spending over half of their income on rent or mortgage payments.

In America, where we have no government health coverage, there are over forty million people who are uninsured. I am discovering that many of these are young people. They are betting they won't need health coverage. When they are wrong, the result can be financial ruin; the leading cause of foreclosure is inability to pay medical bills. In other words, today's young in many Western countries—certainly in America—will never have the economic lifestyle they were raised with.

The decline in generational income is documented in a book titled *The State of Working America 1996–1997*. "The average income of families headed by someone under 25 declined at an annual rate of 2.4% from 1979 to 1989 and 1.8% from 1989 to 1995. These young families in 1994 had $6,148 less income to spend in real dollars than their 1967 counter parts had when they were starting out."[30] In fact, there is growing concern that because many of these young people have so little left for savings, they will have few resources on which to retire. This means that those under thirty-five are likely to have significantly less time and money to contribute to the work of God's kingdom than did older generations.

Coming Soon: A Blended, Borderless New Generation

Blending of the West

This generation will also be the most racially blended, borderless generation we have ever seen. Birmingham, England; Auckland, New Zealand; and Los Angeles, California, are cities that are examples of the blended future into which all Western countries are headed. However, the United States is well on its way to becoming the first truly universal nation. Non-Hispanic whites made up 73.1 percent of the population in 1996. That proportion is likely to fall to 52.8 percent by 2050, and after that it won't be very long until the United States becomes the first predominantly nonwhite Western nation.[31] And generation Y is the front edge of this demographic wave. We need to prepare the young and the church for a blended future by raising our young in multicultural communities and developing close relationships with families and congregations from other ethnic backgrounds.

McWorld Celebrating the Creation of a Borderless Youth Market

The marketers of McWorld are celebrating the fact that for the first time in history they have created a borderless youth market in which they can sell their Nikes, Marilyn Manson videos, and Coke anywhere on the globe. Shampoo Planet is a book by Douglas Coupland that describes this generation as the first borderless generation. The reason for the marketers' brilliant success in "evangelizing" this borderless youth is that they have found ways not just to sell the young their products but to change their values so they want to buy their products. "These kids have the same interests whether they're in New York, London, L.A. or a small town in Indiana," says Jeanine Misdom, a youth marketing consultant.

This class of young consumers is being heavily conditioned to acquire appetites for homogeneous McWorld products that transcend local customs, values, or tastes. Marketers gleefully report that "they are all increasingly prone to the same influences in music, food and fashion—easily transported across national boundaries through CDs, MTV, Hollywood and multi-national franchises. The Internet has only hastened the shift."[32]

What isn't generally realized is that we are going backward, not forward, in world evangelization. Peter Brierley of the Christian Research Association reports that 28 percent of the world's people identify themselves as some brand of Christian: Protestant, Catholic, or Orthodox. Because population growth is outstripping our best efforts, this proportion will decline to 27 percent in 2010 and continue to decline after that.[33] The people who are doing a brilliant job at world "evangelization" are the marketers of McWorld, who are persuading the young everywhere to change their values so they will all buy the same soda, watch the same MTV videos, and wear the same clothing.

As my wife and I travel in Britain, Australia, and New Zealand, it is astonishing to see the success that McWorld is having in blaring American pop culture into every corner of the world. The Golden Arches are everywhere. Billboards scream the latest Hollywood hit. American cultural colonization for a new borderless youth market is relentless.

Gail Griffith, writing about this troubling global phenomenon, wonders aloud, "When policy analysts in the coming century look back on this final decade of the 20th century, they will wonder how our leaders could have so underestimated the impact of popular culture on the rapid pace of social and cultural change around the globe. How could we have missed the clues—some measured in decibels—as the younger generation came to embrace wholesale the values espoused in Western pop culture?"[34]

McWorld and the Graying of the Middle Class

Cutting Back Support for the Middle Class

Not only does McWorld want more of our time and money, and that of our young; this new globalized economy is bringing pressure on governments in the United States, Canada, Britain, Australia, and New Zealand to reduce their funding for programs that serve the middle class. In this brutally competitive race to the top, all Western nations are cutting back their programs intended to serve the middle class, which means we will all be forced to use more of our shrinking discretionary time and money to provide for the costs of education, health care, and retirement.

As we have seen, governments throughout the West are shifting more of the cost of public education back onto the middle class. Therefore, it is reasonable to predict that Western young will continue to graduate with heavy debt burdens.

Commonwealth countries still have government-financed health care programs for all their citizens, but those are on the chopping block as well. "In Britain an aging population, more expensive and sophisticated treatment and the Conservative Government's systematic cost-cutting have stretched the health service's budget to the breaking point. Last year Dr. Sandy Macara, the medical association's president, compared the health service to the Titanic, and said it would need billions more pounds in Government financing to keep it from sinking."[35]

Contending with the Challenges of the Graying of the West

The rapid graying of the population is hitting both the health and pension systems hard in all industrialized countries. In America and most industrialized countries, the boomer population is by far the largest generation. In the United States there are seventy-seven million boomers. The most terrifying word in the boomer vocabulary is *bifocal*. They live in absolute terror of moving into the bifocal phase of life. Really, the aging of the boomer generation is going to be a terror for all of us.

The boomer population will begin retiring in 2010, which will make the problems in Social Security and Medicare acute if we don't get them fixed before then. By the time the last boomer retires in 2030, the situation could be calamitous. Politicians are trying to avoid the issue because trying to fix it could prove unbelievably expensive.

Martha Phillips, executive director of the Concord Coalition, offers one forecast of how bad it could become in the United States. She states that the trustees of the Social Security system are now predicting a $233 billion deficit in 2030 between benefits paid and income to the fund. Covering this deficit in the present system would require that a 38 percent increase in FICA taxes be dedicated to Social Security. In 2013 Social Security's annual expenditures will begin to exceed the annual tax income. Phillips says that if we wait this long, "there will be only three choices, none attractive: raise taxes, reduce government spending, or borrow approximately $7 trillion between 2013 and 2033."[36]

Without major alterations, none of our Western pension systems will be able to survive the onslaught of the graying of the boomers. And younger generations could get stuck with the bill. As with health care cutbacks, I think we will see Western governments encouraging their citizens to assume increasing responsibility for creating their own private retirement schemes, which will have an additional negative impact on people's discretionary time and money.

In his 1996 sci-fi novel *Holy Fire,* Bruce Sterling envisions a future world ruled by an all-powerful gerontocracy. This group appropriates most of the world's wealth to design ever more expensive life-extension technologies. We already live in a world in which those over forty-five control the lion's share of the world's wealth. And they are thoroughly enjoying spending it on love-boat cruises, luxury automobiles, and high cuisine. While the majority who are enjoying a privileged retirement are white, the young who will be asked to pick up the tab are increasingly going to be nonwhite.

You can be sure that boomers, the so-called youth generation, will not go easily into the night. They are already setting records in turning to hormones, nutritional supplements, and plastic surgery to hold back the aging process. Nutritional and lifestyle research has demonstrated that individuals can achieve modest gains in life extension by taking better care of themselves. And the boomers are going for it.

Recent breakthroughs in cellular research indicate that it could be possible to reset the aging clock. Essentially, the aging process is brought on by the failure of human cells to keep dividing. This leads to the onset of disease and eventually death. Biologists at the Geron Corporation in Menlo Park, California, and the University of Texas's Southwestern Medical School altered human cells in a way that enabled them to break the limit of their natural life span. This technique could lead not only to the extension of human life but to the growth of new tissues, arteries, or even new retinal cells for a person afflicted with blindness.[37]

You can imagine how excited many boomers are by this news. But imagine the economic chaos it will mean for health care and pension systems that are inadequate for the challenges of existing mortality rates. The science fiction scenario might turn out to be more on target than the author intended. The rapid graying of America and other Western countries could cause a major downturn in our economies.

Those of us on the middle rungs of the economic ladder are undoubtedly going to benefit in terms of affluence if the long boom continues. But I am afraid that affluence could come at a high price for many of us, particularly the young. Many people will get busier, become more locked into the consumer culture, sink more deeply in debt, and stray farther from their spiritual moorings. For many of us, the race to the top may well be a race to the bottom.

Planting a Seed through Movie Decoding

To counter the media blitz of pop McWorld culture, we need to become skilled at decoding the messages that constantly bombard us. Teaching a Fuller Seminary class in leadership development, I invited students to view three movies from three generations to unpack the cultural values implicit in each film. First we viewed *The Wizard of Oz,* which was from the "silent generation" (those over sixty). The students did an excellent job of unpacking the values of Oz: the importance of looking good, and "There's no place like home." The film we watched from the boomer generation was the Beatles' *Yellow Submarine.* The students, most of whom were from generation X, were able to identify the sixties values of love, peace, and tranquility, but they expressed frank hatred for them and missed a lot of the symbolism. The final film *Lawn Mower Man,* was from their generation. They all loved this dark fantasy, even though they identified the values of power, destruction, and ego displayed in the film. This exercise proved to the students that it's useful for all of us to decode the messages that come at us through popular media, so we can deal with them.

Planting a Seed in Seattle

One of the many reasons Americans are running up such large debt loads is that many of us spend an excessive amount at Christmas. Reportedly, half of all Americans were still paying for 1996 Christmas spending in 1997, and 28 percent were still paying off those bills in October 1997. Scott Jones in Seattle was concerned about how much his family spent not only at Christmas but throughout the year. As an orthopedic surgeon, he was also concerned about the amount of time he spent at work. Scott decided to cut his schedule back to three-quarter time, and he and his family decided to stop spending money on Christmas consumerism. The Jones family found resources, such as the Alternative Celebration Catalogue, that helped them learn alternative gift giving at Christmas and throughout the year, so they made gifts for those they cared about.[38] In the same spirit, one Christmas I gave my two grown sons a family history including video recordings of both of my parents sharing their stories about growing up in the twenties and thirties, getting married, and starting their families.

Planting a Seed in New Zealand

The major debt most families struggle with is the mortgage, and for many Christian young, as we saw, it is becoming a huge burden. Two Baptist churches in Whakatane, New Zealand, came up with a creative way for the body of Christ in their community to work together to help members, not only so they can be free from the mortgage trap but also so they can have more of their lives back to invest in mission work to assist those in need.

The seeds of the Liberty Trust were sown in 1988. Essentially, families who join this cooperative contribute $10 (New Zealand dollars) weekly per $25,000 of their unpaid mortgage. As the fund grows, a ballot is held to determine which family receives an interest-free loan for the balance of their mortgage. Once a family receives an interest-free loan, they continue to make contributions to the fund until the loan is paid off. The average waiting time to win a loan is eight years. Over that time, a family would typically invest about $20,000 in the fund, but when their turn comes, they wind up saving roughly $100,000 in interest. To date, the cooperative has given out fifty interest-free mortgages.[39] For information, you can contact John Bartley at: jbartley@wave.co.nz. There are countless creative ways in which we can help the people of God join the mustard seed conspiracy, if we use our imaginations.

A Christian Disconnection between Materialism and Faith

William J. Bennett, former U.S. secretary of education, raises serious questions about whether this economic race to the top is able to satisfy our deepest longings or whether it is destructive to our lives and spirit. "More than ever before, thanks largely to mass marketing, to television, and to the unbridled and omnipresent market capitalism, we are constantly pushing our children and adults to buy things— things they don't need. As a result we are not living at the center. We are misreading the essential human condition, because if we are actually moral and spiritual beings . . . then we ought to act in ways which are consonant with that reality." Tony Campolo shares similar concerns. "I believe we will be likely to find that capitalism's corrosive materialism will destroy us every bit as much as the materialism of Leninist Communism."[40]

I think they are both right. I think that in some fundamental ways, this race to the top is a race to the bottom. While Christians may on occasion rail at consumerism and materialism, research shows there is almost no connection between our religious faith and how we steward our resources. In 1995, in fact, the Pew Charitable Trust funded a study of American Protestants. "Most striking were Protestant attitudes about materialism and television," said Chris Smith, professor of religious studies at the University of North Carolina, in Chapel Hill. While respondents consistently decried materialism and consumerism, they defined problems in such a way that excluded their own behavior.[41]

Robert Wuthnow, in his book *God and Mammon in America,* found much the same result. There appears to be a major disconnection between people's religious beliefs and how they use money. It is an expression of Western dualism and reflects a failure of the church of virtually all traditions to enable believers to develop a biblical view of stewardship. Wuthnow writes, "If a single word had to be used to describe the relationship between religion and money, however, it would be compartmentalization. . . . There is a kind of mental or emotional gloss to contemporary religious teachings about money that prevents them from having much impact on how people actually lead their lives."[42]

One major reason for this crisis is that there are virtually no forums in our churches to help people connect how they use their time and money to their faith. There are no forums in which we can help one another make biblically informed decisions about how much time to spend at work, how much income to spend on the latest consumer novelties, or how many activities our kids should sign up for. We seem content to let modern culture dictate the terms of our lives, and the church gets the leftovers.

Opportunities for Christian Leaders

Christian leaders have the opportunity to prepare middle-class members of churches and organizations and their young to live in a future in which the promoters of McWorld are going to want more of our time and money. And these marketers know that the only way they can increase our appetite for more is to persuade us to change what we value. Therefore, Christian leaders have the opportunity

1. to recognize that we are in a battle for the hearts and minds of a new generation outside the church that is powerfully attracted to the seductions of the McWorld macromall. We will need to create new approaches to evangelism that recognize and counter the seductions of this borderless consumer culture.

2. to enable church members, and particularly their young people, to recognize that we are also in a contest with a secularism we seldom discuss. We need to institute courses in our churches to help people decode the messages, reduce consumption, and get out of debt as quickly as possible so they have more of their lives to invest in the work of the gospel. As part of this initiative, we will need to help people reevaluate their life priorities in light of faith and create communities of resistance to enable them not only to resist the seductions of McWorld but to discover in Scripture an alternative to the aspirations and addictions of modern culture.

3. to create forums to enable Christians to fundamentally reinvent their lifestyles so they can not only resist the pressures of modern culture but also create a more festive way of life in which they are able to free up more time and money to invest in the work of God's kingdom.

4. to enable particularly the Christian young to develop a plan, before they graduate, as to how they can intentionally put God's purposes first in deciding where they work and how many hours they work, as well as how they steward their time and money.

5. to reexamine the expectations of local churches regarding how much time their members can give to church services, to insure that these expectations are essential to the nurture of faith and the advance of God's mission in our communities.

6. to persuade Christian organizations that they can no longer simply ask constituents for their leftovers and expect giving to be constant or to grow. The only way to expand giving in the third millennium, I am convinced, is to conduct stewardship education that challenges the seductions of our consumer culture and offers creative alternatives.

7. to enable churches and Christian organizations to get ready for the rapid graying of our societies in Europe, North America, and Down Under. We need to create ways to use the growing volunteer capability of graying boomers while preparing for the economic impact of their reduced economic support for the church after 2010.

Questions for Discussion and Action

1. In what specific ways are you overcommitted and overbooked, and what are some creative ways in which you can reduce the pressure?

2. In what specific ways are the messages of McWorld influencing you and your children to increase your appetite for more? What are ways in which you can counter these messages?

3. How can the local church create a curriculum to enable members to steward their lives to put first things first?

4. How can we help the Christian young, while they are in high school or college, to develop a life plan that enables them to create a less expensive way of life so they have more time and resources to make a difference for God's kingdom?

5. How can we enable the growing number of seniors in our society to reorder their lifestyles to use the remainder of their lives to put God's purposes first?

6. What resources should churches and Christian organizations design to help Christians counter the messages of the consumer culture and learn to steward their lives in a way that more authentically reflects the aspirations of God's mustard seed instead of the addictions of McWorld?

A Race to the Bottom
for the Global Poor

A GIGANTIC ORANGE SUN begins its descent into Lake Victoria as John Otieno stands patiently in line at the back door of the Euro Fish Factory. John, his wife, Beatrice, and their four children live on the edge of Lake Victoria in Uganda. He has just completed twelve hours of hard work on a road construction project, moving boulders and preparing the roadbed. In a good month, when work is regular, he makes eighty dollars. In addition to caring for her young children, Beatrice works in a community garden plot to grow vegetables for her family's diet. She also does chores for neighbors, which brings in another ten to fifteen dollars a month to help the family income.

The Otienos live on the edge of an urban slum in a small two-room hut that costs them twenty-five dollars a month. A single lightbulb suspended from the ceiling costs them seven dollars a month, and kerosene for their cooking stove costs another eight to ten dollars a month. They spend an additional three to four dollars a month to purchase water from a neighborhood standpipe. In other words, this family spends roughly half their meager income for shelter and utilities, leaving little for food, medicine, and the education of their two oldest children, who are in a public school.

The Otienos attend a local Anglican church and have been praying for God's help to make ends meet. But in the last three years, their situation seems to be steadily getting worse. One of the major changes for them is a serious decline in the quality of their diet. Until three years ago they budgeted their funds to buy fresh fish twice a week from local fishermen. This enabled Beatrice to supplement their sparse rice-and-vegetable diet with a little protein. But globalization has changed all that for the Otienos and thousands of their neighbors who live near Lake Victoria.

The local fishermen used to sell their Nile perch filets for one dollar a kilogram (2.20 pounds). But in the past three years the price of fish has increased more than fourfold, and the Otienos and many others can no longer afford to buy it. They are concerned about how to provide an adequate diet for their four children.

The reason fish prices have soared beyond reach is no mystery. After the 1986 takeover of Uganda by the forces of Yoweri Museveni, the new leader developed some close relationships with European investors. A number of these investors live in areas of northern Europe in which, over the past four decades, fish supplies have been depleted by overfishing. When these investors learned of the bountiful resources in Lake Victoria, they entered into an agreement with the Ugandan government to build fish factories on the edge of the lake. Reportedly, they are buying, processing, and flying two hundred tons of fish a week from Lake Victoria to dinner tables in Europe.

John stands in line at one of these fish factories with his neighbors to buy the bones and fish heads, since they can no longer afford the fish harvested by their own fishermen from their own lake. One of the cardinal doctrines of the new religion of free trade is that everyone on the planet has to be allowed to fish in everyone else's pond. The advocates of this doctrine insist that if everyone is allowed to own the banks and phone systems and harvest the fish in other people's countries, eventually it will work out to everyone's benefit.

But it is difficult to understand how this will work. For example, America's preference for white chicken meat has produced a glut of chicken legs that United States producers can't sell in the United States. So they are dumping them at low prices in Haiti and other countries. This practice is threatening to destroy the local poultry industry in Haiti because it can't compete with these giveaway prices. How will this kind of globalization ever work out for the Otienos in Uganda or for the chicken growers in Haiti?

Finding the Focus

In the last chapter I examined the ways globalization is likely to impact the lives of those of us in the middle class and looked at new challenges and opportunities it presents the church. In this chapter I will focus on how those on the lower economic rungs of our global economic ladder, such as the Otienos, are likely to be impacted by globalization. I will specifically try to identify new needs, challenges, and opportunities that are likely to confront the global and American poor as we rush into a new millennium, and to identify the implications for a Christian response.

Starting with the Good News

There is a great deal of good news that we need to celebrate regarding the global poor. Child mortality rates have been steadily improving since 1960. As a result, life expectancy is rising in almost every country on earth. Immunization is on the threshold of eliminating diseases such as measles and polio. Per capita global income is also beginning to rise in most countries, and global population growth is beginning to slow. God has been influencing people, churches, and organizations all over the world to help our poorest neighbors to help themselves. Over and over it is often the small mustard seed projects that are most effective in enabling those on the margins to not only improve their local economies but also transform their lives and communities.

One of the positive aspects of globalization is that the United Nations and a number of Christian organizations are beginning to build new partnerships with corporations to enable poorer communities to participate in the global economic liftoff. World Vision is one of the first to experiment with such collaboration.

It is important to stress that those who are spearheading the globalization of the economy have no interest in seeing anyone excluded from the global economic liftoff. And there is mounting evidence that recent global economic growth has benefited many poor and marginalized people in the Two-Thirds World. However, millions of those who benefited from the liftoff in Asia are struggling for their very survival again as most of Asia struggles to overcome the recent economic meltdown. In spite of the global liftoff, many of the world's poor are being left behind. And we will see that the global race to the top seems to favor those with assets; it is a tough race for those without them.

A Rising Tide Lifts All Boats?

"A rising tide lifts all boats, they say. But America's soaring stock market has inevitably benefited the rich, who own more shares of stock. The richest 1 percent of Americans, who earn over $225,000 a year or have assets of more than $3 million, have enjoyed an increase of 70 percent in the value of their shares since 1993. This has helped raise their net wealth by 43 percent," according to the *Economist*.[1] The leaders of

McWorld continue to insist that this race to the top will indeed raise all boats. But the evidence consistently shows that the shareholders who have benefited most from this global liftoff are the very wealthy.

Forbes provides an annual snapshot of those who are thoroughly enjoying this race to the top. When the magazine started this annual feature in 1982, there were thirteen billionaires in the United States. In 1997 there were 170. Over the same period, the net worth of those who are admitted to what is called the Forbes Four Hundred has quintupled to over $475 million each. "If wealth isn't compounding . . . it is certainly growing at a faster clip than at any other time in history. Last year on average Bill Gates' net wealth grew by an astounding $400 million every week. Michael Dell's net worth increased five fold, to $5.5 billion."[2]

Before his latest retirement, Michael Jordan took over $65 million to the bank every year. CEOs are bringing home outrageously high salary packages that often seem to have little relationship to job performance. Glenn Pascall reports that "thanks to stock options, chief executive officers at the 1,000 largest companies receive compensation equal to 336 times the average employee, according to the latest *Business Week* survey. That's up from 240 times a decade ago. The survey found no link between CEO pay and performance."[3]

We are witnessing the creation of a two-tier society in Western countries. The very wealthy new elite from Britain, the United States, and Australia increasingly live in gated communities of extravagant affluence. They often vacation in the same luxury resorts in France, Mexico, and the Caribbean. Reportedly, they have more in common with one another than with those in their countries of origin. When they share a bit of their wealth in philanthropy, typically they give to the arts and medical research that directly benefits their own select community. What is particularly troubling is not only the enormous disparity between the global rich and poor but also that the race to the top seems to be widening that gap.

According to the *New York Times,* 358 billionaires now "control assets greater than the combined incomes of countries with 45 percent of the world's people."[4] The World Bank predicts that the gap between richer and poorer nations will continue to widen in the next ten years, and there is little real hope of moving toward convergence any time in the near future.[5]

The United Nations development program is particularly concerned about the long-term consequences of this troubling trend. They state that thirty years ago the poorest 20 percent of the world's population earned 2.3 percent of the world's income. Now they earn only 1.4 percent, and that amount is still declining. At the same time, the richest 20 percent increased their share of global income from 70 to 80 percent.[6] The point is that the race to the top seems to be dramatically expanding the wealth of the richest 20 percent while at the same time shrinking the resource base of the poorest 20 percent.

Joining the Race to the Bottom in Haiti

Louie Enel returned home late one humid evening with his head down. He had just come back from the rice merchant in Cayes with bad news. Seven months earlier he had sold half his rice crop to the merchant to make enough money to buy beans, oil, salt, and sugar to feed his family for the rest of the year. He thought he had held enough rice back to make it until the next harvest. But rats destroyed a third of the rice.

The merchant offered to sell Louie some of his rice back to him—at ten times the price he had been paid for it. Louie had no other option. But he had to sell the family milk goat to purchase enough rice to keep his family fed for the next three months. After that he didn't know what he would do to make ends meet. Louie, his wife, Lorraine, and their family are typical of many in the bottom 20 percent of our planetary community who are being passed over by the global economic liftoff. Without assets, they simply have no capacity to compete in this race to the top.

While global population is indeed beginning to level off, that isn't the entire story. Population growth is still soaring among the world's poorest inhabitants. Today we share the planet with six billion neighbors. By 2050 that number could reach between 9.5 and 9.8 billion.[7] And for poor families like the Enels, growing numbers in their communities likely means declining resources.

For instance, the population of Africa is slated to double by 2020; however, the AIDS epidemic could change that forecast. The future of many in the poorer regions of Africa are imperiled because they don't have the resources to join the race to the top. And for too many of the poorest nations on that continent, as elsewhere in the Two-Thirds World, population growth is exceeding both economic growth and food production.

Debt, Unemployment, and Lack of Education Greasing the Skids

The global debt crisis makes it virtually impossible for many of the poorer countries to ever join the race to the top, because such a high percentage of their income has to be used to pay for the interest on their loans. For example, Nicaragua and Algeria are using over half of their export income to service interest on their debts. Recently, the Anglicans had their worldwide communion, in which one of the major issues was debt among the poorer countries. "The Lambeth Conference has demanded action on international debt and economic justice, not only from governments and banks, but also from churches. The resolution asks bishops to take money from their own budgets to help pay for international development and to cooperate with other faiths in advocacy programs."[8]

Add to this the fact that today's high unemployment rates in the Two-Thirds World are escalating as the Asian crisis threatens to go global. It is projected that the global economy will have to come up with two billion new jobs by 2020 to meet the burgeoning population of young people who will be entering the workforce in these poorer countries. However, job creation isn't enough. We must make an effort to educate not only young men but also young women so they will be qualified to work in tomorrow's world. This is a major opportunity for those involved in mission work.

One of the other formidable problems confronting the global poor is that population growth is outstripping the carrying capacity of the environment in countries like Haiti and Bangladesh. A growing number of these regions will be in peril. Every mission initiative in the twenty-first century must include a component to care for creation.

The message regarding the twenty-first century is loud and clear. The poor are unable to play in this game without assets. We must all make a greater investment to help the poor help themselves. But the globalization of the economy is happening in a way that is not only benefiting those with resources but influencing many governments to sharply reduce their investment in economic aid to enable the global poor to join the liftoff. Which means the church and voluntary organizations must do much more.

Reducing the Drag: Cutting Assistance to the Global Poor

As the industrial nations join this brutally competitive race to the top, they are doing everything they can to reduce the drag on their economies and thus be more competitive, including reducing humanitarian aid to the poor.[9] David Beckmann, president of Bread for the World, stated, "The trend in cutting back foreign aid is global. But the United States is the leader of the trend, which will mean increased hardship for poor people in poor countries."[10] (The religious right in the United States has consistently supported legislation to cut back humanitarian aid to the world's poor, without explaining how this advances a pro-life, pro-family agenda.) In other words, since many of the world's governments are cutting back their humanitarian aid to the growing ranks of global poor, the church, voluntary organizations, and the private sector will need to do much more.

What Will It Take to Raise All Boats?

As we saw in the opening story, the economic globalization lifting the boats of European investors is swamping the boats of poor Ugandans. The reason? Those with financial means can always outbid the poor, even for resources in the country in which the poor live. The world's poor are simply not playing on a level field, because they have virtually no assets with which to participate in this competitive contest.

As we saw in the story from Haiti, the poor aren't playing on a level field even in their own country or in doing business with their own people. Louie Enel has no leverage to improve his family's lot economically. But the rice merchant is fully enjoying the race to the top because he has leverage. Louie is having difficulty feeding his children, and he cannot afford to send them to school. It is a different story for the rice merchant and his family, however. His six children are well fed, and they go to a private, church-related school. Indirectly, the Enel family is helping to make a more secure future for the rice merchant's children.

You see, the very greed that makes the free-market economy work so brilliantly in efficiently producing goods and services is what undermines its capacity to work justly on behalf of the poor and the marginalized. You can count on anyone who achieves wealth and power in a fallen world to use it to acquire more wealth and power, often at the expense of those who are at an economic disadvantage. That's the name of the game. The free market and free trade will never improve the lot of the marginalized unless people of faith and compassion make it happen.

Enabling the Global Poor to Enjoy a Taste of the McWorld Banquet

Plowing the Sea[11] is an important book that makes a compelling case that the standard economic prescriptions of McWorld are not adequate to address the real-world challenges of poor countries. How can a poor nation join this race to the top? The standard economic prescription is simple: Educate your people, reduce inflation, open your economy to free trade and investment, and watch your gross domestic product soar.

But from Bangkok to Barranquilla, the poor declare that it isn't that simple. Thailand's economy took off like a rocket, only to wind up with huge trade deficits, a currency devaluation, a clampdown by the IMF, and now major recession. In Peru the economy is growing. The wealthy are doing well. But unemployment is high and the gap between rich and poor is growing while inflation rates are dropping.

Essentially, the authors of *Plowing the Sea* argue that the standard prescriptions aren't adequate. There must be a commitment to major change at the microeconomic as well as the macroeconomic level. Corporate executives, politicians, and church leaders must create a broad spectrum of microeconomic opportunities down in the bowels of the economy. Poorer countries must reevaluate how they operate economically if their people are to have any hope of benefiting from, rather than being victimized by, the globalization of the economy. And the actions of IMF often come at the highest cost to the poorest citizens of a nation.

Too many Andean companies are trapped into being suppliers of inexpensive commodities. Since these companies compete on the basis of price and quantity instead of quality and innovation, they pay meager wages and keep living standards for their workers depressed. Many Andean countries are also trapped in a dead-end form of economic growth. They are becoming increasingly dependent on the export of natural resources to grow their economy. Then the more highly industrialized countries use those resources to produce goods with higher profit margins, which they sell back to the nations from which the resources came.

Clearly, the global race to the top will, for many of our poorer neighbors, become a race to the bottom if people of compassion don't take action. The global poor need the education and economic opportunity that will enable them to achieve a decent way of life. Poorer nations need to create regional microenterprise ventures that are more innovative in transforming their resources into higher quality economic goods.

In light of escalating challenges and declining government programs, it is essential that we Christians wake up to the biblical call to work for justice for our most vulnerable neighbors. The people of God have a unique opportunity that we dare not pass up: to partner with churches in poorer communities to increase educational and economic opportunity as an expression of God's new order.

Opportunities for Christian Leaders

In response to the mounting challenges facing the growing numbers of global poor, the debt crisis, decreasing government aid, and the failure of the global economy to include many of our poorest neighbors, those in leadership have opportunities

1. to enable those involved in mission work with the poor to assist them to develop strong local and regional economies that include the poorest residents, while helping the poor to work for the spiritual and cultural transformation of their communities and for the care of creation, in a way that reflects the values of the mustard seed more than those of McWorld.

2. to encourage local communities, where possible, to develop a high level of self-reliance in the production of basic foods, to reduce vulnerability to the ups and downs of the global economy.

3. to enable Christians to address the needs of the most vulnerable, including: education for the poor, especially for female children (to promote community development and improve the quality of family life); land-reform projects to help landless families secure

a way to support themselves now and in their retirement years; empowerment programs for abandoned children to help them grow spiritually, educationally, and in all their relationships.

4. to fashion a range of new cooperatives and partnerships to maximize the impact of our efforts to transform communities of need. These partnerships first of all need to include churches in these communities collaborating with churches abroad. We need to create new opportunities for Christian relief and development agencies to partner with church-planting agencies to work for the common goal of community transformation. But we also need to experiment with mission organizations collaborating with UN agencies, corporations, environmental organizations, and national governments.[12]

5. to work through agencies such as Bread for the World to work for structural change that promotes justice for our poorest neighbors.

6. to celebrate the inbreaking of God's kingdom among the poor and have them help prepare those of us who are more affluent to live and serve God in a more demanding future.

Planting a Seed in a Coffee Cooperative

Thousands of people shouted and praised God as the prayer meeting around the old truck loaded with bags of coffee beans concluded. It was a bright spring morning, and people had come from all directions to the market square in Plaissance de Sud in Haiti. A week earlier thousands of people from this rural Haitian community had pooled their resources to purchase the truck so they could take their coffee beans to market.

The buyer in Port-au-Prince had already quoted a price for their first truckload. Bypassing the middle man had increased their income by 250 percent. This additional income would mean that thousands of families who, like the Enels, were constantly on the edge of survival would be able to feed their kids and send them to school, and they would have enough economic leverage to start a business selling small items, such as homemade soap, in the market.

This story began seven years earlier when leaders from the valley invited those of us at World Concern to partner with them and their churches to improve the quality of community life. World Concern turned the development project back over to the valley leaders after the organization helped them attain their initial goals in three years. This was the second phase, and they had every reason to celebrate the success of this cooperative mustard seed venture.

Planting a Seed in Mozambique

Mike Morris is a Christian leader in Great Britain who has taken the initiative to challenge the church to address the tremendous debt load that is making it impossible for many poorer nations to fully participate in the global economic liftoff. He is bringing together support from a number of Christian groups to secure the resources to pay off the debt of smaller Two-Thirds World countries for the year 2000 as part of a celebration of God's jubilee, when all debts will be forgiven.[13] Part of the terms to pay off the debt for a small nation like Mozambique would be that the debtor nation contribute $2 million to local nongovernment organizations (NGOs) for every $8 million they save in annual debt servicing. These faith-based organizations would use this money to implement programs in education, community health, and infrastructure reform.

Planting a Seed for Global Awareness

A group of twenty-year-olds in the United Kingdom have started a unique ministry called CRED (Christian Responsibility Education Development) to raise awareness in churches regarding the growing global plight of the poor and our Christian responsibility. They promote fairly traded products such as coffee, tea, nuts, and crafts that are produced under just working traditions.

McWorld and the Future of the Western Poor

Stacey Jackson gave Carol Johnson a tearful hug as the judge read his ruling in the Chicago municipal court. She and Carol had been on a three-year journey together. It all started when Stacey, age twenty-nine, was arrested for possession of crack cocaine. At the time, she had a twelve-year-old daughter and a nine-year-old son, and she was pregnant. The court ordered her into drug treatment at Leland House, and her children were placed in foster care with their grandmother. That is when Stacey first met Carol, a volunteer from Jesus People USA who was working at Leland House. Carol became her mentor and friend and saw her through a lot of ups and downs.

Carol reported to the judge that over three years Stacey had attended ninety meetings of Narcotics Anonymous. She was clean of any drug use, which was periodically checked by random testing. She had successfully completed a course in parenting. And she had also taken a course in basic computer training while she was at Leland House. During this rehab time Stacey recommitted her life to Jesus Christ. Carol noticed a profound change in her attitude. At one point Stacey confided to Carol, "Without the Lord in my heart, I know I wouldn't be alive today!" Also, Stacey's church has begun to take an active role in helping her get her life back together.

So when the judge ruled that Stacey Jackson had completed all the conditions to regain custody of her children, there was a lot of hugging and celebrating. Stacey got a job working at a burger franchise at an entry-level income of under seven dollars an hour. But like a lot of single moms coming off welfare, she is at a loss as to how she can make that income stretch to cover basic living costs. The least expensive rental she can find for herself and her three kids is a two-bedroom apartment for nine hundred dollars a month, right on the edge of an area where crime and drug use are high. She and the baby share a room. Her daughter has the other bedroom, and her son sleeps in the living room. It is not a neighborhood in which she wants to live, but she can't afford anything better.

As Stacey prepared to move, she figured out her budget, and it dawned on her that with her entry-level salary, after she paid rent and utilities and bought food and clothes from Goodwill, there wasn't any money left for other things. She had no money left for medical insurance, food stamps, or child care. And she had no idea who would watch her baby daughter and look after her other two kids when they got home from school at 2:30 in the afternoon.

Stacey is one of millions in many Western countries who are making every effort to get their noses above water but are a long way from enjoying the bounty of the McWorld liftoff. Not only the global poor but also the American poor are discovering that for too many, the race to the top is in reality a race to the bottom.

Counting the Heads of the Western Poor

The globalization of the economy has created a new class of millionaires in Poland, Bulgaria, Romania, and throughout Russia. But millions of Russians are finding that their standard of living is plummeting as their economy is in free fall. In Holland, Germany, Denmark, and other European societies, the middle class is living comfortably in the main. But these countries too are experiencing high levels of unemployment, particularly among the young and among immigrant groups.

Down Under there are high rates of unemployment among Pacific Islanders, Aboriginals in Australia, and Maoris in New Zealand. Many of the unemployed have become chronically dependent on government welfare. In Britain, as in America, there is less unemployment, but many, like Stacey, are trying to make ends meet on entry-level jobs and are not having a lot of success.

Nowhere is the gap between rich and poor wider than in America. According to a United Nations survey, the United States has the highest rate of child poverty among eighteen industrialized nations. In 1996, 36.5 million Americans, including Stacey Jackson, didn't earn enough to rise above the poverty threshold. That is 13.7 percent of the population. One child in five is born into poverty in America, but closer to 40 percent of American children experience poverty at some time in their lives.[14]

While employment among African-Americans is slowly increasing, that isn't the case for black teenagers. Only 14.5 percent of white teens are unemployed, but the Department of Labor's Bureau of Labor Statistics reports that 32.7 percent of all black teenagers are out of work. Some of these young people graduated from schools in which they haven't learned basic literacy skills, which hinders their ability to participate in a highly technological society.[15] The poorest of the poor in America are still Native Americans, who experience more than 30 percent unemployment. A third of Native Americans who worked earned less than ten thousand dollars a year in 1995.[16]

According to the U.S. Census Bureau, recent research indicates that the gap between our richest and poorest citizens is wider than it has been at any time since the end of World War II. From 1964 to 1994 the income of the wealthiest 20 percent of Americans jumped 44 percent after being adjusted for inflation. During the same period the bottom 20 percent only saw a 7 percent increase, which resulted in a reduction of purchasing power during this period.[17] The economic liftoff is not raising all boats in America either.

Assessing the Future of the Working Poor

The Annie Casey Foundation reported a dramatic increase in the number of children living in poverty in a home in which one or more parents worked. Between 1989 and 1994 that figure swelled by 30 percent, with 5.6 million children—more than a third of all poor children in America—living in working-poor families.[18] What is particularly concerning is that while the race to the top has seen a steady improvement in real GNP, increased worker productivity, and the rapid creation of new jobs between 1989 and 1995, the number of children in America starting out poor and with serious disadvantages is growing.

During the late sixties a breadwinner could work full-time at an entry-level job and earn enough to support a three-person family above the poverty line. By 1995 someone working full-time at an entry-level job fell 30 percent below the three-person poverty line. And many of the new jobs that have been created in the last few boom years don't pay a living wage.

One of the reasons for the widening gap between rich and poor in a number of Western countries is the way in which this new McWorld economy is designed. John Challenger, who heads up a Chicago-based outplacement firm, says, "The advent of free trade and deregulation is causing American companies to increasingly view the world as their playing field. We see the jobs that require no skills as jobs that can go overseas."[19]

One of the major reasons the working poor don't seem to become any more competitive in the global marketplace is that they don't have access to the educational opportunities that can help them break out of poverty. Like the global poor, they aren't playing on a level field and therefore have little leverage to improve their situation.

In America children of the poor and working poor are at a particular disadvantage because of the way we fund public schooling. Jonathan Kozol, in his disturbing book *Savage Inequalities*,[20] describes in vivid detail how we have inadvertently kept millions of children locked in poverty by creating a discriminatory public school system in which quality is largely determined by the local tax base.

Schools in some poorer urban districts can scarcely afford textbooks, let alone the new computer learning tools abundantly available in wealthier districts. Recent legislation in the United States to do away with affirmative action programs will make it even harder for kids from the poorer communities to get out of situations of entrenched poverty, because their opportunities are shrinking.

Since in a McWorld economy the primary commitment is to maximizing benefits to shareholders, there is an inherent bias to keep labor costs as low as possible. We are in serious danger in the West, especially in the United States, of creating a permanent underclass that will be largely excluded from the opportunity to participate in the affluence of the McWorld liftoff.

Cutting Back Assistance to the Western Poor

To reduce the drag on Western countries in this competitive race to the top, governments are cutting back not only aid to the poor in the Two-Thirds World but assistance to the poor and marginalized in their own countries as well. The United States, Australia, New Zealand, the United Kingdom, and even Sweden are cutting back their social benefit programs for the poor to reduce the drag on their national economies. For example, Austria has recently attacked its welfare program because the program gobbles up 28 percent of the country's GDP, and if the program continues at the present rate, it will consume 40 percent of Austria's GDP by 2020.[21]

Of course, the United States has made the most draconian cutback in its social welfare programs, limiting mothers with children to two consecutive years, or five years over life, and these funds are now administered at the state level.[22] A number of people leaving welfare are finding jobs, but many of those, like Stacey, can only find entry-level McJobs that don't pay enough for moms coming off welfare to afford child care, health insurance, or in many communities even rent.

New York State tracked those coming off welfare from July 1996 to March 1997 and discovered that only 29 percent found full- or part-time jobs in the first several months after they were cut from welfare. Early evidence seems to indicate that this kind of welfare reform, while helping some Americans out of chronic dependency, is driving other Americans into another kind of chronic poverty, that is, the lot of the working poor in the United States.[23] And millions of others coming off welfare never find any work.

Having been a social worker in a former life, I know firsthand that it just doesn't work in all cases to cut back social welfare and tell people to go to work. It isn't that simple. Twenty-eight million Americans can't read and write. Many of them are products of woefully inadequate urban schools. Those people cannot fill out an employment form at McDonald's or KFC, let alone find an employer that would hire the illiterate. Many more have no work experience or job skills. Millions of others are addicted to alcohol and drugs or are emotionally disabled, and they cannot join the workforce without rehabilitation first.

Cutting Back Funding to the Caring Edge

The cutbacks aren't just in direct assistance to the poor; they are also in government funds to help voluntary agencies that are supposed to pick up the slack from government cutbacks. Catholic charities across the country predict they will receive $200 million less from Washington for social services by 2002. The Lutheran Social Services organization will be set back at least $200 million by the same date, and the Salvation Army expects a $50 million cutback.[24]

Here again, the race to the top could, for many of the poorest residents in Western countries, particularly in America, become a race to the bottom if people of compassion don't find ways to join with others in creating genuine opportunities for the excluded. The Bible convinces me that we Christians will face the judgment of God for the calloused way so many of us ignore the plight of the poor and vulnerable who live in our communities and our world.

Listen to God's warning to the children of Israel regarding the sins of Sodom: "Now this was the sin of your sister Sodom: She and her daughters were arrogant, overfed and unconcerned; they did not help the poor and needy" (Ezek. 16:49). And we will be without excuse when we find ourselves reciting the words "When did we see you hungry, naked, alone or in prison and didn't respond?" In light of the mounting challenges, it is essential that our middle-class congregations don't fail to partner with churches in communities of poverty to increase educational and economic opportunity in the twenty-first century as a witness for God's love for the poor.

Opportunities for Christian Leaders

Christian leaders in the Western church have the opportunity

1. to focus on community restoration, which includes not only economic empowerment but also the transformation of the spiritual life and relationships in communities to reflect the values of the mustard seed more than the values of McWorld.
2. to help churches in suburban and small towns as well as in urban areas provide inexpensive child care for single moms coming off welfare or for families of the working poor.
3. to encourage many more churches and Christian agencies to start literacy and job training programs (such as training in computer skills) to enable the young and the poor to secure jobs that pay a living wage.
4. to learn, from microloan and microenterprise projects in the Two-Thirds World, how to help the poor start small businesses to break out of poverty. Also, leaders have the opportunity to help enable the poor become more self-reliant through urban agriculture projects and possibly even the development of fishponds and small livestock projects.
5. to develop new collaborative relationships between urban and suburban churches, between urban ministries, government agencies, and corporations.
6. to develop new capabilities to deal with sudden need among the poor during times of economic crisis in our volatile McWorld future, as well as to lobby for just social policies in America that reflect Christ's compassion for the poor.

Planting a Seed in Liverpool

A friend encouraged Tracy to visit a Christian ministry in Liverpool called Training into Jobs. Tracy graduated from high school three years earlier but had never been able to find work. Like Stacey, she had no job skills or work record. She also had a low sense of self-esteem, and it took all of her courage to visit the Training into Jobs offices, since she had experienced many rejections in her efforts to apply for work. The worker at the center listened to Tracy's story and enrolled her in a training program in the hospitality industry. Nine months later Tracy not only had her first job in a hotel near her home but had become a Christian and had taken a course to help her develop her confidence and leadership skills. As a result, her church asked her to lead a women's Bible study group. Her entire life has been transformed because some Christians found they couldn't ignore any longer the large number of unemployed youth in Liverpool. The seed they planted is bearing good fruit.

Planting a Seed for Partnership in Ohio

A rural Methodist church in Ohio developed a partnership with a Methodist church in an inner-city area in Cleveland. The creative part of the partnership was that the rural church was growing and grafting fruit tree seedlings they planned to bring to the inner city so the two churches together could plant them in parking strips and backyards throughout the neighborhood to take a step in promoting local food self-reliance.

Planting a Seed in Habitat Belfast

Habitat for Humanity Belfast made history in 1997 when Catholics and Protestants gathered together to dedicate an eleven-house development in the Catholic part of Belfast. Then they prayerfully walked to a groundbreaking ceremony in the Protestant side of town. This was the culmination of three years of hard work by hundreds of volunteers from both parts of Belfast who are committed to giving peace a chance.

Planting a Seed in Down Payments for Urban Housing

Nehemiah Ministries is a creative black-run national ministry in the United States that provides down payments for poor families so they can purchase their own homes. And the group is creating collaborative ventures with other urban organizations to rapidly expand this form of economic empowerment.

Planting a Seed in National Advocacy for the Poor

"On June 1, Call to Renewal convened a daylong 'Capitol Preach-in' to bring the message of God's concern for the poor to the U.S. Congress. Hosted by Rep. Tony Hall [D-Ohio], a dozen of the best-known preachers in America participated in the event. . . . Jim Wallis concluded the day: 'In our discussions of public morality, it is important that we remember that morality is also about how we treat the poor. On June 1, we reminded Congress about what is important and called America to a new moral awakening about its responsibility to our nation's poorest families.'"[25]

Call to Renewal is an effort in the United States to bring African-American, Hispanic, Catholic, evangelical, and mainline Protestant churches together with the government and corporations to promote community economic empowerment and social justice for God's kingdom. And God is using this movement to help the poor help themselves. They are looking for those who are ready to learn from and partner with our neighbors living in poor communities in America. Christian magazines that can help you and your church work with the poor are: *Sojourners* (202-328-8842), *Transformation, Prism,* and *Creation Care* (610-645-9390; esa@esa-online.org).

Questions for Discussion and Action

1. How could the rapid movement into global free trade benefit or penalize the poor?

2. How are the needs of the global and Western poor likely to change as we enter a new millennium?

3. Why are many Western governments cutting back their assistance to the poor at home and abroad?

4. What is our biblical responsibility to the poor and the vulnerable, and what are some creative ways in which your church could become more directly involved in helping the poor help themselves and in lobbying for just social policy?

A Race to the Bottom for the Incredible Shrinking Western Church

SARAH LIVED IN A SMALL FLAT in Buffalo, New York, barely scrimping by on her Social Security check. Her only living relative, her thirty-five-year-old daughter, Natalie, was permanently institutionalized with schizophrenia in a hospital sixty miles away. There was no public transportation to the hospital, and Sarah didn't own a car. She discovered that Concerned Ecumenical Ministries conducted a senior citizen support program. Sarah applied and twice a year was shuttled to visit her daughter. One day the phone rang and Sarah got the bad news—the transportation she had come to rely on had been canceled due to a sudden cutback in funding by the American Baptist Church in that region.

Now let me give you the story behind the story. In 1984 I had the opportunity to lead a two-day consultation with the executive council of the American Baptist Church, regarding the future of the denomination. We presented projections that made it clear that the ABC would have to do more to respond to the growing human needs at home and abroad.

Then I showed them demographic projections of how their denomination was changing. Black and Hispanic churches made up about 30 percent of the membership and were slowly growing. But white membership was graying and declining at a rate that would undermine giving and the ability of the ABC even to sustain its present level of mission to those in need. It was clear that this was the first time most of these leaders had seen these figures. And they immediately understood the implications for the future of their denomination and its mission. Before we finished the consultation, ABC leaders developed a plan to increase church growth and giving to respond to this projected decline.

Almost ten years later I was asked to meet with the executive council again. I discovered that no one had followed up on the recommendations that the council had made ten years earlier to get the church growing. Regrettably, my projections proved to be valid. While ethnic membership had grown to over 35 percent, white membership and giving had declined. As a consequence, many districts of the ABC were forced to cut back funding to important ministries, including Concerned Ecumenical Ministries in Buffalo, which provided that shuttle ride twice a year for Sarah to visit her daughter.

I have been able to identify few major denominations or mission organizations that make any effort to anticipate either how the larger context in which they operate is changing or how changes to their demographics and funding will affect their ability to carry out their mission in a new millennium. We have seen how we are racing into a future that is changing at blinding speed, a future of growing human need, in which the church is going to be called on to do more. But we have also seen how the forces of globalization are likely to decrease the amount of discretionary time and money that members are able to invest in the church and its mission, given our present models of discipleship.

Finding the Focus

The question I want to raise in this chapter is, How effectively will the church be able to address the mounting challenges of the third millennium, given changes taking place in attendance and giving patterns within the Western church? I will share an overview of these changing patterns in the church in Britain, Australia, New Zealand, Canada, and the United States, to predict the future of the Western church and its mission. Finally, I will describe creative ways in which those in leadership can take decisive action if the Western church is even going to sustain its present level of mission between now and 2020. I will begin by looking at the changing character of religion in the future.

Globalization of Religion

As we race into a new global future, everything is changing at time-warp speed, including the religious character of our global village. Religions that once had geographic boundaries in various parts of the world are now going global, as Christianity has done. For example, recently when we flew into Auckland, New Zealand, we saw the completion of the first Hindu temple. Hinduism and Buddhism are currently the fastest-growing religions in Australia. For those living in Western countries, people are no longer limited as to what brand of Christianity they want to choose. As a result of globalization, individuals now have access not only to all the historic world religions but also to an explosion of alternatives.

In the musical *Sweet Charity* there is an intriguing song titled "The Rhythm of Life," in which people are invited to join the Religion of the Month Club. For those interested in shopping around, there has never been such an astonishing array of the weird and the wild. Reportedly, over five hundred new religions are created each year in southern California alone.[1]

As we enter an uncertain new global future, everyone from George Gallup to *Time* magazine has documented a growing hunger for spirituality throughout the Western world. One thing that is clear in the nineties is that cults requiring a high level of commitment aren't nearly as popular as they were in the sixties. Many people seem to be looking for a postmodern faith offering a form of spirituality that makes little demand for serious change in their lives. That is why various New Age religions and Scientology are more popular today than the more demanding religions of the Moonies or the Hare Krishnas.[2]

The ultimate in low-demand new religion is perhaps the annual ritual of the Burning Man Festival in Black Rock Canyon, Arizona. From small beginnings in southern California, this ritual burning of a huge male form now attracts 3500 participants from many different religious and cultural backgrounds. It is the ultimate example of religion without dogma or demand. Every participant is free to interpret the Burning Man in any way that makes sense to them. One guy in a military helmet with Mickey Mouse ears said, "When you burn the man, you recognize the past is ashes, and that is significant—everyone recognizes that—it's all gone."[3]

Graham Cray, a lecturer at Cambridge in the United Kingdom, is particularly concerned over the extent to which Christians in the West are embracing a form of religious pluralism in which, like those outside the church, they are picking and choosing those elements they want to embrace as true. Cray is alarmed that this postmodern relativism is spreading particularly among the Christian young.

Religion is also rising in pop culture. Television shows such as *Touched by an Angel, Soul Man,* and *Nothing Sacred* are beamed into our homes. Christian music is crossing over into the mainstream. Books on religion and spirituality have increased sales 112 percent between 1991 and 1996. They are the only form of adult nonfiction whose sales have been rising.[4] A growing number of patients in hospitals are requesting alternative therapies, including prayer and spirituality.[5] The question is, How can people of Christian faith respond to this growing spiritual hunger?

Back to the Future One More Time

Remember that we are going backward, not forward, in global evangelization. Twenty-eight percent of the world's people identify themselves as Protestant, Catholic, or Orthodox today. By the year 2010 that will decrease to 27 percent and continue to decline from there because global population is growing more rapidly than the global church while the marketers of McWorld are doing a brilliant job of "evangelizing" the global young.[6] Human needs at home and abroad are going to mount and Western governments are cutting assistance. The question again is, How well will the church be able to respond to these mounting challenges, given the changing demographic and giving patterns in the Western church?

First the good news from the church worldwide: Dudley Woodberry, who heads the School of World Mission at Fuller Theological Seminary, notes that "through the efforts of the Lausanne Committee for World Evangelization AD 2000 and Beyond and the World Evangelical Fellowship, coordinated efforts are being made in church planting, especially in the 10-40 window . . . with considerable church growth."[7]

Patrick Johnstone, in his new book *The Church Is Bigger Than You Think,* documents the remarkable growth of the church in much of Africa, Latin America, and parts of Asia. Through DAWN and the AD 2000 movement, new churches have been planted in regions with little gospel witness. Johnstone states that while the Bible was translated into only 537 languages at the turn of the last century, by the time we reach the twenty-first century, it will have been translated into 2,800 languages.[8]

Interdev, a Christian mission organization based in Seattle, predicts that 95,000 missionaries will be sent out from non-Western churches by the year 2000.[9] *Christianity Today* celebrates the emergence of a truly global church, in which Episcopalians in America recruit leadership from the Anglican Church in Uganda, and in which Australian churches are adopting Korean cell groups to nurture spirituality.[10]

The recent Lambeth Conference for those in the Anglican tradition has signaled a shift in the axis of the global church. The church of Britain and America is no longer defining the direction of the global Anglican church. Anglican bishops from Africa, Asia, and Latin America have taken leadership of the Anglican parade, much to the dismay of many old-line liberal bishops in the north, who are used to framing the faith and setting the course. I think we will continue to see the church shift to Two-Thirds World leadership in many traditions as we enter a new millennium.

Another one of the hopeful trends is reverse missions. In the future we will see missionaries from Asia, Africa, and Latin America bring a more vital faith to many Western communities. For example, a small, vibrant Pentecostal church in Concepción, Chile, sent its pastor as a missionary to an affluent, stiff United Church of Christ congregation in Massachusetts. The pastor said that as he worked with this group of old-line Congregationalists, "we could sense a spiritual hunger."[11]

Ian Douglas, who teaches at the Episcopal Divinity School, contends "that what God is about in the world today is a genuinely new thing and is not simply an extension of the old. . . . What we are witnessing today is not so much the globalization of a Euro-American church but the advent of a new church of the southern hemisphere, the third church."[12]

Scoping Out the Future of the Western Church

While there is robust growth in much of the church in the Two-Thirds World, regrettably that isn't true in much of the Western church. I will describe many positive ways in which God is at work in the Western church. But I will also share some concerning patterns in Western church attendance and giving patterns.

In describing the Western church, I will focus principally on English-speaking nations because they are most relevant to the intended audience of this book. These countries include Britain, Australia, New Zealand, Canada, and the United States. My research and travels in continental Europe suggest that in the main the church there is in even more serious decline than the church in English-speaking nations. In all these countries, we are witnessing the rapid emergence of a "postdenominational church."

As I profile the church in the English-speaking Western countries, I think you will see that the trends in these countries are remarkably similar. A word of caution before I begin. This analysis will not be fully satisfying to those trained in statistics, because the data I will be sharing was not all gathered in the same way or organized in a consistently parallel fashion. Therefore, this analysis is offered not as a scientific study but rather as an impressionistic examination of the best data I have been able to locate. Even so, I hope this information will be useful.

First, I will look at how the changing attendance patterns of the church in Great Britain, Australia, New Zealand, Canada, and the United States will affect the ability of the Western church to respond to the challenges of a new millennium. Then I will explore how changing attendance patterns by age are likely to determine the future of the church in the West. Finally, I will examine how changing giving patterns are also likely to impact the ability of the Western church to expand its mission thrust to respond to the mounting challenges of tomorrow's world.

Recently I sent to a number of evangelical magazines in the United States an article about the future and the church, which cited examples of what God is doing in Australia, New Zealand, and Great Britain. One editor said he wouldn't be able to use my article, then added, "Why in the world did you mention examples from Great Britain, Australia, and New Zealand? They are all a part of a post-Christian culture where the church is no longer vital or growing. What do we possibly have to learn from them?" I have found that his viewpoint is fairly common in the United States. But as I will show, in many ways I have discovered a more vital, creative faith in these countries than in the States.

The Future of the Church in Great Britain

I believe that in many ways the church in Britain is a much healthier church than in North America, even though its attendance patterns are lower.

Clive Calver, now head of World Relief in America, collaborated with other leaders in the United Kingdom for almost twenty years to create a remarkable informal network of Anglican bishops, Pentecostal pastors, leaders of parachurch agencies working in world mission, and leaders from the full spectrum of Protestant denominations—Methodists, Baptists, and Reformed. I have not seen another country in the West in which such a collegiality of Christian leaders are working together for the gospel of Christ.

In the past twenty years, Christians in the United Kingdom have spearheaded efforts in church planting and evangelism that I believe have outstripped anything going on in the United States during the same period. Hundreds of new churches were planted, from Ichthus Fellowship to Revelation House churches. Tens of thousands of Brits came to vital faith in Jesus Christ during this period of Christian expansion and renewal.

Also, in the United Kingdom I have found per square mile more creative approaches to advancing God's kingdom than in the United States, particularly among those under age thirty-five. This movement to plant churches, evangelize neighbors, and work with the poor is still growing strongly in the United Kingdom. The only problem is that the established old-line denominations such as Methodist, Anglican, and Reformed are graying and declining more rapidly than others are able to grow the church.

As a consequence, adult church attendance in England, which was 10.2 percent of the population in 1980, declined in 1995 to 8.1 percent and is projected to decline to 7.7 percent by the year 2000.[13] According to the Christian Research Association, the decline has even been steeper for the church in Scotland and Wales. Imagine what the rate of decline would be if there weren't so many Christians working at growing the church. Even more concerning than the steady declining and graying of the church in Britain is the drop in church attendance among those under age thirty.

Attendees over sixty-five compose a greater portion of churches than English society (25 percent more), while attendees twenty to twenty-nine years old compose a smaller portion of churches, 30 percent fewer than of English society.[14] Peter Brierley and Heather Wraight at the Christian Research Association track demographic change not only in the United Kingdom but throughout the larger world. Their email address is 100616.1657@compuserve.com.

As you will see as we visit the church in Australia, New Zealand, Canada, and the United States, there is a consistent pattern. All the old-line denominations are graying and declining and slowly going out of business. The charismatic movement has largely plateaued in all Western countries. Evangelical and Pentecostal churches are often showing growth, but the overall pattern is still one of decline, as it is in England, and the missing generation is consistently those under age thirty-five.

The Future of the Church in Australia

In the past twenty years in Australia, as in the United Kingdom, one can point to a period of energetic growth in church planting and evangelism. A number of new Pentecostal and charismatic churches have been planted during this period. The Sydney Diocese of the Anglican Church is conservative theologically and has been in the forefront of church planting and evangelism. As a result, they have grown, unlike most Anglican communions in Britain, Canada, and the United States.

John Smith, a prophetic Australian Christian leader, has started a network of ministries called Care and Communication Concern to address the growing urban needs in Melbourne and Newcastle. In one ministry, Hand Brake Turn, young men caught stealing cars are trained to rebuild cars by CCC. For graduation CCC arranges for the young to race their rebuilt cars with the police.

But again it's the same story as in England. The old-line denominations are graying and declining. And the growth among charismatic, Pentecostal, and evangelical churches is not enough to offset the overall trend. Peter Kaldor and his colleagues at the National Church Life Survey report, "Sample survey data can provide a picture of trends over the past 40 years for all denominations including the Catholic church. During the '50s, over 40% of the population attended church at least once a month. By the '90s this had dropped to around 25% of the population."[15]

While people under thirty compose a greater portion of smaller Pentecostal groups than they do of Australian society, they compose a significantly smaller portion of larger Protestant groups than of Australian society. Peter Kaldor states, "Around 40% of mainstream attendees are over 60 years of age. If patterns continue as they are, in 20 years there will be a significant decline in numbers."[16] Philip Hughes and Peter Bentley state that their research indicates weekly attendance is only about 10 percent for adults.[17]

The Future of the Church in New Zealand

The charismatic renewal vitalized many traditional denominations in New Zealand, such as the Presbyterian, Congregationalist, and Anglican denominations. The same winds of the Spirit stimulated a tremendous growth of church planting and evangelism among Pentecostal churches. For example, the New Life Center in Christchurch planted over a hundred new churches in the seventies and eighties. Evangelical denominations such as the Baptist denomination also experienced vigorous growth in recent years.

Christians in New Zealand are more respectful of the indigenous Maori culture than Christians in the United States are of our native peoples. They design Christian ministries in a way that not only respects but includes elements of Maori culture. Youth for Christ is active in trying to find new ways to reach a new generation with interest-based clubs and performance-oriented cafés. The church in New Zealand sends more missionaries overseas percentage-wise than any Western country other than Norway.

During the past two decades there has been growth in church planting, evangelism, and the creation of innovative Christian ministries. Perhaps the most significant development is an umbrella organization called New Vision New Zealand. Headed by Bryian Hathaway, it is committed "to the growth of the kingdom of God by all means possible."[18]

In spite of all the good things God is doing in this beautiful country, the pattern is identical to that of Great Britain and Australia. The oldline churches are graying and declining, and the growth among evangelical, charismatic, and Pentecostal churches doesn't offset the trend. In the fifties 40 percent of Kiwis were attending church once a month. In the early nineties that proportion had declined to 29 percent. And a survey by New Vision New Zealand indicated weekly attendance rates of 17 percent. Again the graying and declining of the Anglican, Presbyterian, Lutheran, and Methodist congregations is primarily responsible for the overall demographic decline.[19]

It is important to report, however, that both the Anglicans and the Methodists began to see a bit of growth again starting in 1993. The groups that have experienced robust growth in the eighties and nineties in New Zealand are the Assembly of God churches, the Apostolic churches, the Elim churches, and the Vineyard churches.[20]

One researcher, Hugh Dickey, reported that only 12.7 percent of the nation's children are on Sunday and church school rolls. And of this number, he states, on average only 73 percent attend. There has been a precipitous drop in Sunday school attendance since the early sixties, which threatens the church's future.[21] Not surprisingly, 81 percent of those in New Zealand who identify themselves as having "no religion" are under age forty.[22]

The Future of the Church in Canada

In the nineties, Toronto was a mecca for charismatics from all over the Western world. But in spite of the "Toronto blessing," Canada has experienced less growth in the church than has the United Kingdom and Australia. However, in Canada, as in New Zealand, an umbrella organization was developed to promote evangelism and church planting to grow the church. In the late eighties this organization, the Evangelical Fellowship of Canada, started a thrust called Vision 2000. And they have seen fruit from their initiatives.

While there has been growth among conservative Protestants in Canada, there is also an array of emerging expressions of the church that is encouraging. Regent College is, in my opinion, one of the finest centers for Christian learning in North America. InterVarsity in Canada is doing a brilliant job in preparing a new generation of high school and university students to serve God. One Hundred Huntley Street television productions and Brian Stiller Reports produce Christian television with more substance and taste than most of what is offered south of the border. And Canadian Christians, like those of other Western countries, are involved in a broader range of social issues—including creation care and opposition to land mine production— than are many of their American Christian neighbors.

Reginald Bibby has been writing about the demographic profile of the church in Canada since he published his first book, *Fragmented Gods*. Bibby reports that in 1957 you would have found 53 percent of Canadians in church on Sunday morning. By 1990 this proportion had declined to 23 percent and is reportedly still declining.[23] Bibby discovered that one of the reasons for declining attendance in Canada is mobility. He explained that half of the Canadians who move stop attending church regularly.[24] But again the major problem is the graying and declining of the United Church and the Anglican Church. Between 1957 and 1990 the membership patterns of these mainline denominations declined from 80 percent to 30 percent.[25]

If we want to know where the church is going in the future, our best indicator is the involvement and commitment of the Canadian young. In the early eighties 23 percent of Canadian teenagers were weekly attendees, and 39 percent described themselves as religiously committed, according to Bibby. By the early nineties the proportion of weekly attendees had fallen to 18 percent, and that of the religiously committed to 24 percent.

Even more stark are the contrasting attendance and membership patterns for eighteen- to twenty-nine-year-olds between 1957 and 1990. In 1957 36 percent of this population would be found in attendance at church. By 1990 that proportion had fallen to 14 percent. In 1957 68 percent of these young adults were church members. By 1990 that proportion had plummeted to 17 percent.[26] If the church in Canada is to have a future, it must find ways to reach and keep its youth.[27]

The Future of the Church in the United States

The church in the United States has enjoyed a period of growth in the last two decades. We have witnessed the emergence of megachurches like Willow Creek and Saddle Back. Alpha programs in evangelism, imported from Britain, are resulting in thousands coming to vital faith in Jesus Christ. Prayer initiatives are involving millions of American believers. Promise Keepers is not only calling men back to a vital faith but also promoting racial reconciliation. And we are seeing significant levels of growth among black, Hispanic, and Asian congregations in the United States.

However, I am concerned about the future of the mainline Protestant churches in America. I am seeing a small but growing number of mainline churches buying into a religious pluralism in which they are openly embracing all forms of spirituality the mind can imagine, from neopaganism to New Age. As they move away from biblical orthodoxy and Christology at warp speed, I am wondering how they can retain any genuine sense of Christian identity.

We evangelicals have another problem. Nowhere else in the Western world do evangelicals have to be right-wing Republicans or the equivalent to be considered born-again Christians. I believe many people have unwittingly confused their faith with American nationalism and a narrow political ideology.

I am also concerned about the future of the evangelical movement in the United States because of a growing disconnection between middle-of-the-road evangelical organizations (such as World Vision, InterVarsity, and the spectrum of evangelical colleges and seminaries) and the evangelical rank and file. These organizations tend to understand Christian life and social responsibility in broader terms than do many of their constituents, who often don't read broadly and who tend to rely on talk radio and Christian radio to help them understand the world. I urge evangelical organizations to launch new initiatives to do much more, using Christian radio, to educate their constituents to a broader vision for Christian social responsibility to avoid a potential schism in American evangelicalism.

In the United States, while the Catholic church is still experiencing a bit of growth, virtually all mainline churches are graying and declining, as in other Western countries, as we move into a postdenominational future. In 1968 eleven mainline Protestant denominations represented 13 percent of the U.S. population. By 1993 this proportion had plummeted to 7.8 percent, a 40 percent decrease. If the present trends continue uninterrupted, these denominations will be out of business by the year 2032.[28]

Add to the problem of declining numbers that of aging congregations. For example, of all people over seventy-five, twice as many are members of the Evangelical Lutheran Church than not.[29] The Presbyterians, the United Church of Christ, the American Baptists, and the United Methodists are all dealing with the twin blows of declining numbers and graying congregations. The 2.5-million-member Episcopal Church lost one million members from 1965 to 1989. And as we will see, declining membership has already begun to hit the pocketbooks of a number of major denominations.

Wade Roof and William McKinney, in their important book *American Mainline Religion,* stated that "the churches of the Protestant establishment, long in a state of relative decline, will continue to lose ground both in numbers and in social power and influence. The proportion of the population that is Protestant will continue its gradual decline in the decades to come, and within Protestantism denominations and revitalization movements will continue their contest for power and influence."[30]

However, Gustav Niebuhr, religion editor for the *New York Times,* has recently reported that there is a bit of good news. Several mainline denominations, including the Episcopal Church, the United Methodist Church, the ELCA, and the Presbyterian Church USA, saw their rate of decline begin to slow in the past three to four years. However, this doesn't alter the reality that they are slowly going out of business.

Even the Southern Baptist Church, which has enjoyed strong growth since the end of the Second World War, is in trouble. Fraught with internal conflicts, it has seen its growth almost come to a halt at 0.5 percent or less from 1994 to 1997.[31] The major growth in the Unites States, as elsewhere, is among conservative Protestant groups, including black and Hispanic congregations, Assemblies of God, the Vineyard churches, the Evangelical Free churches, and the Covenant Church in America.

John and Sylvia Ronsvalle state that fifteen conservative and evangelical denominations have grown between 1968 and 1993, but that isn't the whole story. They point out that between 1985 and 1993 this rate of growth slowed and the portion of the U.S. population involved in the church declined.[32] In the past ten years I have seen several conservative denominations such as the Mennonite Church shift from slow growth to no growth.

Figure 1.
Trend in Membership as a Percent of U.S. Population, 29 Protestant Denominations, Linear and Exponential Regression Based on Data for 1968–1985, with Actual Data 1986–1995

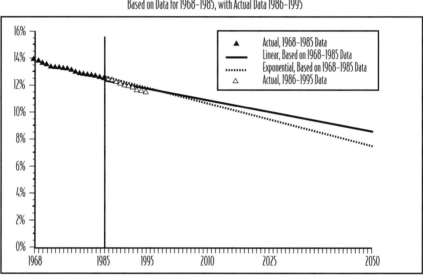

Sources: Yearbook of American and Canadian Churches, adjusted series; U.S. Bureau of Economic Analysis

© empty tomb, inc. 1997

It is essential to mention that the church in the United States is the only one that appears to vary from the attendance pattern of the church in other English-speaking Western countries. As we have seen, in spite of often significant growth in evangelism and church planting, Britain, Australia, New Zealand, and Canada have over the past three to four decades all suffered a steady erosion in attendance, which threatens their future.

However, George Gallup researchers insist that in spite of the graying and decline of the old-line churches, attendance of American Christians since the fifties has remained fairly constant, between 40 percent and 45 percent. George Barna, who has been tracking attendance patterns only since the early eighties, puts average U.S. attendance nearer 40 percent.[33]

In the past decade, other demographers have begun questioning the validity of surveys showing that American church attendance patterns are remaining constant when there seems to be anecdotal evidence to the contrary. Kirk Hadaway, chief statistician for the United Church of Christ, believes that Americans are overreporting their attendance. Hadaway states, "Interest in spirituality is up. But active participation in a faith community or institution is dropping." He points out that mainline churches have lost one-fourth of their members in the last thirty years. Roughly 48 percent of the children in Episcopal families leave church at age eighteen. Since 1965 the United Methodists have lost almost one thousand members a week. To check the validity of self-reporting methods, Hadaway had his research team count cars in church parking lots in a small Ohio county over a period of several months. His finding: "Americans overreport their actual church attendance by a marked degree. Actual attendance is closer to 24 percent," according to Hadaway, "and is falling slowly."[34]

If Hadaway's observational research is more accurate than the self-reporting approach, U.S. attendance patterns are more similar to the kind of attendance patterns we find among churches in other English-speaking Western countries. One trend that is identical in all these countries, including the United States, is that the more theologically conservative, evangelical side of the church is the lively and growing edge. "For both the United States and Canada, evangelicals—whether defined by denominational attachment, personal beliefs and practices, or both—now constitute the largest and most active component of religious life in North America," state Mark Noll and Lyman Kellstedt.[35]

To the question, How many evangelicals are there in the United States? Kellstedt responds, "If you mean—how many claim a conversion experience of being 'born again'?—the answer is that nearly a third of the population is evangelical. If you mean—how many believe that the Bible is true?—the total rises to nearly half the population. If you mean—how many Americans are adherents to a church in the evangelical tradition?—we find that about one fourth of Americans are evangelicals."[36]

Those of us from the evangelical tradition in America, rather than celebrating our growing numbers, should be asking how we can be such a large part of the population and apparently have so little influence. In the next chapter I will argue that the reason we have so little influence on the larger, modern secular culture is that we have allowed that culture, instead of our faith, to define what is important and of value. Most social science research I have read reports that we evangelicals are simply not that different from our non-church-going neighbors. We will need to place more emphasis on quality growth instead of simply celebrating numerical growth.

There is another trend in the American church that is identical to what we have seen in all other national profiles. Those under age thirty-five are the missing generation within the American church, too. In a recent survey of college freshmen in the United States, 15 percent indicated no religious preference. This is the highest proportion ever for college freshmen, and two and a half times that of the nation as a whole.[37]

In his seminars George Barna says that the buster generation (those age eighteen to thirty-two, born between 1965 and 1983) is the first generation in America that is starting life without some kind of clear Christian heritage. Barna Research reports that over the past ten years, while older generation attendance patterns range roughly from 40 to 60 percent, busters come in dead last with about 34 percent attendance.[38]

The Incredible Shrinking Western Church and the Future of Christian Missions

The cold, hard fact is that the welcome growth of the evangelical church in North America and other Western countries isn't the entire story. As we look into the future, we are witnessing the incredible shrinking Western church. And within two decades the Western church is likely to see even more rapid decline because of our inability to reach and keep the young. While the human needs in our McWorld future mount, how will it be possible for the Western church to expand missions at home and abroad, if the church continues to gray and decline?

It is my reluctant conclusion that unless something dramatic happens to change the present trends, the church is not only likely to become significantly smaller in the first two decades of the twenty-first century; it will also have significantly less time and resources to invest in mission work to meet the growing needs likely to fill tomorrow's world.

The problem with a decline in numbers, of course, is that it will automatically reduce the amount of time and money available to be invested in the advancement of God's kingdom. Simply put, a decline in numbers inevitability means a decline in resources. In the second section of this chapter I will examine specifically how the giving patterns of the church are likely to change as we gallop into a new millennium. Because of the limited availability of research on this topic, I will have to limit this examination to giving patterns of the church in North America.

The Incredible Shrinking Western Purse

It is becoming more and more evident that in an increasingly competitive McWorld future, many middle-class people will have to work not only harder but longer. So we are likely to continue to see a steady erosion of our discretionary time available for family, relationships, prayer, Scripture study, service, and being involved in our churches. As we have seen, there will also be growing pressure to persuade us, and particularly our young, to relinquish an increasing percentage of whatever is left of our discretionary time and money at the McWorld macromall.

Fund-Raisers Frozen in a Time Warp

As I work with Christian fund-raisers in North America, they all seem to work from unstated twin assumptions: (1) that the Christian giving pool in Western countries will be at least as large in the future as it is today; (2) that the new generation will have at least as much discretionary time and money to support the church as did older generations.

We have already seen that the first assumption isn't valid. The donor pool is shrinking, and there will be significantly fewer of the under-thirty-five to lead the church into the twenty-first century. The second assumption isn't valid, either. Those under age thirty-five have hit the economy at a much tougher time than did those over age forty-five. Because, as we have shown, the relationship to what the young earn to what they can afford to buy has changed, they will have both less time and less money to invest in the work of the church than did older generations. The declining purchasing power of those under age thirty-five is documented in *The State of Working America 1996–1997.*[39] And if the young succumb to the growing pressures of McWorld to work longer and consume more, they could have even less left to invest in the cause of the kingdom. Therefore, given these trends, I believe that those under age thirty-five will not even be able to sustain their present giving levels to the church and its mission, let alone increase them.

At the core of this emerging crisis is the dawning reality that my generation sold their generation the wrong dream. For all the talk about the lordship of Jesus, my generation sold the young the American dream with a little Jesus overlay. For all the talk about lordship, the real message to the Christian young is the message that drives McWorld. Agenda one is getting ahead in your job, getting ahead in the suburbs, getting your upscale lifestyle started; then, with whatever you have left, follow Jesus. As we have seen, if the new generation puts the American dream first, they will have little time or money to invest in the mission of the mustard seed.

Future of Fund-Raising in the North American Church

Dean Hoge, in his important study *Money Matters: Personal Giving in American Churches,* informs us that twenty thousand to forty thousand professionals plus support staff are on the front lines of the competitive field of fund-raising in the United States.[40] Even with the economy slowing now, many of them are having a good ride. Research indicates that for the last seven years, income is up for charitable organizations, including the church. However, the rate of increased giving is not keeping pace with the rate of economic growth in the United States in the last seven years.

But there is another concerning trend. While corporate profits have been soaring during this boom time, corporate giving has declined. In 1980 corporate donations were 2.1 percent of pretax profits. In 1996 they had fallen to less than 1 percent.[41] In their efforts to maximize profits for shareholders, corporations are not only scaling back their contributions but increasingly tailoring them in a way that focuses on advancing corporate objectives rather than addressing the most urgent needs in their communities.

Since governments everywhere are likely to continue to cut back services for those in need, people of faith must persuade not only the church but also the business sector to increase, not decrease, its funding of programs to enable our poorest neighbors to participate in the liftoff of the McWorld economy.

My greatest area of concern in terms of church giving is how much time and money Christians invest in God's mission to our poorest, most vulnerable neighbors. Hoge tells us that in 1994 Christians gave a total of $1.41 billion. But of that amount, total giving to foreign missions was only $109 million.[42] And as I work with mission executives, frankly they aren't all having the same levels of success at raising money in these boom times as are other organizations. Let's look at the future of giving in the U.S. church and discuss the implications for the future of the church in America and its mission into the third millennium.

Giving, American Style

Buoyed by recent economic growth, donations to all kinds of charities in the United States, adjusted for inflation, increased 7.8 percent. However, giving to social services such as youth, family, and employment services declined by 3 percent. For those counting on the private sector to pick up the slack, this isn't welcome news. If giving to social services is declining in economic times as good as these, what will the future hold if we enter a full-blown recession? Giving to religious organizations, including the church, increased by only 2.5 percent.[43]

The Empty Tomb, which does some of the most helpful research on giving patterns in the American church, has some concerning information on giving over the last twenty-eight years. They report that the real growth in the United States per capita income, after taxes and inflation have been factored out, increased by 68 percent between 1968 and 1995. However, during the same period the percentage of per capita income contributed to the church declined 21 percent, from 3.11 percent to 2.46 percent.[44] Even more concerning is the decline in benevolent giving in the American churches that are designed to address human needs outside the church building. Between 1968 and 1995 income given to benevolence declined 38 percent.[45]

The researchers divided the American church between those mainline churches affiliated with the National Council of Churches and

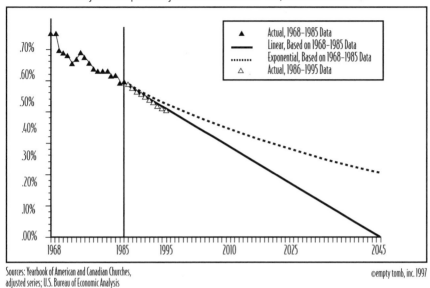

Figure 2.
Projected Trends for 29 Denominations, Giving as a Percentage of Income to Benevolences,
Using Linear and Exponential Regression Based on Data for 1968–1985, with Actual Data 1986–1995

Sources: Yearbook of American and Canadian Churches,
adjusted series; U.S. Bureau of Economic Analysis

©empty tomb, inc. 1997

those evangelical churches affiliated with the National Association of Evangelicals. Both groups reflected the decline. The NAE group's giving declined from 6 percent in 1968 to 4 percent in 1995, a 33 percent drop. The NCC group's giving declined less sharply, from 3.3 percent in 1968 to 2.9 percent in 1995. Particularly concerning was the rate of decline in benevolent giving. Between 1985 and 1995 giving to benevolence by NAE-affiliated churches declined by 18 percent. During the same period benevolent giving declined by 14 percent in NCC-affiliated churches.[46]

The Empty Tomb's forecast for the future of benevolent giving in the United States is truly alarming. "If the giving patterns of the past 28 years continue in an uninterrupted fashion, then per-member giving as a portion of income to the category of Benevolence will reach 0% of income . . . in 2045."[47] While this linear forecast seems improbable, the downward trend of giving should concern all those in Christian leadership.

We need a wake-up call! While the challenges of the twenty-first century are escalating, the capacity of the Western church to be part of God's compassionate response is declining at a disturbing rate. If the dual trends of declining attendance and declining giving continue uninterrupted, by the year 2020 the Western church and our mission initiatives could be a shadow of what exists today. I pray that this assessment will sound an alarm among leaders in the Western church. I urge Christian leaders in local churches, denominational offices, and mission organizations to convene forums with missiologists and demographers and develop innovative strategies to grow and fund the mission of the church into a new millennium.

Opportunities for Christian Leaders

To reverse the trend of decline in attendance and giving will take a major new initiative in all countries. This presents an opportunity for leaders

1. to strategically target our evangelistic efforts to reach those under age thirty-five. Much of the leadership for this initiative will need to come from younger leaders. However, for this initiative to be successful, we must create a new spectrum of church plants and mentoring programs and genuinely bring the young into leadership, inviting their creativity to help reinvent the church for the twenty-first century.
2. to call Christians of all ages to embrace a more biblical form of whole-life discipleship and stewardship, in which we are sharing much more than the scanty leftovers of our lives in the advancement of God's kingdom.
3. to reinvent not only our lives but our communities of faith so they more authentically incarnate the values of God's kingdom and so we will dedicate a larger share of resources to advancing God's kingdom in ministering to the growing needs of the third millennium.
4. to replace the flawed secular humanist critique of how we got off the tracks with a new critique that takes seriously the extent to which McWorld and the aspirations and values of modern culture have seduced many American Christians.
5. to enable our members to find in Scripture a compelling new alternative vision for their lives, to replace the one offered by McWorld.

Questions for Discussion and Action

1. How are attendance patterns changing in the churches in your country and in your denomination or local congregation? What are some creative ways in which you can respond to these trends?

2. In particular, what are the attendance patterns of those under age thirty-five, and what are some creative ways in which you might reach this population in your community?

3. How are giving and volunteering patterns changing in your church or denomination? What are some innovative ways in which to increase these figures?

4. What are some specific ways in which you and your church could alter your priorities in the use of time and money to invest more in evangelism, church planting, and mission efforts to the poor to grow the church again?

Part 2

A Crisis of Vision

Learning to Take the Future of God Seriously

WESTERN PROGRESS IS THE CENTERPIECE of modernity, and
the powerhouse propelling McWorld into a new millennium. And more than we recognize, it defines for
many of us our notion of home and our image of the better future. Richard Middleton and Brian Walsh state,
"The progress ideal functions as an article of faith, the
unifying commitment or civil religion of the Western
Civilization. . . . Just as the story of Babel [Gen. 11:1–9]
summarizes the primordial cultural aspirations of the

143

human race . . . of the building of 'a city with a tower reaching to the heavens,' so we could characterize the modern Western dream of progress as the building of a vast, towering civilization."[1]

Postmodernists have in recent years busied themselves deconstructing everything they don't like about modernity. One of the things they particularly don't like is the orchestrating vision of modernity, Western progress. They do a brilliant job of dismantling the vision of inevitable economic and social progress, but by the very nature of postmodernity, they are incapable of offering an alternative vision of home or hope. As a consequence, Brian Walsh describes postmodernists and a postmodern generation as wandering homeless through the universe in search of something more.

Walsh pictures postmoderns as Arthur Dent, a cosmic nomad from *The Hitchhiker's Guide to the Galaxy,* and as Lily Tomlin's character Trudy the Bag Lady. Arthur wanders through an apparently meaningless universe, homeless and alone. Somehow he realizes that reality is not what it ought to be, so he travels in search of counsel. He meets a prophet who encourages him to solve his problem by creating his own universe, his own reality. But Arthur realizes that there is an inherent problem with this postmodern solution. If anything goes awry in his self-created universe, it is essentially his fault.

This answer doesn't solve Arthur's deepest longings. The narrator says, "He so much wanted to be home. He so much wanted his own home world. . . . He so much wanted that when he opened his eyes again he would be standing on the doorstep of his little cottage in the western country of England, that the sun would be shining over the green hills, the post van would be going up the lane, the daffodils would be blooming in the garden, and in the distance the pub would be open for lunch."[2]

Trudy the Bag Lady is trying to help some aliens from outer space, who are in search of intelligent life in the universe, consider relocating on planet Earth. "The prospects do not seem too promising!" Walsh intones. "But not only do we have the alien's cultural perspective, Trudy herself sees things aslant." Speaking of her own madness, Trudy exclaims, "I refuse to be intimidated by reality anymore. After all, what is reality anyway? Nothin' but a collective hunch. My space chums think reality was once a primitive method of crowd control that got out of hand. In my view, it's absurdity dressed up in a three piece business suit. I made some studies, and reality is the leading cause of stress among those in touch with it. I take it in small doses, but as a lifestyle I found it too confining."[3] Trudy figures that being out of touch with reality isn't such a bad idea.

More and more of the Western young are, like Dent and Trudy, homeless in our world, left to define their own reality and manufacture their own hope. They have joined Trudy in rejecting the dominant reality and live in an increasingly tribal world in which everything is morally relative. But like Dent, they also share a tremendous longing for home. But they have no idea how to get there. Postmodernity is highly skilled in dismantling the dominant reality but is impotent to offer us a home or a hope.

And since much of the Western church is locked into a dualistic worldview that accepts unquestioningly modernity's view of reality and the better future, we aren't able to offer much hope to a postmodern generation, either. Middleton and Walsh conclude, "While modern culture was self-assured in its control of the world and taming of nature in order to make a human home, postmodern culture is plagued by a profound sense of homelessness."[4]

A Crisis of Vision

I am convinced that the number one crisis in both society and the church today is a crisis of vision. It isn't just a postmodern generation that is having difficulty finding its way home. We all seem to be struggling in many ways to find purpose and meaning in our existence.

When I use the term *vision,* I am not talking about anything hyperspiritual in the clouds. I simply mean the image of the better future that we want for ourselves and those we care about. Kenneth Boulding, a Christian and a scholar, said, "No people, society, or organization can long exist without a compelling image of the better future that calls us forward into tomorrow." The Bible says, "Without a vision the people perish." Not only are we perishing, but the people we are called to serve in Christ's name are perishing because we lack a compelling image of the better future that comes from our faith instead of from modern culture.

A Crisis of Reflection

I believe that this crisis of vision is at the core a crisis of reflection. We simply don't spend enough time reflecting on why we do what we do. As a consequence, at many levels the images and values of modern culture subvert our lives, families, and Christian organizations, and we scarcely seem to notice. Charles Silberman has charged that "what is wrong with elementary or secondary education—or for that matter higher education, journalism or television . . . has less to do with incompetence or indifference" than with "mindlessness" and "venality." He added, "We must find ways of stimulating educators . . . to think seriously about what they are doing and why they are doing it."[5]

When I lectured for seven years in the doctoral program in educational policy studies at Seattle University, I was repeatedly astonished at how difficult it was for professionals who had worked their entire lives in education to explain what they were doing and why they were doing it. These professionals were brilliant at curriculum design, reading computer spreadsheets, and "matching teaching styles and learning styles." But when I asked them what their assumptions were regarding what learning is (is it information transfer? the systematic reinforcement of desired behaviors? demonstration of the ability to work critically and synthetically with ideas? or something else?), they visibly blanched and often became speechless.

A Crisis of Reflection in the Church

I believe this is a particular problem in the American church. As Mark Noll documents in *The Scandal of the Evangelical Mind,* there is a strong strain of anti-intellectualism in American Protestantism, particularly in the conservative or evangelical tradition.[6] When I ask Christian leaders to explain to me their assumptions underlying their programs in church planting, youth ministries, or missions, I receive the same kind of response I get from educators. The leaders can describe in detail the latest approaches in planting "user-friendly churches," but they are often at a loss to define their ecclesiology (their theology of the church).

A few years ago I attended an international evangelical conference that had a single task: to enable participants to define the relationship between church and parachurch. When the conference ended, we were more confused than when we began, largely because as evangelicals many of us had never biblically defined for ourselves what the church was.

In a course on Christian worldview that I teach for Fuller Theological Seminary, we spend a good deal of time discussing how we Western Christians tend to appropriate the secular models of almost everything, baptize them, and employ them in Christ's name. Virtually all of our Christian schooling, for example, is simply an appropriation of secular Greek models of education into which we plug chapel and a few Bible courses. We don't seem to recognize that a lot of the assumptions that come with the secular models are often in tension with biblical assumptions.

The problem isn't just with education. When Christians set up counseling programs, establish health clinics, or work with the poor, we tend to appropriate the secular models without ever critically evaluating the assumptions that are part of the package. And in our effort to reach the unchurched, too often we plant consumer-oriented churches that are more reminiscent of an upscale shopping mall than of that first informal band who followed Jesus.

Os Guinness observes in his incisive book *Fit Bodies Fat Minds* that "failing to think Christianly, evangelicals have been forced into the role of cultural imitators and adapters rather than originators. In biblical terms, it is to be worldly and conformist, not decisively Christian."[7]

One of the major reasons I believe we fail to think Christianly is that many evangelicals operate as though all the questions have been answered regarding what it means to be the church, do the mission of the church, and be followers of Christ, and now it's our responsibility to simply go out and put it into practice. I am not convinced we have answered all these questions or that all our answers are bibilical. In the next two chapters I will argue that we need to fundamentally rethink why we do what we do.

Nowhere is this situation more critical than in the extent to which we have unquestioningly embraced modernity's notion of the good life and better future for ourselves, our children, and our communities of faith and made it our home. This crisis of vision is subverting our ability to provide an authentic witness of God's new order and is fostering a culturally accommodated view of faith, church, and discipleship. And it is also making us more vulnerable to the marketing messages of McWorld, which in turn directly contributes to our declining attendance and giving patterns.

I am persuaded that for many of us the reason for both our crisis of vision and our crisis of reflection is our failure to take Scripture seriously for *all of life*. We have learned to use Scripture devotionally and liturgically in worship. But we seldom use it culturally to help us define an alternative vision to the American dream. The black church in America is much more in touch with the rich biblical imagery of the promised homecoming of God than is the white church. Unless we take dramatic action to deal with this crisis of vision in the Western church, we will become little more than a culturally compromised shadow of what God intended. And we will have little ability to offer a hope or a home to others. Ravi Zacharias Ministries is one of the few organizations that help us think biblically about why we do what we do. The ministry is a valuable resource to the North American church and can be reached at: rzim@rzim.com.

In chapter 7 I will ask, How did we get off the tracks? And in chapter 8 I will ask, How can we find our way home? How can we find, in a renewal of biblical imagination, a vision for our lives, families, and congregations that offers a compelling alternative to the aspirations of the American dream? How can we find our way to a home that looks more like Jerusalem than Babylon?

How Did We Get Off the Tracks?

THE LARGEST CROSS I HAVE EVER SEEN soared twenty stories in the air above the Valley of the Fallen outside Torrejon, Spain. An elevator took me down twenty stories into the bowels of the mountain on which the cross stood. As the elevator door opened, I was ushered into a Benedictine abbey built in the depths of the earth. We were in time for morning vespers. I could hear the haunting sounds of a boys' choir singing Gregorian chants that echoed through the corridors. We entered the sanctuary and took our seats in the back as the service began. During this trip in Europe, I had visited a Cistercian abbey in Switzerland and a Franciscan community in Italy, but I was unprepared for what I experienced in the depths of this mountain in Spain.

As I sat down, I found myself in a sanctuary chillingly different from any I had ever visited before. The severe gray vaulted chamber looked as if it had been designed as a railway tunnel by fascist architects of the thirties. It came complete with heroic sculptures of biblical figures that resembled the women of war that decorate some structures I had seen in Germany.

In the center of the somber chamber, where two gray tunnels intersected, was a breathtaking sight. There suspended above us was the most human Christ figure I have ever seen. It was carved out of a single piece of wood firmly nailed to a rough-hewn log cross. Jesus' body shone with a warm golden glow that seemed out of place in that dark fascist cavern.

I found the contrasting images and the emotions they provoked so disturbing that I was unable to focus on the Mass. As the abbott led me out of the sanctuary, I questioned him regarding the images, in an effort to make sense of what I had just experienced. He explained that the Valley of the Fallen was the site of one of the most brutal battles of the Spanish Civil War. The cross and the Benedictine abbey were dedicated to the victory of the Nationalists in that war.

He paused and then said, "You have been worshiping in the midst of thirty-five thousand soldiers from both sides buried in this mountain. Franco not only ordered the construction of this religious shrine to celebrate his victory, he personally cut down the tree on which the figure of Christ is hanging. We Benedictines hope this place can somehow be a center for reconciliation." As he said that, a chill went down my spine.

I found myself reeling with the warring images of a national monument dedicated to the victory of a brutal dictator and his fascist government . . . a sanctuary dedicated to reconciliation . . . the thousands of young men forever entombed in the walls of that sanctuary . . . the sight of young Spanish lads in the choir—some of whom undoubtedly were related to those who had fallen—chanting the praises of the Almighty . . . and this most human Christ forever nailed to Franco's cross and eternally entombed with the fallen in this monument to war, fascism, and nationalism.

I struggled because I found everything I had come to treasure as a follower of Jesus co-opted by images and agendas that not only bore no similarity to his peaceable kingdom but in so many ways violated everything that the servant Jesus represented. The obsessions of nationalism have dominated the twentieth century and created this disturbing specter. However, as we cross the threshold of a new millennium, the forces of nationalism are rapidly losing ground to the forces of globalism. But I believe that the aspirations and values that power McWorld's intentions for our common future are no less alien to the aspirations of God's kingdom than are the images in the bowels of that Spanish mountain.

Babylon Revisited

Finding Our Way out of Town

Once when my son Clint and I were touring England, we tried to drive out of York at rush hour so we could get to London and start our trek back home. For an hour and a half I tried unsuccessfully to get out of town. Every road I tried brought us right back into the center of

York. And we tried yet again to get out of town. It was like the film *Groundhog Day*—déjà vu all over again. In many ways that is reminiscent of our common human journey. We tend to get stuck in a place that isn't home and seem to have a lot of trouble finding our way out of town.

Finding Our Way Home

Walter Brueggemann tells us that the children of Israel, when they were in captivity in Babylon, came down with another problem regarding home. They contracted a serious case of amnesia. Somehow they forgot that Babylon was a place of bondage. They forgot that Babylon had defied the authority of the Creator God by declaring itself to be absolute reality. They forgot that they were in exile in a "strange land and they came to regard it as home. They assimilated."[1]

They assimilated into the dominant reality of their time and apparently even forgot their God and their home. It is to these victims of cultural amnesia that the prophet Isaiah speaks. He not only invites them to come back home to Jerusalem; he announces that Yahweh will bring down the arrogance and pretensions of Babylon to make it clear that God, and God alone, is the Lord of history.[2]

Finding the Focus

In this chapter I will explore how we seem to continually get off the tracks and become seduced by Babylons that keep us from finding our way home. I will explore why we do what we do in the way we seek to follow Jesus Christ in our contemporary society. I will particularly examine how, I believe, we North American Christians have often unwittingly allowed modernity, Western dualism, and the American dream to shape our lives and trivialize our faith. I am convinced that at the core of our crisis is a misplaced allegiance.

I will attempt to show that many of us have inadvertently given our primary allegiance to the aspirations that power McWorld instead of to those that motivate the mustard seed movement. I believe this misplaced allegiance can explain why we have so little of our lives and resources left for the things that really matter.

Essentially, I will argue that we have discipleship dead wrong. We have settled for a dualistic discipleship and have exported this flawed model all over the planet. To get discipleship right requires discovering a new sense of biblical purpose for our lives—all of our lives. Therefore, at the center of a biblical call to whole-life discipleship is a reawakened imagination of the Creator's vision for coming home that is different from the vision promised us by McWorld.

Naming the Powers and Finding Our Way

Our deepest human longing is to find our way home to all we are called to be. But too often we keep winding up right back in Babylon. As we saw, many people in Spain, including those of Christian faith, accepted the definition of ultimate reality that was offered them by a fascist state. The fascist state succeeded in fabricating a feeling of national brotherhood. And even many in the church accepted and celebrated its pretensions and its brutal use of power. But I think the abbot knew that the shrine to Spanish fascism constructed twenty floors below ground wasn't home.

After the Soviet empire imploded, Orthodox clerics acknowledged that they too had allowed faith to be co-opted by the agendas of a brutally repressive communist state. Even Emilio Castro, the former head of the World Council of Churches, belatedly admitted that the WCC, in its efforts to support the Orthodox Church, had often been co-opted by the agendas of the Soviet state. They all confessed that they had lost their way and that the communist state wasn't home, either.

The arrogant human pretension of defining for ourselves what is ultimate is still alive and well. It simply continues to take on new forms. Hendrik Berkhof traces this arrogance to what Paul described as the "principalities and powers of the earth." Berkhof states, "The powers are no longer instruments, linkages between God's love, as revealed in Christ, and the visible creation. In fact they have become gods [Gal. 4:8], behaving as though they were the ultimate ground of being, and demanding from men appropriate worship. . . . No longer do the powers bind man and God together; they separate them."[3]

Lesslie Newbigin adds, "The principalities and powers are real. They are invisible and we cannot locate them in time or space. They do not exist as disembodied entities floating above this world, or lurking within it. They meet us as embodied in visible tangible realities—peoples, nations and institutions. And they are powerful."[4]

In *Engaging the Powers,* Walter Wink states that the "Powers," while essentially good, have become bent on control and degenerate into the "Domination System." The domination system is not only intent on defining what is ultimate but is also determined to insert itself into every arena of human existence. In the process, the powers even redefine the destination of human life.[5]

The arrogant fascist and communist states, like the original Babylon, have fallen. But Babylon lives on. As we will see, the principalities and powers are still in the business of creating domination systems that, like the Babylons before, seek to define what is absolute and the values that should direct our lives and shape our institutions.

Today modernity, as expressed in a fiercely competitive global economic order, is the domination system that is, I believe, playing the lead role in subverting our lives, families, and congregations. Os Guinness offers a helpful definition of modernity. "Put simply, modernity can be understood as the character and system of the world produced by the forces of development and modernization, especially capitalism, industrial technology, and telecommunications."[6]

While we are all benefiting in many ways from globalization, in other ways, as we have seen, it is putting our future at risk. Whatever may be the respective costs and benefits of globalization, I will argue that the aspirations and values that power McWorld are in many ways in direct conflict with those that motivate the mustard seed movement. We need to find a way to be in this new one-world order without being a part of it.

How Did We Get Derailed?

In every age Christians battle against those forces that would subvert our faith and secularize our lives. I believe that one of the major reasons why we have discipleship wrong is that we haven't accurately named the principalities and powers with which we struggle. We haven't named the forces of secularization that are having their way with us. And as a consequence, we haven't been able to describe clearly why our attendance and giving patterns seem to be declining. Exactly how have we been derailed in our desire to follow Christ in a foreign land, and how has that influenced us to reduce our levels of involvement?

Derailed by Worldliness?

When I attended an evangelical Christian college in the fifties, everyone knew what would derail a vital faith: "worldliness." Therefore, the way to maintain a vital Christian life was simply to abstain from worldliness. The only problem was that the list of worldly activities differed from group to group, which was confusing for serious young Christian college students. Some churches had a short list that included abstaining from the basics: dancing, movies, and drinking. Others included cosmetics, jewelry, and playing with face cards. I don't believe that any of the groups that are still promoting the old-fashioned legalism can make any clear connection between this view of secularism and why Christian involvement in the work of God's kingdom is in decline.

Derailed by Secular Humanism?

By far the most popular notion of how we in the contemporary church have become secularized is something called secular humanism. Today it is virtually the only game in town when it comes to explaining how we got off the tracks. Francis Schaeffer gave us the term. He said the roots of modern secularism were to be found in the Renaissance, when "man became the measure of all things." Of course, there is some truth to that, but I am convinced that the secularism that bedevils us has its roots more deeply imbedded in the Enlightenment than in the humanistic period.

As popularly understood in the United States, secular humanists are those people who are for abortion, gay rights, and a liberal political agenda. Evangelical Christians in America not finding themselves anywhere on this list mistakenly assume we are as pure as the driven snow. Of course, nothing could be further from the truth. We are being eaten alive by a secularism we haven't named.

It is my contention that the secular humanist critique doesn't hold water either biblically or historically. Since this critique sees the problem as something largely external to the community of faith, it doesn't offer much help in explaining why levels of Christian involvement are declining. The only way in which we can hope to overcome the secularizing influences of contemporary culture is to do a better job of defining how Western Christians are being derailed. I urge church historians, biblical scholars, pastors, and the rest of us to join together in an effort to develop a fresh critique of the forces of secularization with which we struggle. Here's my beginning attempt to add to the conversation regarding a quest for a new critique.

Derailed by Modernity?

As we have seen, postmodernists have in recent decades launched a major intellectual critique of modernity. They busy themselves deconstructing everything from modernity's assumptions about the objectification of knowledge to the belief in Western progress. A number of generally younger Christians in Britain and the United States find that they resonate with the postmodernists' critique of modernity. For instance, *The Post Evangelical,* written by Dave Tomlinson, has caused a real stir in Britain.[7] It has caused a stir because Tomlinson states that he feels more comfortable with the intellectual insights of postmodernity than with those of modernity and that he no longer identifies himself as a part of the evangelical community.

David Wells is a theologian who also battles with modernity. In his book *Losing Our Virtue,* he writes, "While we feast on the largesse of modernity . . . we are losing our moral bearings."[8] His critique reflects the biggest problem that most evangelicals have with modern culture: the erosion of our moral values. And that is important. But Rodney Clapp is one of a handful of Christian authors who understands that our fight with modernity not only is an intellectual and moral struggle but is a cultural contest as well. In his book *A Peculiar People,* Clapp calls the church to seek the transformation of not only our spiritual lives and moral values but our cultural values too.[9]

Unfortunately, I find few postmodernists, postmodern Christians, or Christian authors, except Clapp and a few others, who offer a serious critique of the way in which we have allowed modernity to fundamentally define both the structure of our daily lives and our sense of what is important and of value. I believe we have permitted modern culture to define why we do what we do both in our personal lives and in how we organize our churches and Christian organizations, and never realized we were caving in to aspirations and values counter to biblical faith.

Speaking at St. Luke's Anglican Church in London, where Dave Tomlinson and his post-evangelical compatriots worship, I said, "You haven't gone far enough in deconstructing modernity. It isn't enough to join the postmodernists in an intellectual critique of modernity. We also need to critique the extent to which we have all allowed modernity to define our notion of the good life and better future and what we are raising our kids for."

Buying Into the Dualistic Discipleship Model

What we have done, I am convinced, is to inadvertently succumb to a dualistic model of discipleship and stewardship. In spite of all the talk about Christ's lordship, everyone knows that the expectations of modern culture come first. Everyone knows that getting ahead in the job comes first. Getting ahead in the suburbs comes first. Getting the kids off to their activities comes first. And we tend to make decisions in these areas pretty much like everyone else does, based on our income, our professions, and our social status.

Essentially, most Western Christians unquestioningly allow modern culture to arrange the furniture of our lives: forty- to eighty-hour workweeks, single-family detached housing, congested time schedules for our lives and children. Over the last fifteen years I have seen Christians becoming busier and busier, which means they have less time left over for prayer, church, ministry, or even family. As we have seen, we are racing into a future in which McWorld wants an even larger chunk of our time and money, which means having even less time for the things of faith.

On the other side of this dualism, following Christ is too often trivialized to little more than a devotional lubricant to keep us from stripping our gears as we charge up the mountain, trying to get ahead in our careers, the suburbs, and our kids' activities. In this dualistic discipleship model, following Christ is for too many of us reduced to little more than fifteen minutes in the morning and two hours on Sunday. In this model, we wind up with a highly privatized and spiritualized piety that is often largely disconnected from the rest of our lives.

- Getting ahead in the job comes first
- Getting ahead in our living situations comes first
- Getting our economic security comes first
- Getting our kids off to their activities comes first

✝ and Jesus too

The problem with this dualistic model is that we not only sanction giving our first allegiance to decisions about where to work, live, and rear our young; we permit modern culture, as part of the deal, to define our notions of the good life and better future. As a consequence, our lives are too often driven by the same manic aspirations that propel McWorld. No wonder we are exhausted. Modernity calls the tune and we dance.

Rodney Clapp observes that we are in serious trouble when we privatize and spiritualize our faith and allow the dominant culture to define the rest of our lives. George Marsden, looking back at the revivalist roots of this kind of culturally accommodated faith, states there was no insistence to "abandon most of the standards of the respectable middle-class way of life. It was to these standards, in fact, that people were to be converted."[10]

The American church, in its many expressions, seems to quietly accept modern culture's demands on its members as a given and then content itself with whatever is left. Virtually all the Christian books I have seen on discipleship—or for that matter, on finances, time management, and career planning—also tend to accept the demands of modern culture as unquestioned givens, and then advise that we simply try to practice our discipleship over the top, as if it all goes together. And of course, it doesn't.

I am convinced that one of the main reasons we American Christians aren't effective in evangelism is that we are so much like the culture around us that we have little to call people to. We hang around church buildings more than others do. We abstain from a few things. We don't practice hedonism as well as the people around us—but we sure keep trying.

Looking Back—Origins of Our Dualism

This dualistic model of discipleship is a product of modern culture, which has its origins in our Hellenistic and Enlightenment past. Plato can take a lot of credit for our drawing a sharp line between the material world and the world of the spirit. He characterized the material world in negative terms, as a realm from which we need to escape to enjoy an ideal existence in the nonmaterial realm of the spirit up there somewhere. Sound familiar? This early Greek dualism has decisively shaped our modern worldview, our Christian faith, and even our notions of God's redemptive initiative.

Francis Bacon, writing in the sixteenth century, drew another sharp line that reinforced this Platonic dualism. He metaphorically took a sword and divided the world in half. He said that on one side of the line are the "words of God," which have to do with the world of the spirit. He assigned this realm to the theologians. On the other side of the line, he stated, are the "works of God"—that's the larger natural world that had his keen attention. In that simple act of dividing the "words of God" from the "works of God," Bacon inadvertently divided spirit from body, evicted the Creator from the creation, and created a dualistic worldview that has come to pervade modern culture and has directly contributed to our dualistic view of life and faith.

A Crisis of Vision: Dualistic Images of Coming Home

Because of the pervasive influence of Western dualism, many of us have embraced two different images of the better future, neither of which is biblical. The first image of the better future is a heaven in the clouds divorced from this material world. The second image is coming home to a life of individual economic upscaling, in which the better future is defined primarily in economic terms, as it is in McWorld.

Coming Home to a Disembodied Future in the Clouds

Many Christians, including those of evangelical faith, envision the future of God in considerably broader, less spiritualized terms than I describe here. But I am constantly astonished at how many Christians of all traditions envision coming home to a highly spiritualized, privatized future up there somewhere, a future completely disconnected from this world.

Speaking at Wheaton College to a class of forty students, I asked, "What is your image of the future of God?" A young man spoke up. He said, "Heaven." I asked, "What imagery comes to mind when you think of heaven?" He thought for a moment and then said, "Clouds, harps, and angel wings." Plato has had his way with us. It is Plato who wrote that little ditty "This world is not my home; I am just passing through."

Remember, it was a Greek philosopher, not a Hebrew prophet, who envisioned the ideal future as going home to a nonmaterial existence in the clouds. In Hebrew literature the image of God's future always includes the creation and is never divorced from it.

Lesslie Newbigin declares that looking forward to having our disembodied souls take up residence in a nonmaterial heaven in the clouds simply isn't biblical. "For a biblical writer, continued existence as a disembodied soul is not something to be desired but feared with loathing."[11] Of course, when we are absent from the body, we are present with the Lord. But as we will see in the next chapter, the future that God is preparing will not be found in a nonmaterial existence in a heaven up there somewhere. Scripture teaches us that because Christ rose, we will also rise, mind, body, soul, and spirit, to be a part of a new heaven and a new earth.

There are a number of problems with this narrow, spiritualized view of redemptive theology. First of all, because it is incredibly individualistic, it tends to reinforce a self-centered, spiritualized form of faith that implies the Creator God singularly exists to meet my needs. Second, since God doesn't care about this world and plans to vaporize it, why should we give a rip about it? Third, if God is only interested in saving our souls, then, as a friend once asked, why should we care about hungry people? It makes no sense.

Finally, for many people this spiritualized view of redemptive theology is wedded to a degenerative view of history and a fatalistic view of the future, in which everything is destined to get worse. Because of the endtimes theories they have embraced, many people are convinced that nothing can get better. As I mentioned in *Cease Fire,* I doubt these good people ever prayed that the Berlin Wall would come down or the Soviet Union would implode, because they couldn't imagine anything on that scale getting better.[12]

As a consequence, many Christians wind up with a dualistic view of God. Their God is active in their spiritual lives and shows up at prayer meetings but is impotent to act in the larger, natural world until the curtain comes down. This God has no power to act in the Middle East peace negotiations, influence the direction of urban planning among the poor in east Los Angeles, or make a difference in the destruction of the rain forest in Belize.

Let's look at the other image of the better future, which seems to play a greater role in determining the focus and format of our busy lives.

Coming Home to a Future of Economic Upscaling on Earth

What gave strong momentum to the Enlightenment was the creation of a new image of what the better future could look like. The storytellers of the Enlightenment told us a new tale and fashioned a new imagination.

They took the vertical quest for God's kingdom that had dominated European consciousness through the Middle Ages and tipped it over on its side. In the Age of Reason it became the horizontal quest for a kingdom on earth largely divorced from the reign of God or anything transcendent.

The storytellers of the Enlightenment assured us that if we cooperated with natural law, all of society would progress. We would gradually gain greater mastery over the natural world, create a future of ever increasing levels of economic growth, and be freed to pursue our individual material happiness.

Francis Bacon, in his book *The New Atlantis,* was the first author to imagine coming home to a future of advanced technology mastering nature, of synthetic foods, and of a society with expanding consumer choice. This is the vision of the better future that is at the core of modernity. Someone has written, "Marxism says all there is, is matter. Capitalism says all that matters is matter." But both are inherently materialistic visions for the future that lack any larger sense of transcendent purpose.

Modernity from John Locke on has also increasingly defined life in individualistic terms. This has given rise to a radical autonomy that Craig Gay, in his book *The Way of the (Modern) World,* describes as one of the most destructive features of modernity.[13] Many in the boomer generation want a life not only of individual economic upscaling but also of self-actualization, whereby they are accountable to no one, including God.

Over time, modern Western society has come to define the good life in largely economic and materialistic terms. Most of us, whether we are evangelicals, mainliners, or Catholics, seem to have accepted without question that the better future means getting ahead in our individual careers, in the suburbs, and in upscaling our individual lifestyles. Like our secular counterparts, we seem to have bought into the notion that the more we own, the more we are.

Leo Tolstoy wrote a compelling short story titled "How Much Land Does a Man Need?" A Russian farmer named Paho'm buys and sells land but is never satisfied. He always wants more. A nomad offers to sell him as much land as he can walk around in a day. Driven by an insatiable appetite, the farmer attempts to make it around a huge piece of land by sundown. As the sun is about to set, Paho'm rushes, exhausted, back toward the starting point. Just before the sun disappears, he reaches his goal. Paho'm's servant runs to congratulate him and finds him dead, with blood flowing from his mouth. How much land does a man need? "Six feet from his head to his heels was all he needed."[14]

According to David Myers, research shows that the average American owns and consumes much more today than in the fifties. We are twice as affluent as we were then. We own twice as many cars and TV sets, plus a spectrum of new technologies that weren't available then, such as VCRs and computers. And on average we are considerably larger and spend two and a half times more money on eating out in restaurants and bars than Americans did in the sixties. But despite the fact that we have more than doubled our level of consumption, the National Opinion Research Center reports that people aren't any happier than they were in the fifties.[15]

Focusing on the Family

In spite of evidence to the contrary, many of us still believe deep in our guts that increased consumerism and having more will result in increased happiness. And for many, like Paho'm, this insatiable appetite for more can cost everything. While Christians on occasion rail against materialism, the aspirations of the American dream still seem to play a major role in shaping the direction of our lives and families. For example, Christian parents want what's best for their kids, as do all parents. But because of the pervasiveness of the American dream, we tend to define what's best, as everyone else does, in largely economic terms. For all the talk about "raising a child up in the way he should go," the real message to the Christian young, which often flies under the banner of "excellence," is, "Get the best you can for yourselves"—a driven individualism.

Robert Cole, a leading psychologist in the United States, observes of the North American young, "Very little is asked of a lot of American children with regards to compassion and thinking of others. The emphasis is to cultivate the individuality and self-importance of each child. One sees home after home where children are encouraged to look out for themselves and get what they can. Very little emphasis is put on pointing a child's eyes and ears away from himself or herself and towards others."[16]

The number one reason given by Christian college students in the United States for not considering a vocation in mission work is their Christian parents. When the subject is broached, their parents typically tell them, "Look, we didn't spend sixty thousand dollars on your college education for you to go bopping off to a refugee camp in Africa. You get your career under way, your IRA pension scheme started, and then after you are established, if you want to vacation in Africa, that is up to you!"

American Christian parents, just like our non-Christian counterparts, tend to surround our kids with things: their own CD player, their own phone, their own TV, and when they get to be a certain age, their own car. Every Christmas it looks as if the department store blew up in the living room. The clear message is that what is important is things. We aren't losing the Christian young to the cults and New Age; we're losing them to the new religious shrines of devotion in McWorld, the shopping malls. Too many American Christians of all ages are succumbing to the idolatry of modern culture, placing the acquisitiveness of McWorld before the servanthood impulses of the mustard seed.

Getting to the Root: Confusing Occupation with Vocation

Frankly, I am convinced that one of the major reasons why we American Christians give the modern secular world so much authority to determine the terms of our lives is the teachings regarding work and vocation that were born of the Reformation. These teachings have been widely and often uncritically embraced as gospel by a broad spectrum of the North American church.

Leaders of the Reformation correctly decried the division of life into the sacred and the secular. Martin Luther called us to a whole-life faith in which all that we do we should do to the glory of God. And of course, he is right. Under the creation mandate, all work is seen not only as legitimate but as advancing the purposes of God. Wayne Boggs explains a Reformed point of view on work: "The reason man works today—not merely to make a living, nor to 'succeed' in the eyes of the world—but because it is God's plan for man to subjugate the earth. . . . All honorable work, no matter how insignificant before men, offers some opportunity to subdue this earth to God's will."[17]

Since in this view all work is advancing the purposes of God, one's work automatically becomes one's calling. Leland Ryken writes, "Viewing work as calling makes it something personal. If God calls us to work, then to do work is to obey God. That is why the Reformers made so much of the attitude of the worker. Work only becomes calling if we recognize God's hand in it and view it as a part of our relationship with God."[18] No one can argue with the fact that we need to recognize God's hand in all we do, but I am not sure our occupation automatically becomes our calling. Many of those first disciples quit their jobs to advance God's purposes.

Let's go back to the starting point, the creation mandate. Frankly, I think it is a serious mistake to look at work and calling only in terms of the creation mandate. I believe we also need to view both from the perspective of God's kingdom purposes. For example, working at Microsoft might enable Bill Gates to subdue his few remaining competitors, but I am not convinced that this has anything to do with the creation mandate to subdue the earth. Undoubtedly there are Christians who are helping to construct cruise missiles at Boeing, but I am not persuaded that this is a Christian calling, even if they do it with the right attitude.

I believe the purposes of God's kingdom are subversive to many of the aspirations and goals of the dominant modern commercial culture. I am convinced the purposes of God's mustard seed movement will ultimately subvert the arrogance of every Babylon that claims the authority to define what is ultimate. Therefore I believe Scripture teaches that the primary vocation for every believer is not what we do to earn a livelihood but how we devote our lives, as Christ did, to seeking to advance the subversive purposes of God's kingdom.

Beyond Christian Dualism: Discovering the Possibilities of a Whole-Life Faith

In light of this discussion, it shouldn't be a mystery to anyone why attendance and giving patterns are declining in the Western church in general and the North American church in particular. In our dualistic faith, many of us have pursued the aspirations of the American dream with a vengeance and tried to work a little faith in around the edges, as if it all fits together. Many of us have permitted modernity, instead of our faith, to define not only our notion of the good life and better future but most of the priorities and rhythms of our lives. And not surprisingly, we find we are stressed.

Let me be as clear as possible. I believe we have got discipleship wrong. While dualistic discipleship has become the normative model for many in the American church, it simply isn't biblical. The solution, which I will present more fully in the next two chapters, is to call Christians back to a radical biblical approach to discipleship—a whole-life discipleship.

Farmers will tell you that you can sit on a three-legged or a one-legged stool to milk a cow, but a two-legged stool is terribly unstable. I believe most of us are practicing discipleship on a two-legged stool. The first leg on the stool is the transformation of our spiritual lives. The second is the transformation of our moral values. Both are essential. But the missing leg on the stool is the transformation of our cultural values. I believe the Bible teaches that God wants to transform us not only our spiritual values and our moral values but our cultural values too.

We cannot practice biblical discipleship over the top of the acquisitiveness, materialism, individualism, and consumerism of modern culture and wind up with anything that bears much resemblance to Jesus and his mustard seed movement. Listen again to Jesus' words: "Do not store up for yourselves treasures on earth, where moth and rust destroy, and where thieves break in and steal. . . . For where your treasure is, there your heart will be also. . . . No one can serve two masters. Either he will hate the one and love the other, or he will be devoted to the one and despise the other. You cannot serve both God and Money" (Matt. 6:19, 21, 24 NIV).

In the New Testament, following Christ was clearly a whole-life proposition. It wasn't something you worked in around the edges. In the first century, being a disciple of Christ meant putting a third leg on the stool. God is interested in changing not just our spiritual condition and moral values but also our cultural values.

In Christ we are crucified to the world. That simply means we are crucified to the secular values and the idols of the age. And we are crucified to the principalities and powers behind those values and idols. Remember that Jesus, in his life and teachings, was radically counter to the culture of his age and ours. And Jesus formed a new community of disciples that began to give people in that day a glimpse of God's new order that was clearly counter to that of the dominant system of his day.

It doesn't seem to have occurred to many of us that we are in no way obligated to accept all the arrangements modernity hands us. We can take charge of our lives, families, and communities. If we can find within Scripture an alternative vision for the better future, we can imagine and create new alternatives for our lifestyles, find new, less-expensive ways to shelter ourselves, and gain greater control of our working lives. Instead of living dualistic lives in which there is little connection between our faith and how we spend our time and money, we can fashion new options for our lives that are both more festive and can free up more of our time to advance God's kingdom.

Beyond the Commodification of the Church

Many sincere Christians have unwittingly allowed modernity to define not only our sense of what is important and of value but also how we do church. In *A Peculiar People,* Rodney Clapp traces our problems to Christianity's accommodation of the Constantinian state. Before that accommodation the Christian community was clearly seen as being beyond the pale of acceptable society, and persecution was a fact of life for believers.

Anabaptists have helped us understand that since the "Constantinian Compromise," we have unwittingly blended the agendas of state and church, and we have never recovered. In the Reformation, according to theologian John Milbank, the dualism we have been discussing was augmented by privatizing, spiritualizing the sacred, and making faith transcendent to the rest of human experience.[19]

Subsequently the contemporary church in the United States has learned from the apostles of McWorld how to package, commodify, and market the church, using sophisticated marketing research. A growing number of megachurches have essentially become "Christian" consumer malls. They include weight-loss programs, weight rooms, saunas, and food courts, just like in the malls—except these symbols of modern culture are all offered in Jesus' name.[20]

Many of the heralded "new paradigm" churches have achieved their growth by becoming skilled at marketing their religious wares to an essentially boomer market. Since we view the church primarily as a place where people go, the marketing challenge is to make your place more attractive than their place by offering a better array of consumer services. In their book *Selling Out the Church: The Dangers of Church Marketing,* Phillip Kenneson and James Street state, "The fundamental question is whether the church and its faith should be viewed as just another marketable commodity."[21] Rodney Clapp calls this form of the church "you deserve a break today Christianity."[22]

We have allowed modernity not only to commodify our faith but also to define how we organize many of our churches. Many churches have embraced a Western, bureaucratic model of organization, complete with a professionalization of ministry. Not only is this an expensive expression of the church; the values reflected in it are more reminiscent of those of a corporation than of that first informal community of itinerant servants, healers, and teachers.

That first community of disciples was known as those "who turned the world upside down." They were constantly challenging the dominant values of their culture and paying the price. The contemporary church often is one of the strongest apologists for protecting the dominant values of modern culture and is uncomfortable with those who challenge these values.

The reason this happens, I believe, is that we not only have settled for a model of discipleship that ignores cultural transformation but also have accepted a model of the church that has too often chosen to silently sanction all the values of the dominant culture, unless they are blatantly immoral. And in the process we have become domesticated. Somehow it has escaped our attention that McWorld isn't really our home, that we are called to be sojourners, "resident aliens" in this world.

In other words, my ecclesiology leads me to believe that the church isn't just a place where we worship and consume activities and programs that "meet our needs." But it is rather called to be a countercultural community that is called to unmask the values of the dominant culture, rather than sanctioning them, and to helping those both inside and outside the church to find a new way home.

Babylon Revisited

We are entering an astonishing new world in which we will benefit from many aspects of globalization. What's new is that Marxism is in eclipse and capitalism has gone global. My quarrel is not with the architects of the McWorld future and their well-intended efforts to improve the human condition or even to make a profit doing it. My problem is that, like Babylon of old, they are making a conscious effort to redefine for all of us what is ultimate. "It's the economy, stupid." As we saw earlier in this book, Francis Fukuyama heralded the triumph of free-market capitalism as "the end of history."[23]

The McWorld economy has taken on a life of its own. There is not a day that goes by when one doesn't see this new globalized economy reaching into every corner of our planet and every part of our lives. It is clear that to grow this new global economy, people must do more than just create an environment for the free exchange of goods and services. They have to develop comprehensive, systematic ways to persuade us all to redefine not only what is ultimate but also what is important and what is of value, to ratchet up our appetites for more.

We are all people who long for a destination that gives all of life a sense of significance and purpose. Even though the postmodernists have deconstructed Western progress and its sense of purpose for our future, they have done little to slow the growth of McWorld. But it has caused many of us, like Arthur Dent, Trudy the Bag Lady, and other postmoderns, to realize that Western progress and the American dream will never be home.

We need to remember that as followers of God, we are exiles in search of a better land. As people called to a whole-life faith, we must in every age unmask the powers, and expose the pretensions, of Babylon. We need to join with other exiles and create new communities of celebration and subversion that have more of the aroma of God's new order than the stench of the dominant reality. In the next chapter we will search for a homeland in an ancient faith and a premodern imagination.

Planting a Seed in San Francisco

The Church of the Sojourners is a church with a difference. The members have bought a number of homes together in the Mission District, where they are seeking to be part of the living, breathing body of Christ in their community. This small congregation of thirty-five finds that by living in a residential setting together, they are able to help one another resist the seductions of the secular culture more effectively than by simply commuting to a church building once a week. Families and singles share meals together in the evening, and prayer before they begin their workday. They worship together on Sunday and meet in small home-groups once a week to study Scripture and pray. They are one of the few communities I have located that invite God to change not only their spiritual lives and moral values but also their cultural values.

Planting a Seed Ministering to At-Risk Youth

David and Mike are a couple of twenty-year-olds who view the call to follow Christ as a whole-life proposition, not something to work in around the edge of their "regular lives." They sense a strong call to make a difference in the lives of at-risk kids in Christchurch, New Zealand, through Youth for Christ. They couldn't find anyone to pay them to do it. So they simplified their lifestyles so they could each get by on a twenty-hour-a-week job. As a result, they could each free up thirty hours a week for the ministry to which God calls them. They are also buying a modest house with some of their other mates to reduce their living costs and provide living space for others involved in the ministry.

Planting a Seed in a Celtic Prayer Retreat Center

Christine and I are planning to build a Celtic prayer retreat center on some land we own north of Seattle. We want to design it so it captures the spirit of a sixth-century Irish monastery. The purpose of the center would be to provide a location where we could enable young people to develop their own spiritual disciplines while learning to live a simpler, more festive, community-based lifestyle that reflects the values of the kingdom more than those of the dominant culture.

Opportunities for Christian Leaders

This critique of dualistic discipleship and the commodification of the church offers those in leadership the opportunity

1. to work with others in our seminaries, colleges, and congregations to engage in a fresh analysis of how we got off the tracks, an analysis that takes seriously the powerful influence that modernity and McWorld have on our lives, our children's lives, and our congregations, to help us become much clearer about why we do what we do.
2. to study the relationship between declining attendance and giving patterns of much of the Western church, in light of the growing pressures and seductions of modern culture that influence the lives of our members.
3. to develop new educational resources regarding whole-life discipleship and stewardship, to enable Christians to deal with the mounting pressures that McWorld exerts on their lives and families.
4. to examine the extent to which the contemporary church has not only accommodated modern culture but also embraced its values, and how we can plant churches that seek to challenge the values of the dominant reality.

Questions for Discussion and Action

1. Why is it important for Christians to think about why we do what we do?
2. What examples have you seen of dualistic discipleship? What ideas do you have for countering the growing influence of modern culture?

3. List where you spent your time last week. How many of your decisions about where to spend your time came out of the expectations of modern culture, and how many came out of the impulses of your faith?

4. What examples have you seen of how the church has apparently accommodated the values of modern culture? What are some ways in which to help the church create models based on biblical values?

How Can We Find Our Way Home?

THEY COULD SMELL THE FRAGRANT AROMA of lamb roasting over an open fire as they walked up the dusty road in Biram, a small village in Palestine. The group of beleaguered Jewish soldiers cleared the final hill and saw a table in the yard of a small, rustic cottage, laden with fruit, vegetables, and freshly baked homemade bread. They saw the lamb on the spit. They saw a Palestinian Christian family preparing to eat. As the soldiers approached the feast, the father of this Palestinian family explained to his children why he had prepared this lavish banquet for these Jewish soldiers. "In Europe there was a man called Hitler. A Satan. For a long time he was killing Jewish people. Men and women, grandparents—even boys and girls like you. He killed them because they were Jews. For no other reason. . . . Now this Hitler is dead . . . but our Jewish brothers have been badly hurt and frightened. They can't go back to their homes in Europe, and they have not been welcomed by the rest of the world. So they are coming here to look for a home."[1] The children from the Chacour family helped load the plates of their guests at this homecoming feast, which took place shortly after World War II.

Longing for Home

I have never met a person of Jewish faith who doesn't look forward to someday returning home to Jerusalem. For many Jews, it would be for the first time. David Swarr, a friend of mine raised in Israel, reports what it is like to come back home to Jerusalem. As soon as planes with Jewish people from other parts of the world land at Ben Gurion Airport, the passengers "all burst into spontaneous applause. First-time returnees descend the steps of the airplane to kiss the tarmac. There are often tearful reunions between family members who have not seen one another, often for many decades. There are stories of families being reunited with loved ones they thought had been lost in the Holocaust."

I have been fortunate enough to travel to the Holy Land several times. The more I study Scripture, the more I find myself looking forward to returning home to Jerusalem, too. As we will see, the prophetic imaginations of Isaiah, Jeremiah, and a number of other Old Testament authors all looked forward to a grand homecoming in a new Jerusalem.

Certainly, one of our deepest human longings is for home. There are some twenty-eight million refugees in the world who have no home, and their numbers are growing. Homelessness is growing in a number of Western countries, including the United States. There are millions more who have adequate shelter but no real home. And hundreds of millions have no sense of the future that God has prepared for God's people and God's world. The Creator built into us all a profound longing to come home.

When I think of returning home, my mind races back to warm summer days at my grandparent's farm in Blackfoot, Idaho. Suddenly I am five years old again, sitting splay-legged on the grass, intently watching a passel of newborn kittens frolicking on the lawn in front of me. Above me, covered with red climbing roses, is a white arbor permanently attached to the old white clapboard house my grandfather built. I can smell the aroma of homemade bread wafting out of the kitchen window. Inside, my grandmother is just now slicing the fresh bread, and I can hear my name being called.

The Creator God has built deep within us all a longing for home, a place where we belong, a place where we hear our name being called, a place that gives all of life a more compelling sense of meaning. The author of Hebrews gives us a list of the great heroes of the faith. The Scripture reads, "These all died in faith, not having received what was promised, but having seen it and greeted it from afar, and having acknowledged that they were strangers and exiles on the earth. For people who speak thus make it clear that they are seeking a homeland" (Heb. 11:13–14 RSV).

In a real sense, we are all exiles seeking a homeland. As we have seen, a lot of folks all over the world, including many Christians, have bought into modernity's notion of what the homeland looks like. We meet so many people who are stripping their gears trying to climb McWorld's mountain, accepting the mythology that the ultimate can be defined in economic terms: if they can only earn a little more or buy a little more, they will be home free.

Like the children of Israel who were taken captive in Babylon, many of the community of God's people today seem to have contracted a case of amnesia. We seem to have forgotten not only whose we are but the homeland to which we are headed. And when we succumb to a dualistic faith in which the future of God is pictured as a disembodied existence in the clouds, the baubles that Babylon offers can start looking pretty good. That is why I argued earlier that crisis number one for the Western church is a crisis of vision. We have unwittingly embraced two different notions of what the better future looks like, and neither of them happens to be biblical.

Finding the Focus

Therefore, in this chapter I am calling for the Spirit of the living God to blow through our imaginations until we are captivated by the astonishing vision of the great homecoming of God. All of us are caught up in a historic contest between the aspirations and values that power McWorld and those that motivate the mustard seed.

I will argue that if we can both understand and embrace something of the Creator's loving purposes for a people and a world, it can help us find what Walter Brueggemann calls "a new reason for being." It can help us find a much clearer and more compelling sense of purpose for our lives, families, and communities of faith. It can help us move from a dualistic faith to a whole-life faith. And it can help us create a way of life that is more festive than anything McWorld can offer.

I am confident that we will be flabbergasted at how much of our time and resources we could free up if we were to decide to put God's purposes first. And I think that we will be even more astonished at how the Creator God will use our mustard seeds to make a difference in our world today and tomorrow.

In Search of a New Way Home

Reports from the front indicate that people are exhausted from long hours of work and are not finding the consumer delights of McWorld nearly as satisfying as they thought they would. Growing numbers of people both inside and outside the church are looking not only for a way to get off the jet skis but for a way of life with a clearer sense of direction and a deeper spirituality. We particularly find that a number of post-modern young are looking for a faith that permeates every aspect of life. If you are among those in search of a greater sense of significance and a faith for all of life, read on.

In Search of a Whole-Life Faith

In other days when my wife, Christine, was a missionary working in Ghana, she found her faith seriously challenged by animism. The spirituality of the people she worked with touched every facet of their lives, from drawing water to harvesting crops. All of life was connected to the spiritual realm. She realized this wasn't true for her or for the other missionaries she worked with. It was through the influence of these animists that her search for a whole-life Christian faith began.

We don't have to look to animism to find a whole-life faith; all we have to do is look to our Judeo-Christian roots. The Israelites understood that their faith was intended to transform every part of their lives, from their spiritual lives and dietary codes to their politics and economics. Clearly, God intended them to be a countercultural alternative to the people around them, not just in their spiritual lives but in every aspect of their lives.

In the first century, being a Christ follower was not something you worked in around the edges of an already overcommitted life. Following Jesus was clearly a whole-life proposition that caused people in that first community to reorder their entire lives to put God's purposes first.

John Alexander writes, "Christians spend a lot of time and energy explaining why Jesus couldn't have meant what he said. This is understandable; Jesus was an extremist and we are all moderates. What's worse, he was an extremist in his whole life—not just in the narrowly spiritual areas but in everything—so we have to find ways to dilute his teachings."[2] I think Alexander is spot on. For all the talk about the lordship of Christ, few of us have much experience of applying his teachings to all of life, including how we use our time and resources.

Look at the monastic movement in Europe. The Desert Fathers, the Cistercians, the Benedictines, and the Franciscans were all creative experiments in whole-life Christian faith. They sought to create a new rhythm that for many of these groups meant a focused four hours a day in prayer, four hours a day in study, and four hours a day in work. And at their best they were compelling witnesses to a whole-life faith. The Desert Fathers had seekers come out to visit them in the Egyptian desert. They characterized those who came with a sincere hunger as "visitors from Jerusalem," and those who were merely curious as "visitors from Babylon."

There is a spiritual renewal going on in many parts of the church in England as members reconnect with their Celtic Christian roots.

One of the reasons they seem to find Celtic spirituality so inviting is that for Celtic Christians, following Christ was very much a whole-life proposition. In fact, the Celtic saints talked about the door into that other realm being constantly ajar. The Spirit of the living God permeated all of life, from banking the fire to milking the cows. There was no division between the sacred and the secular. The faith of the Celtic monks led them to adopt a way of living in which all of life was devoted to the mission purposes of God, and, therefore, God used these Celtic Christians to evangelize Scotland, England, and much of continental Europe.

The Wesleyan lay movement called followers of Jesus Christ to share more than the leftovers of their lives. They participated in communities in which they shared resources and helped one another reorder their priorities to put first things first. One cannot read Howard Snyder's *The Radical Wesley* without being struck by the impact for Jesus Christ this ragtag band of whole-life disciples had on their world in the eighteenth century.[3] Deep down I think we know that we only come home to all we are intended to be when we join this great company of those who have gone before us and choose to become whole-life disciples.

In Search of a Mustard Seed Faith

In 1981 I published a book titled *The Mustard Seed Conspiracy,* which stirred a surprising but welcome response in many who read it. In the introduction I wrote, "Jesus let us in on an astonishing secret. God has chosen to change the world through the lowly, unassuming, and the imperceptible. Jesus said, 'With what can we compare the kingdom of God, or what parable shall we use for it? It is like a grain of mustard seed, which when sown upon the ground, is the smallest of all seeds on earth; yet when it is sown it grows up and becomes the greatest of all shrubs, and puts forth large branches, so that the birds of the air can make their nests in its shade' (Mark 4:30–32).

"That has always been God's strategy—changing the world through the conspiracy of the insignificant. He chose a ragged bunch of Semite slaves to become the insurgents of his new order. He sent a vast army to flight with three hundred men carrying lamps and blowing horns. He chose an undersized shepherd boy with a slingshot to lead his chosen people. And who would have ever dreamed that God would work through a baby in a cow stall to turn this world right side up! 'God chose the foolish things of the world to shame the wise; God chose the weak things of the world to shame the strong. He chose the lowly things of this world and the despised things—and the things that are not—to nullify the things that are, so that no one may boast before him' (1 Cor. 1:27–29).

"It is still God's policy to work through the embarrassingly insignificant to change his world and create his future. He has chosen to work through the foolishness of human instrumentality. And he wants to use your life and mine to make a difference in the world. Just as Jesus invited that first unlikely bunch of fishermen, he invites us to drop our nets, abandon our boats, and join him in the adventure of changing the world."[4]

As we race into a future of economic globalization, ruthless domination, and commercial conquest on a scale never seen before, it is difficult to believe that there is a force in heaven or on earth that can challenge the principalities and powers behind McWorld. But I am convinced that the Creator God is indeed quietly conspiring through the insignificant and unassuming to transform our world to achieve a very different model of globalization. The Bible reminds us that God's agenda is not to create a global supermall but to redeem a people and transform a world. It is a kingdom that is both present and coming, both now and not yet.

Jesus Invites Us to a Subversive Hope

"Hope is the refusal to accept the reading of reality which is the majority opinion," declares Walter Brueggemann. "Hope is subversive, for it limits the grandiose pretensions of the present, daring to announce that the present to which we have all made commitments is now called into question."[5] Brueggemann sees this subversive hope being kept alive in the "ministry of imagination." Jesus was part of this prophetic ministry of imagination. He came proclaiming a vision for the future that was different from the dominant vision in his time or ours.[6]

Jesus Christ walked the streets of Palestine proclaiming a single message: "Good news, good news! The future of God has broken in upon you!" He not only proclaimed it; he demonstrated it. Every time he fed the hungry, opened the eyes of the blind, and hugged the kids, we were given a preview of coming attractions. We were shown a small glimpse of the homecoming that God has in mind for us and for many of our family we have never met. "Jesus rejects 'the world of grasping' and affirms 'the world of the gift.' He comes as an agent of the kingdom of God, dispensing the gifts of the kingdom to those who are dispossessed. His ministry of healing exorcism, table fellowship and teaching restored the broken, freed the oppressed, welcomed the outcast and taught a new pathway home."[7]

Jesus formed a new community intended to be not only counter to the dominant culture but a foreshadow of the future of God that he preached. It was a collection of those who were dispossessed by their culture becoming a new family who were making their way home together. It is through the death and resurrection of Jesus that we are all invited to become part of this new community. And it is through the bread and the wine that we receive a foretaste of that great homecoming banquet.

Through parables, Jesus shows us tantalizing samples of the great homecoming that connect directly to the imagination of the prophets. British New Testament scholar N. T. Wright states that the parables were "subversive stories" to "bring to birth a new way of being the people of God."[8]

For example, in the parable of the mustard seed we not only are shown how God is working subversively through the small and insignificant but also are given a glimpse of the promised homecoming as well. Jesus said that the mustard seed, when planted, "becomes the largest of all garden plants, with big branches that the birds of the air can perch in its shade" (Mark 4:32). Luke said, "It grew and became a tree, and the birds of the air perched in its branches" (Luke 13:19). The imagery of the sheltering tree directly connects to the imagery of the great homecoming of God in Ezekiel 17:22–24.

In Ezekiel 17 God promised to bring down the imposing imperial powers of that day. But God also promised to make the "low tree grow tall." "This is what the Sovereign LORD says: I myself will take a shoot from the very top of a cedar and plant it; I will break off a tender sprig from its topmost shoots and plant it on a high and lofty mountain. On the mountain heights of Israel I will plant it; it will produce branches and bear fruit and become a splendid cedar. Birds of every kind will nest in it; they will find shelter in the shade of its branches. All the trees of the field will know that I the LORD bring down the tall tree and make the low tree grow tall. I dry up the green tree and make the dry tree flourish. 'I the LORD have spoken, and I will do it'" (Ezek. 17:22–24).

Bernard Brandon Scott stated that the imagery of this passage in Ezekiel parallels the imagery in Christ's parable of the mustard seed. It also pictures the mountain of God as a great "world tree" under which the creatures of earth will dwell in the great homecoming.[9] Darrell Bock, in his commentary on Luke, suggests that the birds of the air represent an ingathering not only of Jews who have been scattered but of all God's children, including Gentiles.[10] God intends to bring God's people home to a future made new.

Welcome to the Great Homecoming of God!

Let's take a trip back to the past on the rich images of the prophets to discover a fuller picture of what the great homecoming of God looked like to those early poets. The prophet Isaiah weaves the most breathtaking tapestry of imagery of the Creator's loving purposes for a people and a world. It is not our intent here to do sophisticated theology; rather it is to rediscover some of the powerful imagery of God's intentions for the future of humanity, imagery that can give us purpose today.

First of all, it is important to emphasize that the setting for the future of God is not in the clouds. The Hebrews always saw God's purposes as embracing creation, not divorced from it. As you will see, Isaiah's vision fully embraces the created world while bringing it into complete union with that realm in which God dwells. Isaiah's vision is for all of life and can provide a springboard for us to rediscover a whole-life faith.

In the early chapters of Isaiah, in seventh-century BCE the Assyrians are at the gates, threatening the existence of Jerusalem. But God has mercy and spares Jerusalem. However, in later chapters God allows Babylon to capture Jerusalem, to punish the children of Israel for their chronic disobedience. As a consequence, they wind up in exile in Babylon, and, of course, that's where they begin to treat Babylon as though it were home. We will borrow images from all three parts of Isaiah (Isa. 1–37; 38–55; 56–66).

I will briefly share some of the images Isaiah used to remind the forgetful followers about the hope and the home God had in mind for us. But as you will see, these images were not intended just for those in Babylonian captivity. These images are intended for all the people of God who look forward to coming home to all that God has promised. After we revisit the panoramic vision of the great homecoming, we will be ready to answer two questions.

1. In these passages, what are God's purposes for the human future and the created order?
2. Are the aspirations and values that motivate the great homecoming of God the same as those that power McWorld?

Listen to the vision of the prophet Isaiah: "Behold, I will create new heavens and a new earth. The former things will not be remembered, nor will they come to mind. But be glad and rejoice forever in what I will create, for I will create Jerusalem to be a delight and its people a joy. I will rejoice over Jerusalem and take delight in my people; the sound of weeping and of crying will be heard in it no more" (Isa. 65:17–19). C. S. Lewis writes about how the realm in which God dwells will one day be fused with the created order, and we will come home to a new heaven and a new earth.

Commentator J. Alec Motyer states, "Heaven and earth represent the totality of things. . . . 'Former things' picks up the reference to 'former troubles'" that includes "everything about the old order. . . . The aware-ness will be of a total newness without anything even prompting a rec-ollection of what used to be."[11]

Remember that the author of Revelation also looked forward to a new heaven and a new earth in which the new Jerusalem comes down to earth. Listen to the homecoming welcome: "Now the dwelling of God is with men, and he will live with them. They will be his people, and God himself will be with them and be their God. He will wipe every tear from their eyes. There will be no more death or mourning or crying or pain, for the old order of things has passed away. He who was seated on the throne said, 'I am making all things new!' Then he said, 'Write this down, for these words are trustworthy and true'" (Rev. 21:3–5).

The setting for the future of God is a new heaven and a new earth. But the focal point of homecoming is a new mountain and a new city—Zion and Jerusalem. When Isaiah states that God will "create Jerusalem to be a delight and its people a joy. I will rejoice over Jerusalem and take delight in my people" (Isa. 65:18–19), the prophet is describing a renewed Jerusalem.[12] Earlier in Isaiah is one of the most compelling images of the great homecoming of God. Mount Zion is transformed from a tiny hill to a transcendent peak that welcomes home family from every tongue and tribe and nation. "In the last days the mountain of the LORD's temple will be established as chief among the mountains; it will be raised above the hills, and all nations will stream to it. Many peoples will come and say, 'Come, let us go up to the mountain of the LORD, to the house of the God of Jacob. He will teach us his ways, so that we may walk in his paths.' The law will go out from Zion, the word of the LORD from Jerusalem. He will judge between the nations and will settle disputes for many peo-ples. They will beat their swords into plowshares and their spears into pruning hooks. Nation will not take up sword against nation, nor will they train for war anymore" (Isa. 2:2–4).

The people of God will be drawn home to Jerusalem, many for the first time. The pretentious spokespersons of the dominant reality will be given an early retirement, and Jerusalem will become a center for wisdom and learning. Another passage in Isaiah states that "the knowledge of God will cover the earth as the waters cover the seas" (Isa. 11:9). Paul said, "Now we know in part but then we will know even as we are known" (1 Cor. 13:12). We will finally get it. No more squinting through a glass darkly. And the nations and the ruling economic powers will finally get it, too. Mary was absolutely right: With the advent of God's new order, the high and mighty will be brought down and the poor and humble will be lifted up.

The centerpiece of the great homecoming of God, at the top of the mountain of God, is going to be a huge international homecoming feast. Tony Campolo has it right: The kingdom of God is going to be a party!

Watch the spectacle; enter into the celebration; savor the fare. The best that has ever been will be alive again.

"On this mountain the LORD Almighty will prepare a feast of rich food for all peoples, a banquet of aged wines—the best of meats and the finest of wines. On this mountain he will destroy the shroud that enfolds all peoples, the sheet that covers all nations; he will swallow up death forever. The Sovereign LORD will wipe away the tears from all faces; he will remove the disgrace of his people from all the earth. The LORD has spoken. In that day they will say, 'Surely this is our God; we trusted in him, and he saved us. This is the LORD, we trusted in him; let us rejoice and be glad in his salvation'" (Isa. 25:6–9).

What we are witnessing is not only the great homecoming banquet of God but the consummation of God's great redemptive initiative in Jesus Christ. Through the cross, God's grace is extended to all of us in Christ. The New Testament makes it clear that even as the one whom we follow rose from the dead, at the return of Christ we too will be resurrected in mind, body, soul, and spirit to be welcomed home to a new heaven and a new earth. The prophets picture not only the redemption of a new humanity, including the restoration of those who are disabled, but also the restoration of God's good creation. Even the creation gets in on this incredible homecoming celebration.

"The desert and the parched land will be glad; the wilderness will rejoice and blossom. Like the crocus, it will burst into bloom; it will rejoice greatly and shout for joy. The glory of Lebanon will be given to it, the splendor of Carmel and Sharon; they will see the glory of the LORD, the splendor of our God. Strengthen the feeble hands, steady the knees that give way; say to those with fearful hearts, 'Be strong, do not fear; your God will come, he will come with vengeance; with divine retribution he will come to save you.' Then will the eyes of the blind be opened and the ears of the deaf unstopped. Then will the lame leap like a deer, and the mute tongue shout for joy. Water will gush forth in the wilderness and streams in the desert. The burning sand will become a pool, the thirsty ground bubbling springs. In the haunts where jackals once lay, grass and reeds and papyrus will grow. And a highway will be there; it will be called the Way of Holiness. The unclean will not journey on it; it will be for those who walk in that Way; wicked fools will not go about on it. No lion will be there, nor will any ferocious beast get up on it; they will not be found there. . . . The ransomed of the LORD will return. They will enter Zion with singing; everlasting joy will crown their heads. Gladness and joy will overtake them, and sorrow and sighing will flee away" (Isa. 35:1–10).

"The day of the Lord is coming when the final pilgrimage will be made through a transformed desert. The motif of a transformed world speaks . . . of the end of sin's reign and the reversal of the Lord's curse [Gen. 3:17ff]. . . . The burgeoning wilderness, at long last released from bondage

[Rom. 8:22ff] is actually shouting its welcome."[13] The Pentecostals and charismatics are right: God's will is healing. You can be sure that the pilgrimage through that transformed desert is going to be littered with abandoned walkers, wheelchairs, and white canes. The ransomed will return home to Zion with ecstatic celebration.

The final passage we will use to see Isaiah's vision of the purposes of God is a passage that liturgical churches use during Advent. It pictures the coming of the Chosen One of God, who ushers in this new order. On Christian radio in the United States I have frequently heard commentators, influenced by the dualism that is widespread, state that the first coming of the Messiah focused only on spiritual matters and had nothing to do with economics or politics. In this passage watch what happens to the military uniforms and the rod of the oppressors at the coming of the Chosen One of God.

"The people walking in darkness have seen a great light; on those living in the land of the shadow of death a light has dawned. You have enlarged the nation and increased their joy; they rejoice before you as people rejoice at the harvest, as men rejoice when dividing the plunder. For as in the day of Midian's defeat, you have shattered the yoke that burdens them, the bar across their shoulders, the rod of their oppressor. Every warrior's boot used in battle and every garment rolled in blood will be destined for burning, will be fuel for the fire. For to us a child is born, to us a son is given, and the government will be on his shoulders. And he will be called Wonderful Counselor, Mighty God, Everlasting Father, Prince of [Shalom]. Of the increase of his government and [shalom] there will be no end. He will reign on David's throne and over his kingdom, establishing and upholding it with justice and righteousness from that time on and forever. The zeal of the LORD Almighty will accomplish this" (Isa. 9:2–7).

The zeal of the Lord will accomplish all of this! God will indeed multiply the nation beyond the people of Israel. And the Prince of Shalom will bring this expanded family home to a future of justice, righteousness, and shalom in which the Messiah reigns, exuberance is the order of the day, and the shouts of elation are deafening.

Let's attempt to answer the two questions posed earlier in this chapter. We began this quest to find an alternative to modernity's view of homecoming and to postmodernity's chronic homelessness. It is within the imagination of an ancient faith and a premodern vision that we discover the imagery of the great homecoming of God for the future of humanity.

Question 1

In these passages, what are God's purposes for the human future and the created order?

We are invited into a vast wasteland, a wilderness in which there is not a single blade of living grass. As we look to the horizon, we see small dots coming toward us across the desert. As they get closer, we see that they are people from every tongue, tribe, and nation. There is a family from Kosovo, an older couple from India, and some kids from an inner-city community in the United States, all pressing forward together. Rising out of the desert is a huge mountain. As the throngs start up the mountain, something remarkable happens. Suddenly the wasteland is transformed into an abundant garden. We go up the mountain arm in arm, and crutches are discarded, wheelchairs are abandoned, and the singing in hundreds of different tongues is deafening. When we reach the summit, an incredible banquet is spread before us. The tables visibly sag under the weight of bountiful fare. And God is in the midst of this huge international feast, welcoming us home.

What are God's purposes for the future of humanity and for the created order? The short answer is that God intends to redeem a people and transform a world. God certainly intends to redeem us spiritually. But that's where the redemptive process begins, not where it ends. The imagery makes it clear that at the time of the resurrection of God's new community, God intends to redeem us as whole persons—spiritually, physically, intellectually, and emotionally. The Scripture couldn't be clearer. The blind will see; the deaf will hear; the lame will "leap like a deer."

And we won't be redeemed individually. This is a corporate celebration. The Creator God will redeem us, at the great homecoming, as a huge multicultural family from different times and places. And it is going to be more festive and celebrative than World Cup soccer, Disneyland, and a holiday in the Caribbean all rolled into one.

Clearly, in the stirring imagery of the homecoming initiative, God purposes to bring justice to the poor so those at the margins are no longer excluded or oppressed. In fact, both in Mary's Magnificat and in the Gospels' imagery of the homecoming banquet, the poor and vulnerable are the guests of honor, and the wealthy and powerful apparently find themselves on the outside looking in.

We see weapons of war being transformed into implements of peace. And we see the military equipment that can't be transformed being incinerated. In another portion of the Book of Isaiah we are told that the lion will bed down with the lamb, and a child shall play in a serpent's den. All violence, exploitation, and predation will end. "They will neither harm nor destroy on all my Holy Mountain."

Not only does God intend to bring an end to all violence, but Isaiah reminds us that all suffering, sin, and death will also be vanquished as we come home to a world made new. "The former things have passed away. Behold I am making all things new." And "all things" certainly includes God's good creation. As we have seen, the creation is going to be fully involved in this historic homecoming celebration.

When people of Jewish faith greet one another with "Shalom," they aren't simply saying, "Peace." This Hebrew word means much more than that. Shalom means "May you live in anticipation of that day when God makes all things whole again." What the prophets are describing in the imagery of the great homecoming is really the shalom future of God.

Walter Brueggemann states, "Shalom is an enduring vision. . . . Among the eloquent spokesmen for the vision . . . is this letter [Jeremiah] wrote to the exiles, urging the validity of the vision even among displaced persons: 'I will fulfill to you my promise and bring you back to this place. For I know the plans I have for you, says the Lord, plans for shalom and not for evil, to give you a future and a hope. . . . You will seek me and find me; when you seek me with all your heart, I will be found by you, says the Lord, and I will restore your fortunes' [Jer. 29:10–11, 13–14]."[14]

Question 2

Are the aspirations and values that motivate the great homecoming of God the same as those that power McWorld?

Think about it. How are modernity's aspirations, expressed in the American dream, different from the purposes of God? First of all, the American dream defines the better future largely in individual terms. The vision of the future of God is clearly corporate. While the American dream defines the good life and better future largely in terms of economic upscaling and self-actualization, the imagery of God's great homecoming has a different definition of what the better future looks like. While the biblical vision embraces the material world, it isn't materialistic. It doesn't define the good life primarily in economic terms.

Rather the shalom vision defines the good life and better future in terms of a reconciled relationship with our Creator, with one another, and with the created order. The focus is on giving life away instead of sanctioning the self-interest that propels the market and too often preoccupies our lives. While modernity's aspirations focus exclusively on the here and now, the biblical vision is rooted in the reign of the Creator God and in a forever-after hope. And while modern culture is obsessed with power, the future of God comes on a donkey's back.

The themes of the American dream are accumulating, upscaling, status, power, consumerism, individualism, and self-actualization. The themes of the homecoming future of God are justice for the poor, peace for the nations, the redemption of the people of God, a restoration of community, a renewal of creation, and a celebration of the shalom purposes of God for a people and a world.

These are not two versions of the same dream. These are totally differ-ent dreams. One is born out of an ancient faith. The other is the product of an Enlightenment vision of Western progress.

The Cross and the Empty Tomb Are Our Way Back Home

In the dualistic model, God is active only in the spiritual realm. The God we find in Scripture is the Lord of history and is involved in the totality of human experience. The Creator God has invaded creation in Jesus Christ. And through the brutal crucifixion of Jesus, this God has redeemed all things. The apostle Paul writes, "In him we have redemption through his blood, the forgiveness of sins, in accordance with the riches of God's grace" (Eph. 1:7). Paul goes on to tell us that we are no longer outsiders, but through the death and resurrection of Jesus Christ we have been included in the family of God (Eph. 2:19–22). Through the humiliation of the cross, God has defeated the princi-palities and powers and all the pretensions of our global society. God has forever brought an end to sin, suffering, and death. And it is through the cross and the empty tomb that God invites us home to a future made new.

Jurgen Moltmann writes, "The manner in which God mediates his future through this particular one [Jesus Christ] is the form of substitu-tionary suffering, sacrificial death, and accepting love. If one looks from the future of God into the godless and forsaken present, the cross of Christ becomes the present form of the resurrection. . . . The kingdom of God can only be understood as the real future of the world if it becomes pres-ent in history and as the goal of human striving . . . which we discover in the resurrection of the crucified one."[15]

Jesus Put First Things First

At the beginning of his ministry, Jesus stood up in the synagogue in his hometown and announced his vocation to an attentive audi-ence. "The Spirit of the Lord is on me, because he has anointed me to preach good news to the poor. He has sent me to proclaim freedom for the prisoners and recovery of sight for the blind, to release the oppressed, to proclaim the year of the Lord's favor" (Luke 4:18–19). He rolled up the scroll, handed it back to the attendant, sat down, and then said something quite startling: "Today this scripture is fulfilled in your hearing."

This Scripture, of course, came out of the same compelling tapestry of imagery we have just read in the Book of Isaiah, and that was no acci-dent. What it meant for Jesus to be the Messiah of God was to commit himself not only to God but to God's purposes for a people and a world. In this inaugural address, Jesus announced that the future of God had broken into the present and that he, Jesus, was the one who would usher us home to a future made new. Fred Craddock writes, "When understood literally, the passage says the Christ is God's servant who will bring to reality the longing and the hope of the poor, the oppressed, and the imprisoned. The Christ will also usher in the amnesty, the liberation, and the restorations associated with the proclamation of the year of jubilee [Luke 4:19; Lev. 25:8–12] . . . The age of God's reign; the eschatological time when God's promises are fulfilled and God's purpose comes to fruition has arrived."[16]

Somehow John the Baptist didn't get it. He wasn't convinced that Jesus was the one. So in Luke 7 he sent two of his disciples to find out if Jesus was really the Chosen One of God. What proof did Jesus offer John's disciples that he was indeed the Messiah? "Go back and report to John what you have seen and heard: The blind receive sight, the lame walk, those who have leprosy are cured, the deaf hear, the dead are raised, and the good news is preached to the poor. Blessed is the man who does not fall away on account of me" (Luke 7:22–23).

The evidence Jesus offered that he was indeed the Messiah of God was that he had committed his life not only to God but to working for God's purposes, which directly paralleled Jesus' vocational statement, drawn from Isaiah 61. By the power of God's Spirit, something of God's new order had indeed burst into the present. What greater proof could Jesus offer? People must have been astonished as the blind threw away their canes, the lame danced, cleansed lepers sang, and even those who had died joined in this amazing foretaste of the great homecoming.

Disciples Called to Put First Things First

What did it mean to be a disciple in century one? Something very different than it does today. Today, as a result of many of us buying into Western dualism, we often move things of faith and Spirit to one small compartment of our life. In this compartmentalized faith, everyone knows that your job comes first, your life in the suburbs comes first, getting ahead comes first. Then you work your faith in around the edges.

As we will see in the next chapter, to be a follower of Jesus in the first century, you were expected to do exactly what Jesus did. You committed your life not only to God but to the purposes of God: "sight to the blind, release to the captives, good news to the poor." You were expected to reorder your entire life around this new sense of purpose, to be a whole-life disciple. Mission was not optional. It was the center of life.

Planting a Seed: It All Starts with a Party

Recently Christine and I had the opportunity to work with some students at Messiah College. They read aloud these passages from the Book of Isaiah. Then we divided them into three groups and gave each group a different assignment regarding the great homecoming of God. The first group planned a weekend party called "A Taste of the Kingdom," in which African-American, Hispanic, Asian, and Anglo churches would be invited to bring their food, dance, and music and to invite their entire community. The second group sketched a mural portraying people going up the mountain to the great homecoming feast, arm in arm, with singing and celebration. The third group composed a song about the great homecoming of God that was so compelling that we had them perform it in chapel the next day.

Every time we share the bread and the wine, we are not simply remembering the death and resurrection of Jesus Christ. In the mystery of the Eucharist, we are joining in that great homecoming banquet with our trinitarian God and with all those who have gone before us, in anticipation of the return of Christ and that final great homecoming celebration when we are welcomed home. Frederick Buechner reminds us, "No matter how much the world shatters us to pieces, we carry within us a vision of wholeness that we sense is our true home that beckons to us."[17]

Babylon Revisited

What God offers us as a group of exiles in the world is not just a new destination—the great homecoming—but also a new reason for being. While McWorld comes, as does every Babylon, with power and pretension to establish dominance, the Creator God comes through the small, the powerless, and the unpretentious to turn the world right side up. Incredibly, God can even use your mustard seed and mine to make a difference in some small way now, in anticipation of that day when Christ returns and the Creator makes all things new.

I am convinced that all the upscaling and accumulating of McWorld can never satisfy our deepest longing to find significance in life. But what could give life greater significance than to be part of God's subversive mustard seed movement, which is quietly changing our world and offering people a hope and a homecoming?

Opportunities for Christian Leaders

There is no greater opportunity for those in Christian leadership than to enable believers to discover in Scripture a new vision for the future of God that not only inspires hope but also offers a sense of direction for life. Leaders have the opportunity

1. to enable those with whom we work to discover in Scripture an alternative vision to the aspirations of the American dream and the addictions of McWorld, for all of life; people need particular help in bringing the imagery of God's great homecoming into their lives through celebration, music, and liturgy.
2. to enable members of our churches and Christian organizations to use the biblical vision as a basis to define a new sense of focus for their lives and families, as the first step in putting first things first.
3. to enable members to use their sense of biblical vocation as a basis to help them redefine their notion of the good life, as the first step in reordering their priorities.
4. to examine the assumptions and values implicit in how we live our lives, order our churches, and operate our Christian organizations, in light of the aspirations and values of God's new order.

 ### Questions for Discussion and Action

1. What is your most welcome image of coming home? What is your deepest longing for home?

2. As you read the imagery of the great homecoming, how is it different from the American dream?

3. How could you put the vision of Isaiah and the vocation of Jesus at the center of your life, family, and congregation?

4. Draw a picture, write a song, or plan a party that brings to life the spirit of the great homecoming, and invite some friends over to enjoy the celebration.

Part 3

A Crisis of Creativity

Learning to Take Imagination Seriously

A GRAND OLD-FASHIONED HEARSE drove up in front of the Cascade College auditorium just as we were getting out of chapel one bright spring morning. To my delight, I spotted Paul Byers, a good friend, behind the wheel. As we gathered around, he explained that a day earlier he had spotted the old hearse a couple of blocks from the college, with a for-sale sign in its window. On a whim, he came up with the $250 and was now the proud owner of this stately vehicle with Victorian curtains at each of the windows.

It didn't take long for Paul and the rest of us to realize that this was more than a classic hearse. It represented a challenge to our collective creativity. Just what were the possible uses for an ancient hearse? After about twenty minutes of brainstorming, we discovered that with careful packing, we could get thirteen students lying down in the back of the hearse at the same time. We cut classes and Paul proceeded to drive all over Portland, Oregon. Every time he approached a stoplight or a stop sign, he would accelerate. Then at the last moment he would slam on the brakes, and all thirteen of us would abruptly sit bolt upright at the same time.

Cars drove up on lawns; one guy almost swallowed his cigarette. We would lie back down and wait for the next stop sign. We caused chaos all over Portland. It was very gratifying.

One of God's greatest gifts to us is the gift of creativity. In my book *Live It Up! How to Create a Life You Can Love,* I wrote, "The Story of God begins with creation—with the spectacular, extravagant creativity of God. Before anything existed, the Creator God was; out of nothing God created everything. Our Creator has graciously gifted us, as divine image bearers, with creativity. Though we are not able, like God, to create something from nothing, we are able to imagine and bring into being a lavish array of new possibilities for ourselves and God's world."[1]

Corporate executives tell me that the most satisfying part of their work is not simply increasing corporate profits but the challenge of using their creativity to achieve corporate objectives. I know of no other segment of society that makes greater use of imagination and creativity than the world of commerce. One can see this creativity in some of the imaginative ads.

However, Emil Brunner states that any time we use our creativity autonomously, apart from God, we risk the gravest consequences.[2] Clearly, much of humankind's creativity has added to the beauty and bounty of God's good creation. But human imagination has also been used in ways that undermine our humanity and threaten the viability of creation itself. Harvey Cox charges that the human creature, "while gaining the whole world . . . has been losing his own soul. He has purchased prosperity at the staggering impoverishment of the vital elements of his life. These elements are festivity—the capacity for genuine revelry and joyous celebration, and fantasy—the faculty for envisioning radically alternative life situations."[3]

As we saw in the last chapter, God is clearly at work creating a new heaven and a new earth where we will come home to a future made new. The Creator God invites us, through the mustard seed, to be part of the adventure of creating new ways to manifest something of God's new order.

A Crisis of Creativity

In the American church there is a widespread view that the church is essentially on track as we race into a new millennium. But in Britain, Australia, and New Zealand there is a greater sense that it is in serious trouble and needs to be reinvented to address more effectively the new challenges of an uncertain future. I am convinced that one of the major underutilized resources to help us with the task of reinvention is our creativity.

Everywhere that Christine and I minister, people tell us they feel trapped by the pressures of the modern world and are convinced there is no way out. These sincere believers don't seem to realize that they aren't as boxed in as they think they are. They can, through their imagination, create alternatives that offer a way of life with a greater sense of significance, a way of life that is more festive and less stressed than anything modern culture has to offer. We need to help these good people blow the lids off their confining boxes.

This crisis of creativity not only impacts our lives and families but also impacts how we do church. There are many churches in which there is no shortage of innovation. But much of the innovation we see is faddish. Churches simply attempt to copy other models of what's going on, whether it's buying inflatable playthings for their youth group or jumping aboard the newest church-growth bandwagon.

Candidly, I find that even mission executives and missiologists tend to get caught up in bandwagon approaches to mission instead of being more creative. But we have found that there are few resources available to enable mission organizations, churches, or individuals to create new possibilities for life and mission in a changing world.

Through Mustard Seed Associates (103213. 2024@compuserve.com), Christine and I try to respond to this need by conducting futures creativity workshops. In the final two chapters, I am going to challenge those in leadership to replace random innovation by showing how to get creative on purpose. I will show how to use our creativity for two purposes: (1) to create new ways to advance biblical purposes; (2) to create new ways to respond to tomorrow's challenges.

Creating New Ways to Advance Biblical Purposes

As we saw in chapter 6, there are astonishingly few models of Christian approaches to education, health care, or even church structures that aren't simply dull reflections of modern secular models, sanctified by doing them in Jesus' name. Those in leadership don't seem to notice that many of the implicit values in these models are diametrically opposed to biblical values. We give little thought to why we do what we do. As we saw in the last chapter, while we hold Scripture in great esteem, we tend to use it devotionally or liturgically but seldom use it as a launching pad to create new alternatives.

A group of Mennonites in the United States wanted to have a modest witness for the gospel of Christ in the criminal justice field. Instead of simply borrowing the standard model and doing it in Jesus' name, they created a new model to implement biblical purpose. They started with the biblical call to reconciliation. ("All this is from God, who reconciled us to himself through Christ and gave us the ministry of reconciliation: that God was reconciling the world to himself in Christ, not counting men's sins against them. And he has committed to us the message of reconciliation" [2 Cor. 5:18–19].) And the message of reconciliation is that we are to be reconciled not only to God but also to one another.

Therefore these Mennonites created a modest new ministry called VORP (Victim Offender Reconciliation Program). Essentially, in this program the Mennonites bring together the guy whose house was burgled and the kid who did it. They work for reconciliation and restitution.

Out of this innovative ministry, VORP staff tell me, friendships often emerge. Sometimes the individual whose house was broken into spends money to send the young offender to college and helps him find a new sense of direction for his life. I can guarantee that any Christian leader who moves from bandwagon innovation to creating models flowing directly from biblical principles will be astonished at how God enables him or her to create brand-new models that reflect the values of the kingdom more than those of modern culture.

Creating New Ways to Respond to Tomorrow's Challenges

Christine and I are testing a process with InterVarsity Christian Fellowship in the United States to help prepare a new generation to create new options for their lives to enable them to respond to the new opportunities of tomorrow's world. For example, I talked to a student recently who is studying electrical engineering but feels that God is calling him into mission work. In exploring with him, I found that his view of mission vocations was quite limited, as it is for many students.

He visualized missionaries exclusively as preachers or perhaps educators but had no idea that his training in electrical engineering had any application. I explained that one of the exciting new mission vocations for the twenty-first century is photovoltaic engineering. In other words, he could use his engineering training to help construct solar collectors to turn the sun's energy into electricity in order to start clinics or small businesses in communities of need in the Two-Thirds World. Through this process we are testing, we hope to enable college students to do a better job of anticipating new options in the future and creating new lifestyle and vocational possibilities to take advantage of new opportunities.

In these final two chapters I will argue that business as usual in our lives, churches, and mission organizations will not begin to be adequate to address the escalating challenges of a new millennium. Therefore, in the next chapter I will explore creative new ways we can put God's purposes first in addressing the challenges of a new millennium, in our lives and in our communities of faith. In the final chapter, I will explore how to reinvent our approach to mission in a changing world.

To respond to the mounting challenges of a new millennium, we will need a renaissance of Christian creativity. We will need to invite the Holy Spirit to flood our imaginations to create new possibilities for life and mission for the twenty-first century.

Reinventing Christian Life and Community for a New Millennium

GRAND SPRAYS OF FLOWERS welcome us as we join the throng of people entering the Round Chapel in east London on a warm afternoon in July. A large upholstered bear greets us with huge hugs. In the center of the circular room is the largest fruit-and-vegetable display I have ever seen, surrounded by a ring of flowering plants. Pineapples, melons, oranges, apples, bananas spill out in all directions from a gigantic bowl with a golden centerpiece rising toward the vaulted ceiling. Colorfully decorated tables reach out in all directions from the festive hub, like spokes in a wheel. Medieval banners hang from the ceiling, and multicolored balloons rise above the serving table. The feast includes roast beef, poached salmon, fried chicken, kosher dishes, an array of vegetarian specialties, and rich desserts.

Those pouring in for this lavish feast pay only a pound per head (less than two dollars each). The hosts deliberately priced it so every person in this richly multicultural community could afford to come. And as far as they know, this is the first time anyone has successfully brought together the entire community. We stand in line behind a mom and three kids who are originally from Jamaica. And those behind us are from a local drama group that often performs in this large circular room now primarily used as a center for the performing arts.

As we sit down to join the feast, a local string ensemble begins entertaining the 350 guests. Different local groups take turns performing during the feast. Looking around I can see that members of this London neighborhood are thoroughly enjoying not only the lavish banquet and the music but one another.

Listen to the comments that people wrote as they left: "Simply amazing. Could we have it again, please?" "I thought today was a great innovative idea. To get people from everywhere together is very refreshing." "Felt a bit like a wedding without the bride and groom!" And it reminded me of that final grand wedding banquet that we will share at the great homecoming of God.

Who was responsible for the feast? A lot of people from all over the community and a small group of young Christians were the moving force. They are part of a Reformed congregation determined to creatively reinvent what it looks like to follow Christ in a fragmented, alienated community. At least half a dozen young couples have deliberately relocated to a transitional neighborhood and become united in a common cause as an expression of the reconciling gospel of Christ. And they are finding the satisfaction of creating a way of life with a difference.

They have started a food cooperative that enables those at the margins to buy in bulk a broad array of food at cost. They have also started a community equipment loan scheme to share gardening tools. Their most recent ministry creation is the provision of a place in the community where parents with preschoolers have a drop-in place to come.

Finding the Focus

The Round Chapel Neighborhood Project is not only a sample of the invasion of God's kingdom; it is an example of the kind of innovative approach to life, community, and mission that Christians are initiating all over the world. This is an invitation to discover how the Spirit of God can use your mustard seed, in community with others, to make a difference in the world. The purpose of this chapter is to explore specific imaginative ways in which Christians can both reinvent how we practice discipleship and create communities of faith that advance God's purposes and prepare us to live creatively in tomorrow's world. And it all begins with critically reexamining why we do what we do in nurturing disciples and in growing churches.

Back to the Future One More Time

The challenges of our McWorld future will require that we radically re-create how we, as disciples of Jesus Christ, live our lives, raise our young, and form our communities. Remember, we are heading into a future in which we are likely to come under mounting pressure to work harder and longer. If we experience the future of the long boom, we and our kids are also going to be under growing pressure to consume more to keep the economy booming.

If we experience the future of the slow meltdown, many people in Western societies are likely to face the same dislocations that have caused such enormous pain to millions of people in Asia and Russia. The church needs to prepare people for both boom and bust.

Beyond Christian Dualism: Back to the Bible One More Time

The good news is that we don't have to settle for allowing modern culture to arrange the furniture of our lives or define where we spend our time and money. We don't have to settle for high-stress lifestyles that are disconnected from vital faith and leave us precious little time for prayer, service, or celebration. As with the young people in east London, God can help us create life with a difference.

Call to Biblical Discipleship: Putting First Things First

Think about it! Those first disciples of Christ weren't engaged in Roman culture nine to five with a house church on the weekend. No dualistic, compartmentalized faith for them. They understood that following Christ was a whole-life proposition, unlike the kind of dualistic discipleship offered today. They didn't simply invite God to transform their hearts and forgive their sins, and go about life as usual. For all those committed to equipping Christians to do the work of the church, we must reinvent our programs, calling believers to whole-life discipleship and stewardship, in which they place God's purposes at the center of life. Remember, Christ's call to discipleship is a call to "obey all the things" he taught us.

In the first century you were expected to commit your life not only to God but to the purposes of God as well. As followers of Jesus, you no longer settled for having the dominant culture define the focus of your life. You were expected to make Jesus' vocation—"sight to the blind, release to the captives and good news to the poor"—your vocation.

That's why those first disciples did wild, outrageous things like quitting jobs and leaving homes, because they had a new reason for being. Listen again to Jesus' call to whole-life discipleship: "If anyone comes to me and does not hate his father and mother, his wife and children, his brothers and sisters—yes, even his own life—he cannot be my disciple. . . . Any of you who does not give up everything he has cannot be my disciple" (Luke 14:26, 33).

Dietrich Bonhoeffer, reflecting on this radical call to follow Christ, presents one way in which we often get off the hook. "If Jesus said to someone: 'Leave all else behind and follow me; resign your profession, quit your family, your people, and the home of your fathers,' then he knew that to this call there was only one answer—the answer of single-minded obedience," but we would tend to rationalize away the clear intent of Christ's call by arguing, "Of course we are meant to take the call of Jesus with 'absolute seriousness,' but after all, the true way of obedience would be to continue all the more in our present occupations, to stay with our families, and serve there in a spirit of true inward detachment."[1]

Bonhoeffer is right. In the dualistic discipleship model, it is fascinating to see how we have been carefully nurtured to sidestep the radical demands of whole-life discipleship. We are typically taught to tip our hat to this radical call and give passive assent to Christ's claim on all of our life. In this dualistic model, we are routinely taught to say that everything we have is God's and if he hits us with a blinding vision, we will give it all back. But in the meantime we will continue enjoying for God.

Those first disciples didn't passively wait for a bolt out of the blue to call them to devote their entire lives to Christ and his kingdom, and neither should we. In contrast, we find that many Christian college students are being nurtured in a dualistic discipleship model in which they are too often encouraged to fit into the world instead of changing it.

Message to the Young: Agenda One Is Putting First Things First

Too often the real message to the Christian young, for all the talk about Christ's lordship, is that agenda one is getting your job under way, getting your house in the 'burbs, getting your upscale lifestyle started and then with whatever you have left over serve Jesus. But because many of the young are hitting the economy at a much tougher time than did those of us who are older, they don't have much left over.

When Christine and I speak at Christian colleges, we offer a different message. We state, "Agenda number one is not where to work, where to live, or even whom to marry. Life decision number one is to determine how God wants to use my life to advance God's purposes!" Then, like the first followers of Jesus, they have the opportunity to reorder all of life to put God's mustard seed purposes first.

What I am suggesting is pretty radical. I am suggesting that Christians of all ages need to discover how God is calling us to put God's mission purposes first. Then we can begin the creative adventure of reordering every area of our lives to put first things first, just as Jesus did.[2]

At the beginning of his ministry, Jesus Christ stood up in his hometown and read, "The Spirit of the Lord is on me, because he has anointed me to preach good news to the poor. He has sent me to proclaim freedom for the prisoners and recovery of sight for the blind, to release the oppressed, to proclaim the year of the Lord's favor" (Luke 4:18–19). Then in the remainder of the gospel narrative, we witness Jesus consciously devoting his life to a single focus: to advance the purposes of God.

Remember, Jesus' vocation is directly related to the promise of the great homecoming of God. If we try to follow Christ on automatic pilot, I can guarantee that the values of modern culture will wind up defining the direction and the character of our lives. I am arguing that the call to follow Christ is a call to live out the purposes of God in every aspect of our lives by the power of the Holy Spirit.

Drafting a Mission Statement for a Difference

What does it look like today when disciples seek to put God's purposes first, as Jesus and that first band of disciples did? Recently Jerry Sitzer, who teaches theology at Whitworth College in Spokane, experienced a devastating tragedy. He lost his wife and one of his children in a violent car accident. Left as a single parent to raise three kids by himself, he was overwhelmed by grief. After weeks of prayer and struggle it dawned on him that one of the ways he could honor those who died was to sit down with his three kids and write a family mission statement, to raise his children on purpose.

He sat down with his three kids, and with his biblical training drafted a family mission statement. Jerry told me that they check it every week to ensure that they are finding creative ways to bring faith to every dimension of their life as a family.

Christine and I followed Jerry's example. We have both had the opportunity to work with the poor in the Two-Thirds World, and we will never be the same. As a consequence, we have chosen as a basis for our mission statement Proverbs 31:8–9: "Speak up for those who cannot speak for themselves, for the rights of all who are destitute. Speak up and judge fairly; defend the rights of the poor and needy."

Reinventing Our Lifestyles to Put First Things First

In other days, both Christine and I were out of control in our schedules, and we paid a dear price. We have discovered, the hard way, that Jesus needs our service, not our exhaustion.

Christine and I aren't alone in struggling with highly stressful lifestyles. Speaking at the Greenbelt Festival in England, I asked, "How many are under serious pressure in your schedules?" Virtually all 250 people in the tent raised their hand. We had the same overwhelming response in a Baptist church in Vancouver, B.C., and in a Presbyterian church in Seattle.

Planting a Seed in a Prayer Retreat

What we have found as one way to both get in control of our schedules and focus our lives is to go on a prayer retreat four times a year. Typically we take two days for prayer, biblical reflection, journaling, and refocusing. All we take with us are our Bibles, our journals, and our mission statement.

We usually begin our retreat with an extended time of prayer and biblical meditation, waiting for God to show us where we have gotten off the tracks and become distracted from our sense of calling. After a time of repentance, we prayerfully set new goals for every part of our lives—including our ministry, our spiritual disciplines, our marriage, our relationships, our hospitality, celebrations, and finances—goals we believe clearly reflect our sense of calling.

Then we draft a new schedule that reflects the goals flowing out of our mission statement. Finally, we take a couple of hours every Sunday morning before church and drive to a scenic spot and check in with each other and pray for God's wisdom and strength in the week ahead.

We have discovered that a strong part of our sense of vocation is hospitality. Therefore, we have deliberately set aside more of our time and money to entertain and honor those dear friends whom God has given us. Another part of our sense of calling is celebrating the great homecoming of God with our friends. Every Christmas season, we put on a party called "Advent II—Homecoming," in which we celebrate not only the advent of the King but also the new kingdom of banqueting and celebration. This approach may not work for everyone, but I am convinced that we all need to find a way to discover God's mission call on our lives to enable us to live with greater intentionality.

Opportunities for Christian Leaders
Ten-Week Course on Reinventing Our Lives to Put God's Purposes First

Everywhere Christine and I work, we find people searching for a way of life that is less exhausting, in which they can find the satisfaction of putting God's purposes first. Christians simply don't know how to connect whatever they hear in the Sunday morning sermon with their lives Monday through Saturday. I am persuaded that one thing that could help is a ten-week course to help Christians put first things first. Christine is writing a book on this subject. But I will give you a quick outline that you can use with this book, in any Sunday school class or small group, to discover how, with God's help, you can help others reorder their lives to put God's purposes first.

Week One: Life beyond the Stress Race

I find that it is essential to begin by giving people time to share their sense of exhaustion and frustration with one another, as the first step in a journey toward freedom. It is also essential for leaders to assist people to identify the specific reasons why their schedules are out of control and to begin exploring how they could reduce some of their involvements. And as God's Spirit speaks, people will need time for repentance too.

Weeks Two to Four: Living Life on Purpose

Three weeks is probably a bare minimum in which to enable people to work out of Scripture to draft a personal or family mission statement. You might start by helping them focus on God's passionate purposes for a people and a world. The imagery of the great homecoming of God in the last chapter might help. Like the young people at Messiah College, have your folks plan a party, draw a picture, and write a song that captures something of God's loving intentions for the human future. Next enable them to understand how Jesus and his first disciples deliberately made God's purposes their purposes—and how that sense of biblical vocation shaped every aspect of our Master's life. Finally, help them prayerfully draft a short mission statement that is drawn from a sense of biblical purpose. And then pray for the empowerment and gifts of the Holy Spirit to enable them to act on their sense of calling.

Weeks Five to Seven: Creating a Life with a Difference

The aim of drafting a mission statement is to enable every believer to discover how God wants to use his or her mustard seed to make a small difference in the world for God's kingdom. For example, an attorney could use her training to work for reconciliation in broken families. An engineer could use engineering design and computer systems to help disabled persons become more self-reliant. A mom who stays at home could become involved in the important ministry of foster care for unwanted kids.

Others might even feel called into the huge range of full-time Christian ministries, from working in Scripture translation with Wycliffe in Indonesia to working in urban evangelism among the at-risk young, with Youth for Christ in Glasglow. InterVarsity Christian Fellowship has persuaded hundreds of grads to give God their first year or two out of college to work with the urban poor.

A book titled *Your Money or Your Life* explains innovative ways individuals can simplify their lifestyles for five to seven years and then place a significant amount of what they save into investments and live off the interest.[3] I find few Christians who have ever considered a scheme like this to retire early so they can invest the rest of their lives in their mission vocations.

With the graying of our Western societies, many older Christians have the opportunity to use the second half of their lives to invest in the work of God's kingdom. In his challenging book *Half Time,* Bob Buford writes to those in the middle of their lives, "If you do not take responsibility for going into half-time and ordering your life so that your second half is better than your first, you will join the ranks of those who are coasting their way to retirement. . . . But if you take responsibility for the way you play out the rest of the game, you will begin to experience the abundant life that our Lord intended for you."[4]

But if we are not called to advance God's kingdom purposes through our occupation, full-time Christian ministry, or substantial lifestyle change, we need to enable everyone to change their schedules to free up two to four hours a week to be actively involved in witness or service beyond the doors of the church.

Planting a Seed in Families for Others

One idea from one of our creativity workshops was to have families visit neglected seniors in nursing homes. The creative twist was to have the children read stories to the seniors while the children's parents listened, too. What kind of kids would we raise if instead of providing them with eighteen years of highly indulgent living in the suburbs, we gave our young the opportunity to spend those years being involved with their parents in ministry to others? We challenge every family to find time every week to share God's love with others.

Weeks Eight through Ten: Creating a Life You Can Love

The Christian-lifestyle literature of the late seventies gave the impression that the call to lifestyle change was simply a matter of living a scaled-down version of the American dream. I am arguing that the change to which Scripture calls us isn't primarily economic downscaling but cultural transformation.

You see, the rat race is a fraud! It never was the good life. It is disturbing how many of us, like the children of Israel, have contracted a case of amnesia. We are people in exile who will never be at home in McWorld. We need not only to find a sense of God's call on our lives but to invite God to transform our values from those that pervade the dominant culture to those that motivate the mustard seed movement. Study the Gospel of Luke and compare the cultural values that Jesus taught and reflected in his life with those promoted by McWorld, and help people begin to redefine their notions of the good life. It will help them put a third leg on their discipleship stool.

Planting a Seed in Learning to Party the Kingdom

Speaking in a charismatic church in London recently, I said, "You folks are fun to be with during praise worship on Sunday, but the rest of the week you are a bit of a drag." Of course, I was being a bit facetious. But the point I was trying to make was that in our dualistic faith, we tend to keep our Christian celebrations of faith to one small compartment of our lives. And then, like everyone else, we passively become dependent on McMedia to entertain us.

I encourage people to begin to change their schedules and lifestyles to more authentically reflect God's new order not by cutting back or giving up anything but by throwing a party that begins to express the kingdom of God in Scripture: the wedding feast, the international banquet, the jubilee. Encourage your people to take one of these biblical images and plan a party.

One of the most intriguing aspects of the monastic movement is the way in which it enabled adherents to live out their faith by altering the rhythm of their lives. Try to help one another create an easier rhythm for your lives. We enjoy the annual rhythm of the church calendar.

At the center of whole-life discipleship is the need to set aside generous daily time for Scripture study and prayer. We are called to be people of deep spirituality who are growing in intimacy with our God. In one of Richard Foster's most recent books, *Streams of Living Water,* he introduces us to a rich spectrum of Christian prayer traditions that provide resources to help us deepen our spiritual life. And Foster's organization, Renovare (103165.327@compuserve.com), provides excellent resources to help people in your congregation deepen their life of prayer.[5]

I recommend that you provide a brainstorming time in which people are invited to create new rituals for their lives and families. One particularly helpful resource in this regard is the *Treasury of Celebrations,* which is put out each year by Alternatives for Simple Living (P.O. Box 2857, Sioux City, IA 51106 [800-821-6153]).

We need to enable people to be more innovative in creating not only a new rhythm in the use of their time but also a new pattern of stewardship in the use of their other resources, including money. Once we have biblically redefined the good life, it is time that we all ask the tough question, How much do we really need to spend on housing, transportation, recreation, clothes, and entertainment in a world of growing need?

Part of our problem here is that I believe our view of Christian stewardship is wrong. The standard teaching in most Protestant churches is tithe stewardship. This approach tends to fragment our sense of responsibility. Understanding the Old Testament origins of the tithe, a growing number of New Testament scholars tell us that there is no basis for ten-percent stewardship in the New Testament. The call to follow Christ in the New Testament is a whole-life proposition.

Dualistic Christianity typically teaches that after you bring your tithe (or some part of your tithe) into the storehouse, you can pretty much do what you want with the rest. You can buy whatever toys you want and live as lavishly as you want, as long as you don't get a materialistic hang-up with all your things. It is amazing how many American Christians seem to be able to live palatially without ever getting hung up with materialism. Too often our Christian leaders in the United States are the pacesetters for this upscaling.

What isn't taught very often is that the issue isn't just one of materialistic hang-ups. We are a part of the international body of Jesus Christ. There is something profoundly wrong when some of us live lavishly and other Christians in our world can't keep their kids fed. The only way in which the church has any hope of reversing the decline in our giving patterns is to enable people to find creative ways to become whole-life stewards. I think we all realize if God were controlling all the switches of our daily lives, our time and money would be used very differently.

Planting a Seed in Communities of Support and Accountability

A ten-week course will not be enough to keep us on track in this tough area. We will need community and accountability. In a Mennonite church in Goshen, Indiana, every member is part of a small group that prays and studies Scripture together. And twice a year they do something that terrifies most American evangelicals when I tell them about it. Members bring their time schedules and their budgets to their group. They ask everyone in their group to hold them accountable for how they plan to use their time and money in the next six months in their struggle to put God's purposes first.

I encourage you to have a celebration at the end of the ten-week course as people begin their journey into a more intentional way of life. And we need to remind one another that the decision to follow Christ may also cost us our very lives, as it has for many of our sisters and brothers in other parts of the world. The only way we can possibly be whole-life disciples and stand against the principalities and powers of our age is to be part of a community of faith in which we, like the Mennonites, are known, loved, and held accountable.

Beyond Culturally Accommodated Churches: Reinventing Communities of Faith for a New Millennium

In *Reinventing American Protestantism* Donald Miller identifies the most creative expression of the church in America today as the "new paradigm churches" because they are doing a better job of meeting the needs of their clientele than are mainline churches.[6] While the seeker-friendly churches such as Calvary Chapel, Vineyard Christian Fellowship, Saddle Back, and Willow Creek are often displaying more growth and vitality than their mainline counterparts, I am not sure they are any longer the innovative edge of the church as we enter a new millennium. But they have been the growing edge in the nineties, and we need to thank God for their vitality.

There is a tremendous amount of creativity going on in church planting globally, causing many to rethink and reinvent what it means to be the church. The Web Chapel has a chaplain and a Bible study opportunity and offers counseling and prayer. But is an on-line community really a church?

A new generation of young leaders all over the world are creating some innovative models of the church for a new millennium. For instance, a string of innovative churches for twenty-somethings are being planted all over the United States and are connected and given resources by the Leadership Network, which is providing support without control. This network of churches rejects the user-friendly, highly programmatic megachurch models. They are busy fashioning a more relational, post-modern tribal model of what the church could look like.[7]

Planting a Seed in the Brown Bear Pub

Some twenty-year-olds in Britain planted yet another model of tomorrow's church, the Brown Bear Pub in London, to reach out to Caribbean young people. They created a reggae band to lead worship and opened their doors for witness. One night during a foot-washing service, a Jamaican drug dealer slipped into the back of the worship space. He didn't realize he was in a "church," and when he saw this white guy down on the floor washing his Nikes, it got his attention. He is now the sergeant at arms at the Brown Bear Pub, seriously considering the claims of Christ.

Planting a Seed in the Parallel Universe

Mark Pierson and Mike Riddell created an alternative worship experience for twenty- to forty-year-olds in Auckland, New
Zealand, called Parallel Universe. They rented a nightclub, set
up floor-to-ceiling screens on three sides of the space, and put tables and
chairs in the middle. They have created a highly visual, innovative worship space where everything happens on all three screens at the same
time. One night the focus for this largely nonbelieving audience was on
the grace of God. They started out with limbo dancing: "How low can
you go?"

Rethinking What It Means to Be the Church

What I am arguing is not that we simply need to be more innovative
but rather that we need to be more innovative on purpose. We need to
reinvent the church in a way that more authentically reflects a biblical
theology and equips believers to serve God in the demanding world of
the twenty-first century.

It is past time for Protestants, particularly conservative Protestants, to
do some fresh biblical work on a theology of the church. We need to be
much clearer as to why we do what we do. Avery Dulles, in his classic
book on ecclesiology, *Models of the Church*,[8] offers ten models of the
church, from the church as institution and sacrament to the church as
community and servant.

In *Resident Aliens* Stanley Hauerwas and William H. Willimon compellingly remind us that as we are the exiled people of God, our home
is not in this modern world. They describe the community of faith as "a
colony . . . a beachhead, an outpost, an island of one culture in the middle of another, a place where the values of home are re-iterated and passed
on to the young, a place where the distinctive language and life-style of
resident aliens are lovingly nurtured and reinforced."[9] Part of the problem with our view of the church is that we tend to see it more as a place
to which we go than as an alien community of which we are a part.

Missiologist David Bosch explained that the view of church as a place
to go was an unintentional product of the Reformation. George Hunsberger adds, "This perception of church gives little attention to the church
as communal entity or presence, and it stressed less the community's
role as the bearer of missional responsibility throughout the world, both
near and far away. 'Church' is conceived in this view as *the place where*
a Christianized civilization gathers for worship, and *the place where* the
Christian character of society is cultivated."[10]

In the Book of Acts, the church, that first alien community, wasn't a
building to go to once a week. It was much more a living, breathing com-

munity that was "breaking bread from house to house," sharing life, sharing resources, all centered in the worship of the living God.

I am convinced that the first call of the gospel isn't to proclamation—and I am committed to evangelism. And I don't believe that the first call of the gospel is to social action—and I am concerned for the poor. I believe that the first call of the gospel is to incarnation. Only as we flesh out in community something of the rightside-up values of God's new order do we have any basis on which to speak or act.

Marcus Borg describes this new community of the Spirit as a countercultural community in the dominant Roman-Jewish culture of their day. "Jesus sought to transform his social world by creating an alternative community structured around compassion. . . . Thus Jesus saw the life of the Spirit as incarnational, informing and transforming the life of the culture."[11]

British theologian Michael Green understood that the first church wasn't a place to go. It was an incarnational community in which people found a home and were being transformed in every part of their lives. "They made the grace of God credible by a society of love and mutual care which astonished pagans and was recognized as something entirely new. It lent persuasiveness to the claim that the new age had dawned in Christ. The word was not only announced but seen in the community of those who were giving it flesh. The message of the kingdom became more than an idea. A new human community had sprung up and looked very much like the new order to which the evangelist had pointed. Here love was given daily expression; reconciliation was actually occurring; people were no longer divided into Jews and Gentiles, slave and free, male and female. In this community the weak were protected, the stranger welcomed. People were healed, the poor and dispossessed were cared for and found justice. Everything was shared. Joy abounded and ordinary lives were filled with praise."[12]

Rodney Clapp argues that the church was primarily intended to be not an institution but a family. To follow the Christ of the New Testament requires that we give our first allegiance to a new family, "the first family" of God. "Jesus creates a new family. It is the new first family, a family of his followers that now demands primary allegiance. In fact, it demands allegiance over the old first family, the biological family. Those who do the will of the Father (who, in other words, live under the reign of God) are now brothers and sisters to one another."[13]

In other words, I believe that the church at its best is called to be a new community centered in the worship of the living God, offering a glimpse of the character of the great homecoming of God, and sharing life and resources as would a large extended family. Robert Banks tells us that becoming a part of this family altered how members stewarded their resources. "The principle of mutual financial support . . . lay at the heart" of this new community.[14] And one of the major reasons they formed communities and shared resources was to focus their lives outwardly in witness and service to others.

If we were to begin creating churches that weren't institutions quietly sanctioning the values of the dominant culture but rather communities for "resident aliens," how would we redesign our churches? If we were to start planting churches that weren't places where people worshiped once a week but extended families where believers shared life and resources, how would we reinvent our churches? What kind of churches will we need in order to equip people to live in either the future of the long boom or the future of the slow meltdown?

A Radical Proposal for Church Planting for the Third Millennium

I have a radical proposal. I recommend we experiment in planting some new "churches" that are less buildings in which we worship once a week and more new human settlements in which we live seven days a week and in which we also happen to worship. Much is being written by architects on new village design, new urban community design, and the design of cooperative housing projects.

One of the new design groups in the United States is the Congress for the New Urbanism. In Britain the counterpart organization is the Urban Village Group. What they share in common is a commitment to creating living urban environments that are more than roads, houses, and yards. They are trying to create people-friendly communities that foster neighborliness and community cooperation, both rarely found in suburban communities.[15]

Planting a Seed in a New Christian Settlement

If we were to invent new models of the church that were first of all new human settlements centered in worship and committed to mutual care and mission, what might they look like? To be honest, I am not exactly sure, but let me sketch a bit. Imagine a church plant that is a newly designed intergenerational community for sixty people. Architects, theologians, and Christians committed to whole-life discipleship would design this community from the ground up, in a way that would reflect the values and rhythms of the great homecoming more than the values and rigors of the American dream. The settlement would be designed in a way that facilitated community and mutual care, with residents becoming a large extended family in Christ, committed to mission in the world.

In a Southern Baptist home in Tennessee, a nine-year-old comes home from school and spends an hour every day helping an older woman with her chores before he plays or does his homework. Imagine a community in which every member covenants to barter three hours a week to provide mutual care so we become the body of Christ in real terms and reduce the amount of resources every nuclear family has to set aside for consumer goods, pensions, and disability care.

One of the major benefits of such a model is that monthly living costs could be significantly reduced through building less-expensive dwellings, providing low-interest loans, and providing mutual care. Residents could have more of their lives back to invest in worship, prayer, weekly ministry in their neighborhood, and celebration of their faith. And this community could become highly self-reliant, growing much of their own food and caring for creation as part of their witness. Their entire lives would bear witness to God's new mustard seed order.

I am not suggesting that every believer should be part of this kind of unusual residential church plant. But with the mounting pressures of a McWorld future, we are all going to need to be in communities in which we are known, loved, and held accountable. I am convinced that building strong, mutually supportive Christian communities committed to mission will be one of the most important tasks for the church in the twenty-first century.

Planting a Seed for Cohousing in Denmark

Part of the imagination for designing new residential settlements for mutual support comes out of studying the cohousing movement. Over twenty years ago people in Denmark, who weren't particularly religious, concluded, based on their own experience, that detached single-family housing wasn't necessarily the good life that modern culture contended it was. So they invented cohousing. Essentially, it is condo living with a purpose, and it bears no resemblance to the hippie communes of the sixties.

Envision a two-story dwelling that houses seventy-five people. Instead of every family having their own backyard and front yard, this cohousing complex has one cooperative area where all the kids play together, and another where everyone gardens together. Instead of every dwelling in the co-op having its own large recreation room, the complex has one recreation room for the entire community. They have meals in this common room every evening, at a cost of roughly a dollar per person. Each couple cooks once every two months. However, you don't have to eat there. Everyone has their own kitchen, too.

People who live in these cooperative housing complexes report they prefer a way of life that is more cooperative, in which they share child care, gardening, and meals. Widows and singles state they prefer it to living alone. In fact, they report it is as though they have been engrafted into a larger family in which people care for one another.

This cohousing movement is growing at a rapid clip in the United States, Canada, and Britain. But virtually all of those involved in this kind of experimentation are social progressives. They want to create for themselves and their kids new living arrangements that more genuinely reflect their values instead of those handed them by modern culture. (You can contact *Cohousing* magazine for more info at cohomag@aol.com.)

In our dualistic Christianity, it doesn't seem to have often occurred to us that we aren't obligated to accept all the models that modern culture hands us. The single-family detached house didn't come with the ark of the covenant. And it is among the most expensive ways to live. We do have other options.

Considering Cooperative Stewardship in a Needy World

Let's look at the cost of the single-family detached model in the North American scene. Many Christians will wind up spending over two and a half times what their homes are worth on interest. Many of the couples we work with in the United States and Canada will spend from $500,000 to $2 million (U.S.) over thirty years for shelter.

It costs roughly $350,000 to raise a child in North America. And a report on CNN estimated that the average couple who are age fifty-five will need to put away $1.5 million to retire comfortably in the United States. Calculate the enormous amount that must be taken out of the life income of your congregation over twenty years to meet these kinds of legitimate needs. As we have seen, in a McWorld future the state is likely to shift more of the costs of education, health care, and retirement back to the individual, raising the costs still higher. And these costs are particularly rising for many of our young.

Considering the Possibilities of a Cooperative Stewardship Model

Let's look at the savings realized by Christians who have been sharing the costs of a cooperative model in North America for almost a hundred years. Some thirty thousand Hutterites live in cooperative communities in Canada and the United States. I visited one of these communities and was impressed by how the residents together attempt to authentically live out the kingdom in every aspect of their lives.

The Hutterites explained that as a result of living a cooperative lifestyle, they are able to significantly reduce their living costs compared with the costs of living in a single-family detached model. The cost to construct a three-bedroom home connected to other units is only $32,000. The monthly per-person cost is only $190 for everything, including shelter, food, health care, and retirement. That is less than $800 a month for a family of four, which frees up a lot of time and money for other uses.

This particular community is generous with the resources they free up. They give generously to those in need in Kosovo and to urban ministries in the United States. And families from this community routinely spend a few hours every week outside their community, visiting prisons, working with the poor, and helping seniors and the disabled in their neighborhood with their chores.

I am not for a minute suggesting that we all become Hutterites. But I think that from their cooperative stewardship model, we can learn of ways in which we can, in community, be better stewards of the time and money God has entrusted to us. I am certain we could all find ways to be more a part of God's loving response to the growing needs of tomorrow's world.

Couldn't Christians also create new living arrangements that reflect the values of the kingdom more than the values of modern culture? Couldn't we create not a single model but a range of settlement models that more authentically reflect the biblical values we claim?

Planting a Seed in a Six-Plex to Set the Young Free

I am particularly concerned about the rising costs of shelter for a new generation. For the last six years, I have been presenting a modest diagram of a six-unit cooperative community designed to help those under age thirty-five get out from under the burden of huge mortgages so they have more of their life to invest in the advance of God's mustard seed movement. Assume that this six-plex co-op will be planted in a community in which a two-bedroom fixer-upper sells for $150,000. But remember, a young couple who purchases that house will wind up spending roughly $500,000 for that house over thirty years.

In the co-op I am presenting, a three-bedroom, bath-and-a-half unit could probably be constructed for $60,000 to $70,000 (with some invested labor) on a one-third acre lot. This six-plex would also include a shared recreation room, a shared laundry, and a common garden area the kids could also play in as you can see in the diagram, drafted by Leroy Troyer, a Christian architect. (There are two more bedrooms upstairs in each of the six units.)

I am proposing an alternative mortgage scheme in which six older, well-financed Christian couples in the same church provide six $60,000 no-interest loans to each of six younger couples. The older couples would get their $60,000 back in five years. All they would lose is the interest. For that small sacrifice, their investment would have a double whammy.

These six young couples, instead of spending $500,000 over thirty years, would spend $60,000 over five years to provide a home for themselves and their families.

If these six young couples were willing to keep paying for two more years after payoff to finance the kingdom, that would free up $144,000 to provide housing for a hundred families in Uganda or three to four Habitat for Humanity houses in the neighborhood where the couples live. Do you see the possibilities of whole-life stewardship?

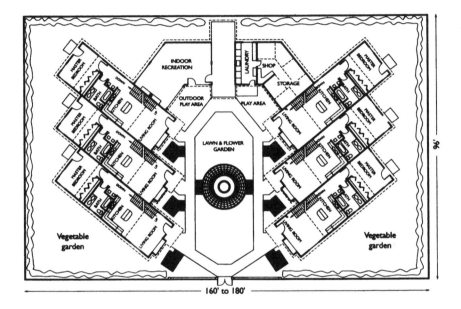

At the end of the seventh year, these six young couples wouldn't have any mortgage left. Nothing in the Bible suggests we are obligated to work for thirty years for a mortgage company. We could set some young people free. Then if they could work it out with employers, both spouses could work twenty hours a week instead of forty to eighty, not just to have more time for their kids and leisure activities but to have some time available to work for "sight to the blind, release to the captives, and good news to the poor."

Reinventing the Church to Put First Things First

Let me share one fresh model of those who are reinventing the church in a way that both compellingly reflects biblical principles and is preparing believers to become more engaged in compassionate response to the challenges of tomorrow's world. Rockridge United Methodist Church is located in a multicultural urban neighborhood in Oakland, California. It began the process of reinventing itself from a typical mainline church that was fairly corporate in its structure to a more organic, relational model of church as family, modeled after the Church of the Savior in Washington, D.C.

While the church-growth movement has largely focused on numerical growth, the leaders of Rockridge Church are more focused on qualitative growth. They are intent on making disciples who attempt to observe all of Christ's teachings. You will remember their primary vehicle for this. They not only call their members to whole-life discipleship and stewardship; they, like early Methodists, institute disciplines to ensure that members grow in every area of their lives. All members are encouraged to become covenant members, which calls for a yearly commitment to the disciplines of a covenant group, including

1. a daily commitment to at least thirty minutes in prayer and Scripture study.
2. a commitment to allow the rhythms of life to be dictated by faith instead of the culture, including keeping the Sabbath holy.
3. a commitment to consistent participation in the worship and educational life of the community, "unless prevented."
4. a commitment to develop and use spiritual gifts, not only in the church but out in the community. They devote one evening a week to be part of a small "mission covenant group." Then they invest an additional two to four hours a week to conduct ministry with their group.
5. a commitment to manifest, with God's help, something of the fruit of the Spirit and strive against sin. It is in these covenant groups where believers are both nurtured and held accountable as they are formed into part of God's new family.
6. a commitment to a form of whole-life stewardship that begins with the tithe and goes up from there. They report, "From this foundation we find God making us more generous. We are becoming aware of the dangers of our society's consumerism, and we can see how to be better stewards of God's creation."[16]

Planting a Seed in a Co-op Community in Oakland

One of the most intriguing mission covenant groups at Rockridge Methodist is the Community Builders. This MCG is committed to planting a new "expression of God's love in . . . North Oakland." These folks are the first Christians I have found anywhere who actually began constructing a cohousing project, called the

Temescal Cohousing Project, to provide another model of how to be the community of God's people in a rapidly changing world. Six church families are designing a nine-unit cohousing project built around a lovely old Victorian house. The common space includes a dining hall, a children's playroom, a workshop, guest rooms, laundry facilities, and a garden.[17]

The Temescal Cohousing project first of all intends to create an intergenerational, multicultural community that will operate as would a large extended family, sharing evening meals, child care, prayer and Bible study, vehicles, and engagement with their immediate neighborhood. These folks are already providing a homework center for neighborhood kids, a computer center for adults and youth, and affordable housing for those in transition. They want to be hospitable with their local neighbors and host community celebrations, as did the young people in east London. And they are designing the whole cohousing project in a way that models sustainable development and responsible stewardship of God's good creation.

I am convinced that this small planting of God's kingdom is going to grow a much larger tree than they realize. I believe it not only will have an impact in their own lives, congregation, and community but also will become a model for many other high-risk disciples who want to put first things first. It is one of the first models of what residential church plants might look like in the third millennium.

Anglican Franciscan Brother Samuel is one of a growing number who are calling for a remonking of the church. Brother Samuel reflects, "Monastic life may seem utterly out of tune with the spirit of our times, yet if we are entering another Dark Age, it may be to the wisdom of such a way the Church of today needs to turn. . . . I sense that the renewal of both the Church and society will come through the re-emerging forms of Christian community that are homes of generous hospitality, places of challenging reconciliation, and centres of attentiveness to the living God."[18]

We are galloping into a future that is changing at breakneck speed. As we race into a globalized future, a little faith worked in around the edges won't begin to equip us for the challenges of a new millennium. We will need to call the people of God to a more biblically radical whole-life faith and to whole-life communities that reflect the mission of the mustard seed more than the addictions of modern culture.

This provides a unique opportunity for Christian leaders who are willing to take some risks to unleash their imaginations. It is an opportunity to create new Christian settlements that draw on the spirit of monastic life, that are rooted in the life of prayer, that provide mutual care and free up individuals and families to spend time together every week in witness and service and to be a planting of God's subversive new order—missional communities for a new millennium.

Opportunities for Christian Leaders

How should leaders prepare Christians to reinvent their lives to put God's purposes first and creatively engage the challenges of a new millennium? Leaders have the opportunity

1. to both call and enable their members to become whole-life disciples and whole-life stewards.
2. to begin this process by assisting individuals and families to use Scripture to draft personal and family mission statements.
3. to design a ten-week course, using the outline in this chapter, to enable people to use their mission statement to reinvent their lifestyles.
4. to help members create small support communities in which they are known, loved, and held accountable. Some leaders then may want to explore creating new cooperative church plants or cohousing communities in which believers can more authentically flesh out the values of the mustard seed in a McWorld future.

Questions for Discussion and Action

1. What is the difference between whole-life discipleship and dualistic discipleship?

2. What was the result of Jesus Christ and that first community of disciples putting the purposes of God at the center of their lives?

3. Working from Scripture and prayer, try to discern how God is calling you to use your life to be part of what he is doing to make a difference in the world. Write down your personal mission statement and share it with your family and your small group.

4. Begin the creative adventure of reinventing your schedule and lifestyle to put your sense of mission purpose first. Ask your small group to hold you accountable, and be sure to add some celebration to your life.

5. If you are not part of a small group in which you are known, loved, and held accountable, prayerfully create one. If you are part of a small group, consider creating a residential model, in which together with others you can more authentically live out the values of faith in an alien culture and reduce your lifestyle costs so you have more of your life to invest in the advancement of the kingdom.

6. Create a celebration for people in your church that helps them enter into the celebration of the great homecoming of God.

Reinventing Christian Mission for a New Millennium

TORRENTIAL RAINS AND FLOODS SWEPT DOWN a steep ravine in Jalapa, Mexico, where the poorest families live in little flimsy shacks hugging the hillside. It was 1:30 in the morning, and Saul Cruz's wife, Pilar, had not come home. He was praying fervently because he feared that his wife had been lost in the floods. She had left home early in the evening to try to help one of her friends who lived in one of those little shanties. Finally, she returned home exhausted at 2:00 A.M. Saul and their children welcomed her with tremendous relief and joy.

In this devastating flood in 1989, hundreds of homes were destroyed and thirty-one people lost their lives. Pilar sat down with her husband and declared that the solution to this problem must be in helping people like her friend in Jalapa build safe houses so they and their families wouldn't be at risk every time the torrential rain and floods came. But Saul knew nothing about construction. He had brought his family to this community to plant a church. But in response to Pilar's passionate concern, he found a man who was a builder and organized a handful of volunteers from the community. Together they built two sturdy basic homes. It was a small beginning—a mustard seed.

If you had seen Jalapa in 1989, you wouldn't recognize it today. "Two million people were living on the sides of a precipitous ravine, often muddy, always dangerous. Raw sewage poured down the hillsides into the streams where children played and the poorest built their shacks out of milk cartons. Now the area has been transformed. Electricity, paved streets, piped drinking water, concrete channels for sewers. Hardly a shack to be seen."[1]

Originally, Saul and Pilar came to this community to bring good news to the poor and plant an evangelical church. But they had no idea of what that good news would be or how God would use their lives to make a difference for his kingdom. Someone gave them a garbage dump and Saul prayed over the dump. For three months Saul prayed over the garbage dump every day for wisdom. God answered those prayers.

One of the leaders of the community volunteered to help Saul and Pilar make a start on their garbage dump, and the community pitched in. Slowly from the rubbish heap emerged a community center that became the hub for the transformation of the entire community. Pilar, working with moms and kids in the community, started homework clubs and a range of other children's activities. Saul solicited help from the mayor to secure resources to rebuild this shanty community. Tearfund England was invited to partner in the project. They not only provided some of the resources for housing construction; they created microenterprise projects, such as producing red roof tiles, to provide income for the unemployed in the community.

During this entire time, Saul and Pilar held a Bible study in their home. But they resisted sponsoring large evangelistic meetings. They wanted to see their demonstration of God's love touch the people. One day a man who was a chronic drunk had a dramatic conversion experience that God used to break things wide open. The people crowded out their home, and they now have a thriving church in the community center on the former garbage dump. The center is called Armonia, which is the closest Spanish word to the Hebrew word shalom. Their dream is to see the continuing transformation of the community through the words-and-deeds ministry of Armonia.

Saul said there are three reasons why they work in Jalapa: "Compassion, obedience, and indignation. Compassion for the suffering people, for their needs; obedience to Jesus Christ, who has sent us to work among the poor; and indignation, because we get indignant when people created in God's image suffer in this way."[2]

Finding the Focus

Saul and Pilar are among a growing number of our sisters and brothers all over the world who are discovering firsthand the satisfaction of

God's working through their mustard seeds to change our world. God invites all of our communities of faith to become instruments of the shalom purposes of God in a world of growing need.

In this chapter I will argue that we need to radically reinvent how we do mission work, both to more effectively address the challenges of tomorrow's world and to more authentically advance the mustard seed purposes of God.

There has been a dramatic growth in short-term mission, more missionaries are being sent by the church in the Two-Thirds World, and more churches have been planted among unreached people groups. But I find that those active in mission tend to focus on the upside and not deal seriously with either the new challenges ahead or the extent to which we haven't worked hard enough to define why we do what we do in missions. And as a consequence, I am afraid that sometimes we get the story wrong and use methods that contradict the faith we claim.

I will begin by taking us back to the future one last time to highlight some of the new challenges facing Christian mission in a new millennium. Then we will go back to the Bible and work to get our story straight. Finally, I will share with you imaginative new ways that Christians all over the world are finding to manifest something of God's mustard seed in response to the mounting challenges of our globalized future.

Back to the Future One Last Time

This book opened with a ride on the wild side that reminded all of us that we are living in a world changing at blinding speed. Too many of us are also experiencing rides on the wet side because we are not paying enough attention to how the church, our world, and the arenas in which we do missions are rapidly changing.

Ray Bakke, a Christian urban specialist, stresses how important it is to understand the urban context, to "exegete the city," before we develop mission strategies. What I am advocating is that mission executives, missiologists, and leaders in local churches make our best effort to anticipate how the context in which we do mission work is likely to change in the future—before we strategize.

The physical needs of people in many poorer countries, particularly on the African continent, are likely to increase significantly in the future. The good news is that the church in the Two-Thirds World will take more leadership in missions and in the worldwide church in the coming century.

Even if the long-boom economy spreads worldwide, it is clear that many of the world's poorest residents will not benefit if they don't receive significant help in becoming competitive players in this tough new economy.

And the forces of globalization are bringing unprecedented pressures on families and local communities all over the planet.

The pressures of global competition are influencing many Western countries to cut back programs to the poor at home and abroad. As we have seen, in the task of world evangelization we are losing ground both to population growth and to McWorld's rapidly expanding borderless youth culture, the marketers of McWorld are proving to be more successful at reaching the hearts and minds of the next generation. So mission organizations need to gear up to do more—much more.

Of critical concern is the growing pressure that McWorld exerts on members of the North American church to work longer and consume more. Which means that if we don't find a way to resist this growing pressure, we will have less time and money to invest in missions.

As we have also seen, the Western church, including the church in North America, is declining at a concerning rate in numbers and in giving. Particularly concerning is the rapid disappearance of those under age thirty-five from our churches, and the declining discretionary time and money of many of those who stay with the church.

Therefore, my reluctant forecast, if we don't find ways to alter these trends, is that the church in the West and many mission organizations are likely to have difficulty even sustaining their present levels of mission investment over the next two decades. The mounting challenges facing us in a global future, and the declining capacity of the Western church to respond, deserve much thoughtful discussion and creative action by missiologists, mission executives, and practitioners.

Back to the Bible One Last Time: Putting First Things First in the Church

Many Western churches are more highly invested in maintaining a place for worship and nurture for folks inside the building than in making a difference in their community or their world.

In fact, it is not unusual to find American churches, with big buildings and big budgets, that don't sponsor a single ministry outside their buildings. Pastors in the United States often tell me "that they don't believe doing ministry in the community is the church's responsibility. But it's fine if their members want to volunteer at the local rescue mission or help out at Big Brothers." In informal sampling, I have found that less than 20 percent of our time or money ever leaves the building in the average American church. I am convinced that our problem of priorities, at its core, is theological. Too many churches have become the protectors of the dominant values of modern culture, not their critics.

British theologian Alister McGrath brings a direct word on the dangers of cultural accommodation. Looking back on Christians who quietly supported the values that were part of Hitler's Germany, he states, "We are doing the same thing today, by allowing ourselves and our churches to follow societal norms and values, irrespective of their origins and goals. To allow our ideas and values to become controlled by anything or anyone other than the self-revelations of God in Scripture is to adopt an ideology, rather than a theology; it is to become controlled by ideas and values whose origins lie outside the Christian tradition—and potentially to become enslaved to them."[3]

The church exists not only to meet our spiritual needs and bring us into faith communities; it is also called to help us transform our values from those of modern culture to those of the kingdom. And the Bible reminds us that the church exists not primarily for itself but for others. We are called to place God's mission at the center of our congregational life, as resident aliens who are intended by God's grace, in spite of our brokenness, to be a rough sample of his great homecoming celebration. And we are called to share the good news of God's new order in word and deed and by unmasking the values of the dominant culture.

Recovering the Theology of First Things

Everywhere I work with the church, I find many Christian leaders who act as though all the questions about what it means to be the church and fulfill the mission of the church have been answered. Now it's just up to us to go out there and do it. I, for one, am not convinced that all the questions have been answered. I believe that too often we operate from a set of "immaculate assumptions." And if we were ever to thoughtfully check out why we do what we do, we would discover that many of us are in serious trouble. And I think we will also discover why God's mission has been marginalized in many of our churches.

Among Christian leaders in Britain and North America, there is a great deal of talk these days about revival and the renewal of the church, talk that sometimes tends to focus us inwardly on ourselves. Wilbert Shenk, a missiologist, wrote a compelling article in the *International Bulletin of Missionary Research,* arguing that the renewal of the church and God's mission are inseparably related. "Authentic renewal of the church cannot be separated from mission; the two are integrally linked. Both arise from the same theological foundation: God's covenant with Abraham was for the blessing of the nations, and this covenant was renewed and reaffirmed in Jesus Christ. The people of God exist because of God's salvific intentions for the nations and the role they are to play in God's mission."[4]

Lesslie Newbigin reminds us that "the church is not an end in itself. The growth and the prosperity of the church is not the goal of history." Jesus instead prepared a community to be "chosen bearer of the secret of the kingdom . . . to embody and announce the reign of God."[5] And the establishment of God's new order is a fulfillment of the blessing to the nations that God covenanted with Abraham and Sarah. Newbigin stresses that this is God's initiative and that the Creator will indeed bring into being the promised new order through the death and resurrection of God's Chosen One.

Reflecting on the North American church's current transition from a modern to a postmodern culture, George Hunsberger states that we must do more than "mere tinkering with long-assumed notions about the identity and mission of the church. . . . There is a need for reinventing or rediscovering the church." Building on Newbigin's call for the people of God to "embody and announce the reign of God," Hunsberger proposes that we reinvent the church to become a missional community, in which mission is no longer a programmatic activity but is at the center of our shared life as a sent community.[6]

The early Celtic Christian community in the sixth and seventh centuries understood that to follow Christ, they were called into God's mission and existed as a sent community that stood against the dominant culture of their time. While the Roman church coming into England from the south was often preoccupied with power and status, the Celtic church coming down from the north was a community of servants identifying with the poor. They were more focused on making a difference than on making a comfortable existence.

Today, Mission America (missionamerica@compuserve.com) is calling the North American church to move mission back to the center of congregational life. As a part of the Lausanne Movement, Mission America is challenging churches to reprioritize resources to invest more time and money in the word and deed ministries of the gospel of Christ. If you are looking for help, move mission to the center of your congregation's life. ACMC (76331.2051@compuserve.com) and the Center for World Mission (mission.frontiers@uscwm.org) also have excellent resources to make your church into a mission-centered church.

Planting a Seed in Christchurch

In Britain, Australia, and New Zealand, the churches I have worked with seem to be more outwardly focused. They typically sponsor several ministries in the community and seem to give a larger share of their budget to missions. For instance, Spreydon Baptist, in Christchurch, New Zealand, is a church that places the biblical call to God's mission at the center of congregational life, not at the margins. Sixty percent of its total budget is invested in mission work locally and overseas. It sponsors twenty-five thriving ministries to single-parent moms, unemployed young people, and those on welfare in Christchurch. And a high percentage of its eight hundred members are involved every week in these ministries.

One of its most creative ministries is called the Kingdom Trust. Essentially, the trust operates much like a credit union in which those on the margins are given small loans so they can start small businesses and become self-reliant. However, Spreydon Baptist not only loans the funds but also makes available free business consultation. Over the years, it has successfully enabled hundreds of people to become self-supporting again.

Planting a Seed in London

Ichthus Fellowship in London is a megachurch without a building. The church relies heavily on home groups and rents a school auditorium once a month so the entire congregation can worship together. This enables the church to invest a greater share of its resources in mission to others. And it sponsors a broad spectrum of ministries in London as well as overseas.

Planting a Seed in La Puente

Casa de Señor is an unusual church plant that exists as a witness to God's love in La Puente, California. It is a Pentecostal Mennonite church. The church is pastored by two men and two women, all nonsalaried. Consuelo Moreno is the minister of prayer. She works at a job from 3:00 P.M. to 11:00 P.M. to support her ministry. She arrives at the church early every morning, and there is a crowd of people from the community, waiting for her to pray with them. Some are seeking prayer for healing, others for work, and still others for discernment. They witness supernatural healings and deliverances, which attracts others to this growing congregation. The church runs a sexual abstinence program for young people in the community that has been so successful that the local school board is exploring adopting it. The church consists of three houses: one for worship, one for community education, and one for transitional housing for those in crisis.

Getting the Story Straight

Sometimes it is hard work to get the story straight. Wycliffe translators working with the Illuit tribe in Alaska were stumped because they could find no word in the Illuit language for joy as they were translating the New Testament. Finally, after weeks of struggle, one of the Illuit elders helped them solve their problem. Now the verse in question reads, "There will be more tail wagging in heaven over one sinner who repents than over ninety-nine who need no repentance."

We all need to work a little harder to make sure we get the story straight. Candidly, I am concerned because some of those I have met who are the keenest for God's mission are, I believe, inadvertently working from the dualistic Christian model I discussed earlier. They are passionately committed to seeing people come to vital spiritual faith and begin to change their moral values. But they are oblivious of the need for disciples of Christ to invite God also to change their cultural values.

While Western missionaries have learned to "contextualize the gospel" when they go into other cultures, we often seem oblivious to the extent to which we bring our cultural values with us. As a consequence, we often wind up unwittingly becoming evangelists for the aspirations and values that power McWorld instead of those that inspire the mustard seed.

Exporting the Wrong Message

And the greater problem is that a number of Christians in the West have exported this narrow spiritual view of the gospel all over the world. Several years ago an American mission organization was working in a supportive relationship with the indigenous Haitian denomination of three hundred churches. The head of this mission organization, wanting to bless the president of this Baptist denomination, invited him to move into the missionary compound with the missionaries, where they would construct a new home for him.

This compound, called the City of Light, was built on a hill above Les Cayes, where it was cooled by the trade winds. The forty or so missionaries who lived there had homes much like they would have had back in the States, complete with electricity, stereo headphones, and Haitian servants, too.

Within three months of the time the president of the Haitian Baptist Church moved into his new American-style home in the City of Light, a remarkable change started to take place in numbers of Baptist churches all over Haiti. Leadership cut back funding to literacy and community health projects. They then began using these funds to build houses for their pastors like the ones the missionaries, and now their president, had.

The missionaries had come preaching Jesus with their lips while their lifestyles preached the good news of the American dream. In his important book *Missions and Money,* Jonathan Bonk documents how insidiously the affluent lifestyles of missionaries from the West have undermined Christian witness throughout the world.[7]

Latin American missiologist Orlando Costas indicted the Western church for exporting a culturally accommodated gospel that calls people to "a conscience-soothing Jesus, with an unscandalous cross; an otherworldly kingdom; a private inwardly, individualistically limited Holy Spirit; a pocket God; a spiritualized Bible," and a church that escapes the gut issues of society. It has conceived the goal of the gospel as "a happy, comfortable, successful life. . . . It has made possible the 'conversion' of men and women without having to make any drastic changes in their lifestyles or world views," guaranteeing thereby "the preservation of the status quo and the immobility of the people of God."[8]

Fulfilling God's Mission on Two Tracks

I believe one of the major afflictions of Protestantism, particularly conservative Protestantism, is that we have often gotten the story wrong. At the core of our dualistic faith is the dualistic vision of the future we discussed earlier. Too many of us have embraced a narrow view of God's redemptive purpose as the saving of disembodied souls for a nonmaterialistic future in the clouds. This has inadvertently given rise to a two-track approach to mission work all over the world.

One of the most concerning aspects of the Christian dualistic model of mission is that it tends to convey the impression that the good news of the gospel only has to do with the narrowly individual spiritual aspects of personal faith. For instance, in 1996 I was invited to participate in a panel discussion of the church's response to the poor, at the Call to Renewal Conference. The other panelists included: Brian Hehir, a Catholic scholar from Harvard; E. J. Dionne, a well-known Catholic author; and conservative commentator Cal Thomas.

Cal Thomas made a forceful statement that illustrates the point I am trying to make. Cal said, "I recently interviewed Ralph Reed [then president of the Christian Coalition] and I particularly liked his response to one question I asked him. I asked, 'What would happen if every member of the Christian Coalition began to live as their leader commanded them . . . and I am not talking about Pat Robertson?' Reed responded, 'Loving their enemies, praying for those that persecuted them, feeding the hungry, clothing the naked, visiting those in prison'"—Cal stressed in his own words—"'not as an end, not as an end, but as a means, because it gives you an entry to their hearts!'"

I responded that I was raised in an evangelical faith that viewed salvation in the singularly personal and spiritual terms that Cal had emphasized. But I said that I had learned that the call to feed the hungry and visit the prisoner was part of the vision of the prophet Isaiah, which clearly reflected the purposes of God. Scripture teaches that God's redemptive purposes aren't just personal and spiritual. They are corporate and touch every aspect of human life. God's redemptive initiative "includes the personal transformation we evangelicals have always emphasized, but the Bible teaches that God also plans to renew a world and create a new community . . . and that is an end and not just a means." The problem is that this viewpoint is not unique with Cal Thomas.

Beyond Two-Track Mission: Recovering the Whole Gospel for the Whole World

This narrowly spiritual approach to the Christian message has inadvertently led to a two-track approach to the church's mission. During the past sixty years there have been those who have defined this mission as simply proclamation evangelism, personal discipling, and church planting. They have planted churches almost solely concerned with the spiritual needs of the members.[9]

Forty years ago other Christians who held a broader view of Christian mission went to many of the same communities in which church planters had been working and began Christian community development projects to help the poor help themselves. World Relief, World Vision, Tearfund England, World Concern, all of which are committed to holistic mission, are a few of dozens of Christian agencies that are still involved in addressing the physical and spiritual needs of the global poor.

As one travels in Africa, Asia, and Latin America, one can still find the legacy of this two-track approach to God's mission. You will still find churches focusing exclusively on the spiritual needs of their members, and an agency such as World Vision working in the same community to help primarily meet the people's economic and physical needs.

When I worked at World Concern, I had a CEO from a church-planting organization ask me, "Do you think my organization should do community development?" I responded, "Absolutely not. Your organizational mission is church planting. But I think you need to plant churches that find ways to address not only the spiritual but also the health care, educational, and economic needs of their congregations so that Christian development agencies never have to come to their villages." I am convinced that if we, like Saul and Pilar, could fulfill our mission on a single track, the witness for the gospel would be much stronger.

Defining Why We Do What We Do: In Search of an Integrated Approach to Mission

To do this, we will need to do some fresh biblical work. For the past forty or so years, there has been an important ongoing conversation among mainline Protestants, Roman Catholics, and evangelicals, regarding what the mission of the church is. Let me mention a few highlights. For evangelicals, the Lausanne Covenant of 1974 is the touchstone for a new movement into a more integrated, single-track approach to the church's mission. David Bosch writes, "[Evangelism and socio-political] involvement are both part of our Christian duty. For both are necessary expressions of our doctrines of God and man, our love for our neighbor and our obedience to Jesus Christ."[10]

At CRESR 1982 (Christian Response to Evangelism and Social Responsibility) the relationship between evangelism and social responsibility was defined as the relationship between two wings on a bird or two oars in a boat. They were seen as being inseparable. I had the responsibility to organize another conference, called Wheaton 1983: The Church in Response to Human Need, in which Christian leaders were invited to define our biblical responsibility to the poor.

Bosch states, "For the first time in an official statement emanating from an international evangelical conference the perennial dichotomy was overcome. Without ascribing priority to either evangelism or social involvement, the Wheaton '83 Statement . . . declared, "Evil is not only in human hearts but also in social structures. . . . The mission of the church includes both the proclamation of the Gospel and its demonstration. We must therefore evangelize, respond to immediate human needs and press for social transformation."[11]

Evangelical leaders in Britain, such as Steve Gaukroger, are clearer about the unity of our biblical mission than many I have worked with in other parts of the Western church. Gaukroger writes, "The Bible consistently describes mission in terms of compassion as well as communication, that is, by works as well as words."[12]

Since the early eighties we seem to have moved into a de facto recognition that mission is broader than simply addressing people's spiritual needs. I say de facto because this growing consensus seems to have come not out of biblical reflection but simply out of embracing the ever changing evangelical worldview regarding the church's mission. However, I still run into numbers of people, including those in leadership, who are still pre-Lausanne '74 in their view of the church's mission.

Let me explain. I believe we need to do some fresh thinking about a theology of the church's mission. When World Vision was exploring getting involved in urban mission in the United States back in the early eighties, Paul Landry asked me to critique one of their earliest proposals for an urban ministry project in Houston, Texas. The proposal presented strategies for meeting the housing needs, economic needs, and nutritional needs of an inner-city neighborhood, but there was no discussion of the theological assumptions undergirding the project. In my response I wrote, "What if you successfully met all these unmet needs for shelter, financial income, and an improved diet in Houston? Would the kingdom of God come on earth? Or are we after something more than simply individual 'need meeting'?"

Many Christians, even those who have a more holistic theology, tend to chronically view the church's mission on two tracks: "individual need meeting" and "individual soul saving." Part of the reason we haven't done a good job of developing an integrated approach to the church's mission is that we haven't spent enough time attempting to define a biblical picture of what God's ultimate purposes are for God's people and God's world.

While serving as a consultant to the leadership team of a Christian mission organization in Britain, I asked, "What are you trying to accomplish in the communities of the poor you work with, in terms of a sense of biblical purpose?" The CEO immediately said, "Our organization works with the poorest of the poor in helping them meet their basic needs, and we work in partnership with a number of different agencies in this mission."

I responded, "I understand your programmatic goals, but what would one village in India look like if you accomplished your sense of what God's purposes are for that community?" He suddenly blurted out, "My goodness, we have never defined biblically what our endgame is! We have never biblically defined what we are trying to accomplish in the transformation of a given community."

Defining Why We Do What We Do: Listening to God through Scripture and Community

Most churches and mission organizations seldom attempt to do the hard work of biblically defining why they do what they do in fulfilling their mission. Most churches I work with are afflicted by what I call chronic randomness, with the men's group going in one direction, the women's group going in another, and all holding a potluck once a year to celebrate the fact that they are still doing some of the things they did the year before. No one knows how it all comes together. Churches typically have mission statements to accompany all their random activity. But it is rare to find a congregation that has developed a mission statement out of Scripture study and then refocused all their activity to reflect that statement.

It is even rarer to find Christian organizations that have done the hard biblical work of defining why they do what they do, organizations that have actually drafted what I call an operational theology of their mission. I can guarantee that when we work largely from unstated assumptions in our personal lives, churches, or organizations, the values of the dominant culture are going to slip in and shape not only what we do but how we do it. And we won't even notice.

Planting a Seed by Listening to Scripture at Luther Place

Luther Place is a largely white congregation in Washington, D.C., that found itself in an increasingly nonwhite and needy community. Like many white congregations in that situation, the members took a vote as to whether to move their church to the all-white suburbs or stay put. To their surprise, the vote was to stay put. In the past, they had been content to simply be a Lutheran church coordinating random activities for themselves. But if they were going to stay in this community, they now felt they needed a clear sense of biblical purpose. Members became involved in a serious Scripture study in the Gospels and received what they believed was God's call on their congregation: "As God is hospitality to us in the bread and the wine of the Eucharist, we feel called to be the hospitality of Christ in this needy community." They followed this up by scrapping some of their random activities for people inside the building and created a range of new ministries in urban housing and tutoring programs that were clearly related to their sense of biblical call. You see, not only do individual believers and families need biblical mission statements; so do churches.

Planting a Seed by Listening to Scripture at World Concern

In the mid-eighties, I helped World Concern (wconcern@crista.org) draft the first operational theology of its mission. We secured the services of New Testament theologian Eugene Lemcio and Old Testament scholar Steven Hayner (presently the CEO of InterVarsity Christian Fellowship in the United States). The mission statement focused on what World Concern understood to be God's ultimate purpose: to reconcile us in Christ, not only to God but to one another and to God's good creation, through nurturing strong churches.

One of the most startling results of making our implicit assumptions explicit was that it changed the mission focus of the organization. In the past, World Concern had been content simply to design water projects and health care projects in Jesus' name.

But once we concluded that a major part of God's endgame was to grow strong churches that God could use to transform the communities in which they were planted, it changed one facet of World Concern's mission strategy. They funded the development of a curriculum for a Bible school in El Salvador to teach people how to plant churches that seek to address not only the spiritual needs but also the economic, health care, and nutritional needs of the community so World Concern would never need to come to that community to initiate development projects.

Planting a Seed in Listening to Community in Haiti

Several years before I helped draft a theology of mission for World Concern, I had the responsibility to initiate a community development project in Haiti. In preparation I invited the team we were sending to Haiti to join me in writing down our biblical assumptions about its mission. One of the assumptions was "that God was alive, well, and at work in Haiti before any of the team arrived." I realized that this principle would be self-evident to many people. But the act of writing it down not only made it explicit but meant that we felt compelled to act on it. The first thing our team did upon arrival was to tour the village, asking people about their felt needs. The team heard people expressing their need for tractors, clinics, and new buildings—expensive stuff.

Determined to act on our assumption that God was alive, well, and at work before the team arrived, we created a strategy to find out not only how God was at work. We did this by asking, What kinds of dreams was God stirring up in the hearts of the people? So the team toured the valley a second time, asking a different question: "What kinds of dreams is God giving you for the future of your family and for the future of your community?"

This time the team got a different response. People shared about a strong rivalry and animosity between several families in the community. They believed that God wanted to see their community reconciled. Over 80 percent of the kids were too poor to attend school, and God stirred up a dream in many to see all the children be able to go to school. And a number of people said that the Lord was leading them to pray for the spiritual renewal of their community. The answers to the second question were more beneficial in helping to focus the direction of the project than were the answers to the first. But you see, we would never have asked the second question if we hadn't first written down our assumptions about mission.

Bryant Myers, in a comprehensive unpublished manuscript on transformational development, states that transformational development is a "convergence of stories." "The story of the community is joined by the story of the development facilitator and . . . they share a story. God has been and is at work in both stories, and God is making an invitation for a better future story. This means the biblical story must become a part of the transformational development process."[13]

Reinventing Our Mission As Though Community Matters

God's purpose for a redeemed community is more than individual "soul saving" and individual "need meeting," which reflect the individualism of modernity. The Bible teaches that God is interested in the transformation not only of our individual lives but also of our communities, including how we relate to one another.

Mennonite theologian Marlin Miller describes God's endgame for the transformation of community as well as of individual lives. "It includes social justice: the protection of widows and orphans, and society's dependents; the struggle against exploitation and oppression; the protection of life and property."[14] James Metzler writes, "From the disruption of *shalom* in the Garden of Eden to its total renewal in the new Jerusalem, the object of all of God's work is the recovery of *shalom* in his creation."[15]

I have found no more compelling imagery of the shalom future of God than that offered us by Richard Foster in his classic the *Freedom of Simplicity*. "This great vision of *shalom* begins and ends our Bible. In the creation narrative, God brought order out of chaos; in the Apocalypse of John, we have the glorious wholeness of a new heaven and a new earth. The messianic child that is born is the Prince of Peace [Isa. 9:6]. Justice and righteousness and peace are to characterize his unending kingdom [Isa. 9:7]. Central to the dream of *shalom* is the wonderful vision of all nations streaming to the mountain of the temple of God to be taught his ways and to walk in his paths."[16] In addition to transforming our individual lives, God wants to transform our fragmented, troubled communities into shalom communities that reflect something of God's new community.

Globalization and the Future of Community

While globalization of the economy is providing some opportunity for numbers of those on the bottom rungs of the economic ladder, it is also homogenizing us into one huge McWorld macroculture in which every place looks like every other place. Local cultures, which often reflect more of the values of God's kingdom than does the invading global commercial culture, are disappearing at an alarming rate. The massive effort to centralize and globalize the economy is also, as we have seen, increasingly devastating local communities, local economies, and the supporting natural environment.

Wendell Berry is concerned that the globalization of the economy is increasingly becoming a threat to many local economies and communities all over our planet. He writes, "The dangers of the ideal of competition is that it neither proposes nor implies any limits. It proposes to simply lower costs at any cost, and to raise profits at any cost. It does not hesitate at the destruction of the life of a family or of the life of a community."[17]

What will be the long-term costs to our families and communities of allowing Godzilla-size corporations to swallow farms, shops, and the economies of whole communities? Do we really need to trust the future of our families and communities to the magic of the marketplace, the forces of globalization, and the centralizing appetites of colossus corporations? My Bible tells me that the people of God are not to sit by and allow centralized political or economic powers to run roughshod over our families and local communities. Aren't we called to work to see the reign of God established not only in our lives and families but also in our neighborhoods and local communities?

Mercy Corps (mercycorps@msn.com) is one of a new breed of Christian organizations working to promote the spread of God's shalom through the creation of civil society in communities from Lebanon to Honduras. It is committed to developing strong communities in which people have a voice in their lives and neighborhoods and are reconciled with their neighbors.

Berry insists that the only response we can make to the forces intent on creating a highly centralized global economy is for us to create "a strong local economy with a strong local culture. . . . A human community, if it is to last long, must exert a sort of centripetal force, holding local soil and local memory in place."[18] I believe that the Creator God is already powerfully at work in all our communities, seeking to provide a place to help nurture families and manifest something of the shalom purposes of God's new order.

Titou Paredes, a Christian anthropologist in Peru, said, "God is in all cultures both affirming and judging." I have never seen a mission project in which there has been any effort to identify the good, the strong, and the beautiful of God's new shalom order already present in that culture and then ask residents, in the face of rapid McWorld cultural colonization and homogenization, which aspects of their culture they want to attempt to preserve and augment. Imagine being involved in a mission project on a single track, working and praying for the transformation not only of lives but of a community as well, cooperating with what God has already been doing in our local communities all over our small world.

Planting a Seed in Community Agriculture in Chicago

As we look into the future and see the growing vulnerability we all face in a McWorld future, it will be essential that we increase our capability for regional and community self-reliance. Wendell Berry states, "In a healthy community, people will be richer in their neighbors, . . . in the health and pleasure of neighborhood, than in their bank accounts. . . . If you have money to invest, try to invest it locally, both to help the local community and to keep from helping the larger economy that is destroying local communities."[19] A growing number of bootstrap agricultural programs are being started to enable the poor to become more self-reliant in providing their supply of nutritious food. Vegetable gardens are being planted in vacant lots, rooftop tomato patches, and backyard beehives. Some 750 cities have community gardening programs.

Perhaps one of the most imaginative urban agricultural projects was initiated with the poor in Chicago by Job Ebenezar for the Evangelical Lutheran Church in America. The food banks in Chicago received half a ton of tomatoes, eggplants, cucumbers, and other vegetables from this project, all grown in four-foot wading pools located on top of a parking garage near O'Hare International Airport. There is even serious consideration being given to working with the International Heifer Project to raise small livestock, including goats and rabbits, in the inner city.[20]

Planting a Seed in Nicaragua

One of the most interesting models I came across in my research was a model not for community transformation but for community creation. The AGROS Foundation in Seattle (miracles@agros.org) has been raising funds to help the landless poor in Central America not only to buy land but also to create new communities on the land. In Nicaragua AGROS has purchased just under two hundred acres of high-quality land that will provide the opportunity to create a settlement for fifty landless families. Mario, who is a member of the leadership council for this project, was a contra soldier during the war. As the war ended, one of his dying compatriots led him to commit his life to Christ. He, in turn, led Alejandro, who used to be a Sandinista soldier, to faith. Alejandro is also on this leadership council, which is composed of both Protestants and Catholics. They not only select the fifty families but help them build homes on the land and create the basis for a civil society, schools and literacy programs, and a worship facility that can be used by both Catholics and evangelicals. AGROS has just received an international award from the World Bank, the United Nations, and the Inter-American Foundation for the creation of one of the most successful antipoverty programs in Central America.

Planting a Seed in Atlanta

"I think what they have done is absolutely phenomenal," said Tiger Woods at the Tour Championship at East Lake Golf Course in Atlanta. Woods was talking about a creative project in which people of compassion in Atlanta raised $93 million to restore not only this aging golf course but the adjacent East Lake community in which people lived in entrenched poverty. With leadership from Christian urban activist Bob Lupton, they have built one of the first urban cohousing projects, complete with a large organic garden, to help these urban residents create a community in which residents work together to improve the quality of their lives.[21]

Planting a Seed in Reconciliation in Mississippi

"One of the most important elements of working for the transformation of our communities is working for the cause of reconciliation. The miracle in South Africa is a witness to the power
of faith to begin the healing process in a nation that has so long been torn
apart. 'The Rev. John Perkins drew applause,' reports Mississippi's leading newspaper, the *Clarion-Ledger*, "from both the Legislative Black Caucus and the Conservative Caucus for suggesting how to help Mississippi
move beyond its past. . . . He suggested lawmakers set up something similar to South Africa's Truth and Reconciliation Commission to bring reconciliation between the black and white community in Mississippi.
Perkins said a new commission can help the state say, 'We're bringing
this to an end, that the war is over and the past is behind us. Now let's
see where we go in the future. . . . Whites have to overcome their guilt
and ask God to forgive them and move forward. We blacks have to overcome our blame and stop being victims.'"[22]

Planting a Seed in Reconciliation Down Under

Aboriginal Christians are seeking not only healing at the massacre sites but justice from the Australian government regarding land claims. An Aboriginal Christian writes to other Aboriginal believers, "Oppressors through violence distort reality . . . they
put forward the 'narrative of the lie.' . . . This lie can only be overcome
by a stronger redeeming narrative. If we, together with many other Aboriginal people, are going to be 'the Exodus people of God down under,'
then we have to learn to walk according to another covenant and learn
to march to a different drum. . . . We are a part of an alternative cosmic
story of what God has done and is doing. And it is never dull to be on
the road with Jesus. . . . I am content to be on the journey and confident
that the creator of this 'precious land under the southern cross' is concerned about all our people and wants all of God's diverse family at the
table in God's future."[23]

Planting a Seed in Reconciliation in the Path of the Crusaders

Perhaps one of the most intriguing efforts at reconciliation is
the Reconciliation Walk. November 27, 1995, is the day that
marked the nine hundredth anniversary of the call of Christen-
dom to retrieve the holy places from the "infidels." This date was selected
by Lynn Green and a group mostly of European Christians as the date to
launch a Reconciliation Walk along the same path the Crusaders walked,

to ask forgiveness of Jews, Muslims, and Orthodox Christians who had been brutalized by the European Crusaders.

The reconciliation message they shared with everyone they met in their journey reads, "Nine hundred years ago, our forefathers carried the name of Jesus Christ in battle across the Middle East. Fueled by fear, greed and hatred they betrayed the name of Christ by conducting themselves in a manner contrary to his wishes and character.

"The Crusaders lifted the banner of the Cross above your people. By this act they corrupted its true meaning of reconciliation, forgiveness and selfless love. On the anniversary of the first Crusade we also carry the name of Christ. We wish to retrace the footsteps of the Crusaders in apology for their deeds and in demonstration of the true meaning of the cross." Muslims, Jews, and Orthodox Christians have warmly accepted the apologies and embraced those who are coming in the name of the reconciling Christ.

Reinventing Christian Stewardship to Put First Things First

If the Western church has any hopes of making a difference in the lives, families, and communities in tomorrow's world, we need to radically reinvent how we practice stewardship, not only in our lives but in our congregations and Christian organizations as well.

Local churches not only need to teach their members to be whole-life stewards; they are going to have to set new goals to focus more congregational time and money on the church's mission. I urge every congregation to set a goal, as Spreydon Baptist did, regarding the percentage of time and money they want to invest in their church's mission, and conduct an annual audit to evaluate progress.

As a part of giving more emphasis to the church's mission, I urge more creativity in stewarding staff and church building costs. A more relational, less bureaucratic approach to congregational life could mean real savings in staff cost. (I am certain more pastors and Christian leaders will need to become bivocational in the future.) A number of churches could go to a more decentralized approach, as did Ichthus Fellowship, that doesn't require new construction. Instead of building facilities, some churches are sharing facilities with Seventh-Day Adventist churches or auction studios.

Puget Sound Christian Center (fax: 255-474-0189) has constructed a two-story warehouse in Tacoma, Washington. Each floor has 35,000 square feet. The church rents out the first floor to small businesses, which brings in enough to pay the mortgage on the building. The church has created a large worship space and an area for recreation on the second floor.

Church planters need a wake-up call. Most under-age-thirty-five congregations will not have the resources to build the expensive church buildings my generation erected. Howard Snyder has long urged the American church to overcome its "edifice complex."

Christian organizations will need to create less-cost-intensive, virtual organizations that rely less on buildings and paid staff to carry out their mission. We won't be able to afford the top-heavy bureaucratic models very far into the twenty-first century, with the high executive salaries paid by a number of U.S.-based Christian organizations. We will need to experiment with webbed and networked organizations that are building-free and in which growing numbers of us work bivocationally in ministry.

Essential to the advancement of the purposes of God will be the creation of new partnerships to maximize the use of limited resources. Increasingly, the leadership for these partnerships will come from the church in the Two-Thirds World. And Christian organizations will also need to learn to create a broad spectrum of partnerships with governments, corporations, and international organizations such as the United Nations.

A wave of the future will be more people-to-people partnerships. Many churches and Christian organizations could benefit from using services, such as those of Interdev (interdev-uk@xc.org), to help broker relationships with churches in other parts of the world. Interdev also helps Christian mission organizations design collaborative ventures within countries to maximize impact and reduce costs.

Planting a Seed in Pecan

When Simon Pellew started Pecan, a Christian ministry to work with the urban poor in London, he took a different approach to staff compensation. He paid everyone the same modest salary he paid himself. He told me, "I thought it was a good idea when we started, but I think it has turned out to be an even better idea than I anticipated. Because we don't have high administrative salaries, we are able to hire more staff and we work together more collegially."

Planting a Seed in Old Tires

In the future we will all need to become creative Christian scroungers doing more with less. During a creativity workshop in Chicago on urban ministry, I gave participants some creativity assignments. I asked one group to find something that was thrown away in the city and do something for the kingdom. They came back with their idea thirty minutes later. I asked, "What do you have?" They responded, "Vertical gardening. We plan to collect old tire casings that you can find all over in an inner-city community. We will stack the tires nine tires high. We will fill the stack of tires with dirt and plant potato seed in the stack. The potato sprouts will grow out between the tires. When it is harvest time, you simply push over the tires, pick up the potatoes, and sweep up the dirt." We need this level of creativity as we seek to expand the church's mission to meet the growing needs of the third millennium.

Planting a Seed in Giving Away Money

Phil Wall, working with Christians in Britain, created a new model of fund-raising from the parable of the talents. He took all of his family's personal savings and asked others in his church to contribute money as they could afford, to help raise money to support AIDS orphans in Africa. They put on a banquet in which they presented the plight of the orphans. Instead of asking people to give money to the cause, Phil gave every person there ten pounds (fifteen dollars). He said, "You can take this money and spend it on yourself if you want. Or you can take a list of ideas of ways to invest this money and multiply it to assist these children in Africa." He handed out the list of ideas and gave a deadline for a response. He has done this three times and each time has received more than tenfold the original amount given out.

Planting a Seed in Brazil

Some conscientious Christian educators in Brazil have created a new, low-cost approach to theological education that costs students only thirty-eight dollars a month in tuition. The Seminario Teologico Sul Americano makes every effort to keep costs at a minimum by using church buildings throughout the country for classes and finding professors who are willing to donate their time to help raise a new generation of leaders who are free to serve God without the burden of school debt. The educators even offer doctoral studies through this program.

This Isn't Your Mom and Dad's Church Anymore

A new generation of leaders is coming on! You will find these leaders planting alternative churches in Glasgow and London and creating new forms of urban ministries in Seattle and Auckland. For example, Simon Chaplin is a twenty-seven-year-old Baptist pastor to the prostitutes and the gay community in the red-light district of Auckland. He and his family live right in the community in which he ministers. You can spot him late at night chatting with his "parishioners," with his camouflage pants and red dreadlocks.

God's Spirit is raising up a new generation of deeply committed young men and women who will lead the church in the new millennium. I am particularly impressed by their keen desire to see God use their lives to make a difference in the world. And much of the cutting-edge innovation I celebrate in this book is the work of twenty- and thirty-year-olds. Those of us who are older need to pay attention to what God is stirring up through their lives and ministries.

Many churches in Britain are encouraging and mentoring a new generation of leaders. Too often in North America you have to be forty before you are invited to use your leadership gifts. I urge every church to begin mentoring the young into leadership and to take seriously the visions, creative ideas, and gifts God has given them.

This postmodern generation is creating a new expression of the church that is more relational, local, and tribal and looks different from the megachurch model of the nineties. The leaders of this generation emphasize the creative character of a God of beauty. Growing numbers of their churches are writing their own music and bringing original art and drama into their services. We need to be open not only to encouraging a new generation but to learning from their commitment and their creativity.

Planting a Seed in *Rolling Stone* Magazine

One of the most creative ventures in sharing the story to a new generation is the production of a new series by International Bible Society. Initiated by CEO Paul Chandler, who is in his thirties, it is titled "Discovering Ancient Wisdom: Practical Words of Insight and Understanding." The International Bible Society has created edited versions of selected Old Testament books, such as Ecclesiastes and Proverbs, in beautifully designed little booklets. It is finding a responsive market for this "Middle Eastern wisdom literature," as IBS has advertised these booklets in *Rolling Stone* magazine and various New Age publications.

Planting a Seed in Red Square

InterVarsity staff seeking to find new ways to share their faith with a secular student population at the University of Washington created an imaginative new approach. There is a huge brick quad, called Red Square, that students cross on their way to classes. These InterVarsity folks wrote the word *hope* in huge thirty-foot chalk letters on the brick. Then they put pieces of chalk down all around the word. Both students and faculty immediately began stopping and using the chalk to write on the brick. Some wrote of their struggle with cynicism and despair. One young woman wrote of the hope that a new relationship gave her. A few wrote statements regarding their faith. Others composed verse. Over the course of four hours, these young Christians found many opportunities to share both life and faith with their peers.

Planting a Seed in Saint Mary's Ealing

Many of the postmodern young from outside the church find that our churches aren't just middle class but middle aged, and they don't connect with their generation. Johnny and Jenny Baker were given the opportunity to plant a new postmodern church in an existing church at Saint Mary's Anglican Church in London. They have created an alternative Celtic Christian Sunday evening service in which they are incorporating their own art, music, and liturgy. This alternative church has drawn large numbers of young people who never would have shown up for a traditional Anglican service. But the leaders of this new church are also finding ways to bring both generations together in common cause.

Planting a Seed on the Road to Canterbury

Matthew 28:20 reminds us that the Great Commission is a call to make disciples by "teaching them to observe everything I have commanded you." Teaching them to observe everything had to do with not just the spiritual compartment of life but all of life. It is a call to whole-life discipleship. But I am persuaded that we need to rethink not only why we do what we do but how we do it. So many of the ways I have seen Western churches practicing discipleship education seem to reflect the modernity lecture model more than the rabbinical one. David Pott invited thirteen students from different countries to come to London for a discipleship training seminar. Always in the past these sessions had taken place in a classroom. But this time David decided to try something different. He had the thirteen students journey together from London to Canterbury, a seventy-mile walk over the course of a week. They journeyed as though they were journeying with Jesus. They read and discussed the teachings of Jesus as they walked together. They gave one another foot rubs and back rubs as they went. In the evenings they would read *Pilgrim's Progress,* about the Slough of Despond and all the other barriers that faced the pilgrim on his way. When they began their journey, they didn't get on very well together. But as they learned to journey with Jesus, they found that it improved how they related to each other. When they arrived in Canterbury, they imagined that they had arrived home to the kingdom of God, and concluded the week with a rousing celebration. I find that a post-modern generation is more drawn to this kind of relational, rabbinical model than to being lectured in a box. God is raising up a new generation to lead the church into a new millennium, and we need to be open to creative new models of education, worship, and missions.

Welcome to the Wedding Feast of God!

Let's return to where we began this final chapter—Jalapa, Mexico. You have just entered the community center that God enabled Saul and Pilar and their church to build on that garbage heap.

Picture the community center transformed, flooded with white balloons, colorful streamers, and ribbons hanging from the ceiling. At the front of the room is an enormous six-tier wedding cake. The buffet table is filled with a festive display of dishes provided by the families of the twenty-eight couples who are being married. The center is packed with hundreds of family and friends, some of whom are standing on tiptoe to see the couples. There are parents, grandparents, and grandchildren all getting married at the same time, not a few with tears in their eyes.

The Armonia community is conducting this mass wedding for poor couples who have never been able to afford the high costs of legal paperwork, medical tests plus the costs of a Mexican wedding. As the final prayer is pronounced and the husbands kiss their brides, an enormous cheer goes up from those assembled, a Mexican band starts playing with tremendous energy, and the celebrating begins in earnest.

Scripture reminds us that the centerpiece of the great homecoming of God is going to be a huge wedding feast. Listen to Jesus making some last-minute changes in the list of invited guests: "The wedding is ready, but those who were invited were not worthy. Go therefore to the main highways, and as many as you find there, invite to the wedding feast" (Matt. 22:8–9 NASB). We dare not be among those who miss out. Like Jesus and those first followers, we need to commit our lives not only to God but also to the purposes of God: "sight to the blind, release to the captives, and good news to the poor."

We are entering a new millennium that will be changing at blinding speed. For the church to faithfully carry out its mission in this world, we will need leaders who lead with foresight, vision, and imagination. We will need leaders who learn to lead with foresight, paying attention to how both the world and the church are changing. We will need leaders who lead with vision, who enable us to find in Scripture an alternative dream to the future envisioned by the architects of McWorld. And we will need leaders who enable us to use our imagination to create new ways to advance God's purposes in response to the challenges of tomorrow's world.

As we have seen, globalization will present us with an array of new opportunities and challenges. I am convinced that if we don't seriously and prayerfully reorder our use of resources in our lives and churches, we won't be able to begin to respond to the new opportunities that God is giving us. We will need to radically reinvent our lives, churches, and mission programs if we have any intention of engaging the challenges of a new millennium.

We also need to pay more attention to the way modern culture pressures us to cave in to the seductions, idolatries, and addictions of McWorld. I am convinced that these pressures are largely responsible for the steady erosion of our investment of time and money in the work of God's kingdom.

At the center of our lives, God calls us to a dream that is different from the American dream. It is the dream of a God who invites us home to a world made new. It is an opportunity to flesh out, in community with others and, by God's grace and the power of the Holy Spirit, something of the hope and celebration of God's great homecoming. And it is an invitation to join sisters and brothers all over the world in allowing God to use our mustard seeds to see his kingdom come, in part, now in anticipation of Christ's return, when the wedding feast will break out in its fullness.

I don't think we have any idea of how God can use our mustard seeds to make a difference in a new millennium if we are willing to take the risk of reinventing our lives and congregations to put God's purposes first. Welcome home to the wedding feast future of God! Welcome home to life with a difference!

Opportunities for Christian Leaders

Christian leaders have the opportunity

1. to make a major effort to reach, church, and mentor a new generation in Western countries and challenge its members to a whole-life, biblical discipleship in which they place the purposes of the mustard seed before the aspirations of McWorld.

2. to challenge all churches to move God's mission to the center of congregational life, setting goals regarding how much time and money they plan to invest in this mission each year (at home and abroad), and to conduct an annual audit to evaluate performance.

3. to enable all churches and Christian organizations to do the hard work of writing down their implicit assumptions about why they do what they do and then to study Scripture and write down a set

of biblically based assumptions to provide a springboard to focus their mission to create new possibilities in Christian missions.

4. to create new ministries that work for the shalom transformation not just of individuals but of whole communities, to reflect something of God's purposes.

5. to reinvent how we steward resources in our Christian organizations, to do more with less.

6. to pay attention to the leadership that is being provided by a new generation and to find ways to collaborate with these new leaders.

7. to create new forms of partnership to maximize impact while reducing costs.

8. to create new celebrations of the in-breaking of God's kingdom as we work with those at the margins to advance the shalom purposes of God.

Questions for Discussion and Action

1. How much of the time and resources of your congregation are presently being invested in ministry in your community or abroad?

2. What are some emerging areas of need in your community, such as child care for moms coming off welfare, activities for at-risk kids, companionship for neglected seniors, that your church could respond to?

3. What are some ways in which you could mentor young people in your church into leadership roles?

4. What are some ways in which your church could partner with churches in communities overseas and at home not only to meet individual needs but to see entire neighborhoods experience the shalom transformation of God?

An Invitation to Share Your Mustard Seeds: We invite you to share mustard seeds of what God is doing in your life, church, and community, or concerns you have regarding the future. We plan to set up a chat room in which Christians all over the world can share creative ways they are finding to put God's purposes first in response to tomorrow's challenges. To join this conversation, all you have to do is go to www.bakerbooks.com, then go to *Mustard Seed vs. McWorld* and click on. I will be looking forward to learning what God is doing in your life, church, and ministry to respond to the new challenges of a new millennium. Should you want to contact us directly at Mustard Seed Associates, please e-mail: tomandchrissine@compuserve.com.

Notes

Introduction

1. Neil Howe and Bill Strauss, *Thirteenth Gen: Abort, Retry, Ignore, Fail?* (New York: Vintage Books, 1993), 105.

2. Jerry Mander and Edward Goldsmith, eds., *The Case against the Global Economy: And for a Turn toward the Local* (San Francisco: Sierra Club Books, 1996), 3.

3. "Excerpts from John Paul's Message about the Poor and the Rich," *New York Times,* 24 January 1999, A6.

4. Peter Menzal, *Material World: A Global Family Portrait* (San Francisco: Sierra Club Books, 1994), 132–38.

5. Benjamin R. Barber, *Jihad vs. McWorld* (New York: Times Books, 1995).

6. Tom Sine, *The Mustard Seed Conspiracy* (Waco: Word, 1981), 11–12.

Chapter 1: *A Ride on the Wet Side*

1. William Shakespeare, *Julius Caesar,* act 3, scene 3, in *The Complete Works of William Shakespeare,* the Cambridge Text established by John Dover Wilson for the Cambridge Univ. Press (London: Octopus Books, 1980), 853.

2. Wayne Burkan, "Developing Your Wide-Angle Vision," *Futurist* (March 1998): 35.

3. Tom Sine, *Wild Hope* (Waco: Word, 1991), 1–2.

4. William A. Sherden, *The Fortune Sellers: The Big Business of Selling and Buying Predictions* (New York: John Wiley and Sons, 1998), 219–22.

5. Richard Kew and Roger White, *Toward 2015: A Church Odyssey* (Cambridge: Cowley Publications, 1997), 38.

6. Sherden, *The Fortune Sellers,* 14, emphasis in original.

7. "Human Relational Concepts for the Emergence of Africa As a Global Power in 2050" (report of workshop held at Beeson Divinity School, February 5–7, 1997), 6.

8. Frank Herbert, "A Future 2000: The Best of All Worlds" (report for the New Business Division of the Weyerhaeuser Corporation, 1974), 2.

9. Peter Schwartz, *The Art of the Long View: Planning for the Future in an Uncertain World* (New York: Doubleday, 1991), 53–54.

10. Ibid.

11. Suzy Parker, "Age of Profits: Gen-X Goal: Be Your Own Boss," *Christian Science Monitor* (March 2, 1998): 1, 4.

12. Mary Lord, "Preparing Managers for the Twenty-first Century," *U.S. News and World Report* (March 2, 1998): 72.

13. Ibid.

Chapter 2: *McWorld: A Race to the Top*

1. Paul MacGeough, "Depths of Despair," *Sydney Morning Herald,* 31 January 1998, 35.

2. Ibid.

3. Kenichi Ohmae, "The Rise of the Region State," *Foreign Affairs* (spring 1993): 77–80. Ohmae's book *The Borderless World* is published by Collins (New York, 1990).

4. William Greider, *One World, Ready or Not: The Manic Logic of Global Capitalism* (New York: Simon and Schuster, 1997), 12.

5. Benjamin R. Barber, *Jihad vs. McWorld* (New York: Times Books, 1995), 17.

6. James L. Tyson, "Behind Those Boxes, a Boom," *Christian Science Monitor Work and Money* (May 26, 1998): 11.

7. Peter D. Sutherland and John W. Sewell, "Gather the Nations to Promote Globalization," *New York Times,* 8 February 1998, 1.

8. Peter Schwartz and Peter Leyden, "The Long Boom," *Wired* (July 1997): 116.

9. Glenn Pascall, "Starving for Time," *Seattle Times,* 5 July 1998, B5.

10. George Soros, "The Crisis of Global Capitalism," *Newsweek* (7 December 1998): 78.

11. "The World's Forgotten Danger," *Economist* (November 14, 1998): 17–18.

12. Michael J. Mandel, "The New Economy: For Better or Worse," *Business Week* (October 19, 1998): 42.

13. John Heilemann, "The Netizen: The Integrationists vs. the Separatists," *Wired* (July 1997): 186.

14. Jeff Gerth and Richard W. Stevenson, "Poor Oversight Said to Imperil World Banking," *New York Times,* 22 December 1997, 1.

15. Charles Handy, "The Invisible Fist," *Economist* (February 15, 1997): 3–4.

16. Vicki Goldberg, "Images of an Economy Devouring the Poor," *New York Times,* 22 March 1998, 44.

17. Jeremy Brecher, "Globalization: The Race to the Bottom" (paper presented at the Community Church, Boston, Mass., April 9, 1995), 3.

18. Eyal Press, "The Free Trade Faith: Can We Trust the Economists?" *Lingua Franca: The Review of Academic Life* (December–January 1998): 30–38.

19. James Goldsmith, "The Winners and the Losers," in *The Case against the Global Economy: And for a Turn toward the Local,* Jerry Mander and Edward Goldsmith (San Francisco: Sierra Club Books, 1996), 178.

20. José Aguayo, "St. Benedict and the Labor Unions," *Forbes* (February 9, 1998): 64.

21. Wendell Berry, *What Are People For?* (San Francisco: North Point Press, 1990), 131.

22. "McWorld," *Economist* (June 29, 1996): 61–62.

23. Barnaby J. Feder, "Cultivating Conagra," *New York Times,* 30 October 1997, C1, C12.

24. Michael Pollan, "Playing God in the Garden," *New York Times Magazine* (October 25, 1998): 44–51.

25. Tom Sine, *The Mustard Seed Conspiracy* (Waco: Word, 1981), 60.

26. Marilyn Berlin Snell, "Bioprospecting or Biopiracy?" *Utne Reader* (March–April 1996): 83, and Andrew Kimbrell, "High-Tech Piracy" *Utne Reader* (March–April 1996): 84–86.

27. "U.S. Food-Safety System Swamped by Booming Global Imports," *New York Times,* 29 September 1997, A1, A8.

28. "The World Health Report 1996: Fighting Disease, Fostering Development" (report of the director-general of the World Health Organization, Geneva, 1996), 20.

29. Harriet Webster, "Stop, Shop and Share," *Parade* (September 15, 1996): 21.

30. Ibid.

31. Stuart L. Hart, "Strategies for a Sustainable World," *Harvard Business Review* (January–February 1997): 68–69.

32. Ibid., 75–76.

33. William McDonough and Michael Braungart, "The Next Industrial Revolution," *Atlantic Monthly* (October 1998): 82–89.

34. Robert H. Nelson, *Reaching for Heaven on Earth: The Theological Meaning of Economics* (Savage, Md.: Rowan and Littlefield, 1991), 2.

35. Lester Thurow, *The Future of Capitalism: How Today's Economic Forces Shape Tomorrow's World* (New York: William Morrow, 1996), 17.

36. Jane Collier, "Contemporary Cultures and the Role of Economics," in *The Gospel and Contemporary Culture,* ed. Hugh Montefiore (London: Mowbary, 1992), 103.

Chapter 3: *A Trek into a Cyber-Future*

1. James O. Jackson, "It's a Wired, Wired World," *Time* special issue (spring 1995): 80.

2. Kristin Spence, "Geo-Cities: Homesteading on the Electronic Frontier," *Wired* (March 1997): 175.

3. Nicholas Negroponte, "The Third Shall Be First," *Wired* (January 1998): 96.

4. Ibid.

5. Youssef Ibrahim, "Finland: An Unlikely Home Base for Universal Use of Technology," *New York Times,* 20 January 1997, 1.

6. Thomas A. Bass, "Dress Code," *Wired* (April 1998): 163–87.

7. Jill Smolowe, "Intimate Strangers," *Time* special issue (spring 1995): 21.

8. Glenn F. Cartwright, "Virtual or Real?" *Futurist* (March–April 1994): 22–26.

9. Douglas Groothius, *The Soul in Cyber-Space* (Grand Rapids: Baker, 1997).

10. Tim Golden, "Sixteen Indicted on Charges of Internet Pornography," *New York Times,* 17 July 1996, A8.

11. Neil Postman, *Technopoly: The Surrender of Culture to Technology* (New York: Vintage Books, 1993), 83, 165.

12. See www.nobel.se.

13. "Devolution Can Be Salvation," *Economist* (September 20, 1997): 53.

14. Benjamin R. Barber, *Jihad vs. McWorld* (New York: Times Books, 1995), 3.

15. Robert Marquand, "Hate Groups Market to the Mainstream," *Christian Science Monitor* (March 6, 1998): 4.

16. Kevin Sack, "Hate Groups in U.S. Are Growing, Report Says," *New York Times,* 5 March 1998, A10.

17. Barber, *Jihad vs. McWorld,* 6–7.

18. Ibid., 7.

19. William Greider, *One World, Ready or Not: The Manic Logic of Capitalism* (New York: Simon and Schuster, 1997), 337–45.

20. Roger C. Altman, "The Force Is with Us: Global Markets Wield Awesome Power," *Seattle Post Intelligencer,* 8 March 1998, E1.

21. Ralph Nader and Lori Wallach, "GATT, NAFTA, and the Subversion of the Democratic Process," in Jerry Mander and Edward Goldsmith, *The Case against the Global Economy: And for a Turn toward the Local* (San Francisco: Sierra Club Books, 1996), 93–94.

22. John Cavanagh, "Global Economic Apartheid" (presentation at Takoma Park, Maryland, September 19, 1996), 1.

23. G. William Domhoff, *Who Rules America Now? A View for the Eighties* (New York: Vintage Books, 1987), 33.

24. Charles Lewis, "The Funding of the Presidency" (paper presented at the National Press Club's "Newsmaker Luncheon," April 23, 1996), 3.

25. Ibid., 1–4.

26. Alle Lasn, "Communications Cartel," *Adbusters* (winter 1999), 20–21.

27. Robert D. Kaplan, "Was Democracy Just a Moment?" *Atlantic Monthly* (December 1997): 76.

28. Steven E. Miller, *Civilizing Cyberspace: Policy Power and the Information Superhighway* (New York: Addison-Wesley, 1995), 384.

29. Edward Bellamy, *Looking Backward* (New York: Penguin, 1982).

30. Horatio Alger, *Ragged Dick and Mark the Matchboy* (New York: Colliers, 1962).

31. Michael Novak, *The Spirit of Democratic Capitalism* (New York: Simon and Schuster, 1982), 112.

32. Rob van Drimmelen, "The Oxford Declaration As a Contribution to the Ecumenical Debate," in Herbert Schlossberg, Vinay Samuel, and Ron J. Sider, *Christianity and Economics in the Post–Cold War Era* (Grand Rapids: Eerdmans, 1994), 140.

33. Mitchell Cohen, "No More Systems: A Leading Sociologist Thinks the New Capitalism Has Some of the Dangers of the Old Marxism," *New York Times* book review, 21.

Chapter 4: *A Race to the Bottom for the Western Middle*

1. United Nations, United Nations Development Program, *The Human Development Report,* 1988, 1.

2. Christine Dugas, "1998 Pace Could Reach Thirty-Five-Year High," *USA Today,* 30 June 1998, 1.

3. Jeremy Rifkin, *The End of Work: The Decline of the Global Labor Force and the Dawn of the Post-Market Era* (New York: G. P. Putnam, 1995), 20–21.

4. Stuart Ewen, "Waste a Lot, Want a Lot: Our All Consuming Quest for Style," *Utne Reader* (September–October 1989), 81.

5. "The Goods Life: How Much Stuff Is Enough? *Sierra* (July–August 1997): 20.

6. Brian Swimme, "How Do Our Kids Get So Caught Up in Consumerism?" *Enough* 1, no. 2 (fall 1997): 1–5.

7. Daniel B. Wood, "Shop Trek: The Next Generation," *Christian Science Monitor* (December 24, 1997): 3.

8. Ibid.

9. Julie Pitta, "Competitive Shopping," *Forbes* (February 9, 1998): 92.

10. Andy Dappen, "When Less Means More," *Hemispheres* (November 1997): 155.

11. Bob Santamaria, "The Global Economy—At War with the Family," *Humanity* (July 1998): 6.

12. Maria Fiorni Ramirez, "Americans at Debt's Door," *New York Times,* 14 October 1997, A19.

13. Saul Hansell, "We Like You. We Care about You. Now Pay Up," *New York Times,* 26 January 1997, F2.

14. Damon Darlin, "The Newest American Entitlement," *Forbes* (September 8, 1997): 113.

15. Ibid.

16. Tamar Lewin, "Men Assuming Bigger Share at Home, New Survey Shows," *New York Times,* 15 April 1998, A16.

17. "Better Off, but Not Much," *Economist* (October 4, 1997): 35.

18. Shelley Donald Coolidge, "Less Leisure: Work and Spend Cycle Makes Company Slaves," *Christian Science Monitor* (April 4, 1995): 9. Juliet Schor's book *The Overworked American* is published by Basic Books (New York, 1992).

19. "Here Comes the Four-Income Family," *Money* (February 1995): 1.

20. "American Economy: Backlash against McJobs," *Economist* (October 19, 1996): 10.

21. The Harris Poll no. 31, table 2, "Work Hours per Week" (July 7, 1997), 3.

22. Coolidge, "Less Leisure," 9.

23. "Affluenza, Warning: Materialism May Be Hazardous to Your Health," *Utne Reader* (September–October 1997): 19.

24. Richard C. Moraise with Katherine Bruce, "What I Wanna, Wanna, Really Wanna Be," *Forbes* (September 22, 1997): 186–90.

25. "Branding," *Adbusters* (spring 1997): 39.

26. Brad Edmondson, "The Next Baby Boom," *American Demographics* (September 1995), 20.

27. Nicole Rosenthal, "The Boom Tube," *Media Week* (May 18, 1998): 44.

28. "5.5 Million Americans Rated Problem Gamblers," *Chicago Tribune,* 19 March 1999, P20.

29. "A Long Way from Flower Power," *Economist* (January 17, 1998): 26.

30. Lawrence Mishel, Jared Bernstein, and John Schmidt, *The State of Working America 1996–1997* (New York: M. E. Sharpe, 1997), 47.

31. Katharine Q. Seelye, "Future U.S.: Grayer and More Hispanic," *New York Times,* 27 March 1997, A18.

32. Rosenthal, "The Boom Tube," 44.

33. Peter Brierley, *Future Church: A Global Analysis of the Christian Community to the Year 2010* (London: Monarch, 1998), 33.

34. Gail Griffith, "10,000 Maniacs Found in Southeast Asia," *Christian Science Monitor* (April 8, 1994): 23.

35. Sarah Lyall, "For British Health System, Bleak Prognosis," *New York Times,* 30 January 1997, A6.

36. Martha Phillips, letter to the editor, *New Republic* (June 22, 1998): 40–41.

37. Nicholas Wade, "Cell Unlocked: Longevity's New Lease on Life," *New York Times,* 18 January 1998, WK1.

38. Ann Scott Tyson, "Christmas without Shopping," *Christian Science Monitor* (December 11, 1997): 1, 9.

39. John Bartley, "Interest Free Equals Set Free! Economics and the Kingdom," *New Zealand Baptist* (December 1997): 6.

40. John Paarlberg, "Questioning Capitalism," *City Gate* (September 1997): 1.

41. Robert Marquand, "Protestant Ranks Become More Secular," *Christian Science Monitor* (December 19, 1995): 4.

42. Robert Wuthnow, *God and Mammon in America* (New York: Macmillan, 1994), 150–51.

Chapter 5: *A Race to the Bottom for the Global Poor*

1. "Rich Pickings," *Economist* (June 6, 1998): 30.

2. Michelle Conlin, "When Billionaires Become a Dime a Dozen," *Forbes* (October 13, 1997): 148.

3. Glenn Pascall, "Starving for Time," *Seattle Times,* 5 July 1998, B5.

4. Barbara Crossette, "U.N. Survey Finds World Rich-Poor Gap Widening," *New York Times,* 15 July 1996, A3.

5. "Disparities in Global Integration," *Finance and Development* (September 1996), 32.

6. "A Global Poverty Trap," *Economist* (July 2, 1996): 34.

7. "World Population Growth," *Global Child Health News and Review* no. 1 (1995): 19.

8. Nan Cobbey, "The Lambeth Conference Speaks Out on Third World Debt," *Episcopal Life* (September 18, 1998), 5–6.

9. "United States Falls to Fourth in Global Giving," *Bread for the World Newsletter* (August–September 1996): 9.

10. Ibid.

11. Michael Fairbanks, *Plowing the Sea* (Boston: Harvard Business School Press, 1997).

12. Jane Sutton, "In Peru: The Means to Serve," *World Vision* (December 1997–January 1998): 15.

13. For more information see: http://reports.guardian.co.uk/debt/.

14. Elia Kacapyr, "How Hard Are Hard Times?" *American Demographics* (February 1998): 30.

15. Ron Scherer, "Whose Boat the Economy Isn't Floating: Black Teens and the Unskilled Are Among Those Still Jobless Despite Buoyant Labor Market," *Christian Science Monitor* (August 1, 1997): 1, 5.

16. Michel Marriot, "Frank Racial Dialogue Thrives on the Web," *New York Times*, 8 March 1998, 1, 22.

17. Stephen Holmes, "Income Disparity between the Poorest and the Richest Rises," *New York Times,* 20 June 1996, 1.

18. Linda Feldmann, "More Children of Working Parents Now Live in Poverty," *Christian Science Monitor* (June 4, 1996): 3.

19. William O'Hare and Joseph Schwartz, "One Step Forward, Two Steps Back," *American Demographics* (September 1997): 53.

20. Jonathan Kozol, *Savage Inequalities* (New York: Crown Publishing, 1991).

21. "Who Remains Left Out of the Economy of the 'Roaring '90s.'" *Christian Science Monitor* (August 1, 1997): 5.

22. "Stakeholder Capitalism: Unhappy Families," *Economist* (February 10, 1996), 8.

23. Raymond Hernandez, "Most Dropped from Welfare Don't Get Jobs," *New York Times,* 23 March 1998, 1, A16.

24. Milt Freudenheim, "Charities Say Government Cutbacks Would Jeopardize Their Ability to Help the Poor," *New York Times,* 5 February 1996, 1.

25. "Putting the Poor on the Map," *Sojourners* (September–October 1998): 56.

Chapter 6: *A Race to the Bottom for the Incredible Shrinking Western Church*

1. Philip Adams, "Faith Healers," *Weekend Review* (April 12–13, 1997): 1–2.

2. Richard N. Ostling, "Kingdoms to Come," *Time* (fall special edition 1992): 61.

3. "Bonfire of the Futilities: Nevada's Burning Man Festival: Ritual without Dogma," *Regeneration Quarterly* (fall 1997): 14–17.

4. Robert Marquand, "Religious Reading Digs Deeper," *Christian Science Monitor* (August 27, 1997): 1.

5. Daniel B. Wood, "New Treatment Showing Up in Hospitals: Prayer," *Christian Science Monitor* (March 8, 1987): 4.

6. "Church and People Worldwide," *CRA: Quadrant* (March 1977): 1.

7. J. Dudley Woodberry, "Toward the Twenty-first Century: Educating People for God's Mission" (paper presented at the Congress on the World Mission of the Church, St. Paul, Minnesota, June 23–27, 1998), 15.

8. Patrick Johnstone, *The Church Is Bigger Than You Think: Structures and Strategies for the Church in the Twenty-first Century* (London: Christian Focus, 1998), 231.

9. "The Power of Partnership" (Seattle: Interdev, 1998), 21.

10. Mark Hutchison, "It's a Small Church After All," *Christianity Today* (November 16, 1998): 48.

11. Rick Hampson, "Missionaries Set Sights on American Souls," *USA Today,* 19 November 1997, 17A.

12. Ian T. Douglas, "The Church and the World in a New Century" (paper presented at Princeton Seminary during a World Vision Conference, "The Church and the World in a New Century," 28–30 October 1999).

13. Table 2.12.1, "Adult Church Attendance in England 1980–2000," Christian Research Association, London, England.

14. Table 14, "English Church Attendance by Age Group 1989," Christian Research Association, London, England.

15. Peter Kaldor, *Winds of Change: The Experience of Church in a Changing Australia* (Homebush West, New South Wales: National Church Life Survey, 1994), 263.

16. Ibid., 280–81.

17. Peter Bentley and Philip Hughes, *Religion in Australia: Facts and Figures* (Kern, Victoria: Christian Research Association, 1997), 52.

18. Bruce Patrick, ed., *New Vision New Zealand: Calling the Whole Church to Take the Whole Gospel to the Whole Nation* (Auckland: Vision New Zealand, 1993), 20.

19. Peter Lineham, "The Condition of the Church," in *New Vision New Zealand,* Patrick, 108.

20. Lynne Taylor, "Denominational Growth," in *New Vision New Zealand II,* ed. Bruce Patrick (Auckland: Vision New Zealand, 1997), 48–53.

21. Lineham, "The Condition of the Church," in *New Vision New Zealand,* Patrick, 107.

22. Bruce Patrick, "Multiplication the Key to Growth," in *New Vision New Zealand,* Patrick, 250.

23. Reginald W. Bibby, *Unknown Gods: The Ongoing Story of Religion in Canada* (Toronto: Stoddart, 1993), 10.

24. Reginald W. Bibby, *There's Got to Be More! Connecting Churches and Canadians* (Infield, B.C.: Wood Lake, 1995), 78.

25. Bibby, *Unknown Gods,* 8.

26. Ibid., 10, 99.

27. Bibby, *There's Got to Be More!* 51–151.

28. John and Sylvia Ronsvalle, "The End of Benevolence? Alarming Trends in Church Giving," *Christian Century* (October 23, 1996): 1012.

29. "Trends Affecting the Evangelical Lutheran Church in America," ELCA Department of Research and Evaluation (December 27, 1966), 1.

30. Wade Clark Roof and William McKinney, *American Mainline Religion: Its Changing Shape and Future* (New Brunswick, N. J.: Rutgers Univ. Press, 1987), 233.

31. Gustav Niebuhr, "Makeup of American Religion Is Looking More Like Mosaic, Data Say," *New York Times,* 12 April 1998, 12.

32. Ronsvalle, "The End of Benevolence?" 1016.

33. "Church Attendance by Generation," Barna Research Group Limited (July 8, 1998).

34. Robert Marquand, "Preaching to Empty Pews," *Chicago Sun Times,* 22 February 1998, 45.

35. Mark Noll and Lyman Kellstedt, "The Changing Face of Evangelicalism," *Pro Ecclesia* 4, no. 2 (spring 1995): 146–64.

36. Lyman Kellstedt, "Simple Questions, Complex Answers: What Do We Mean by 'Evangelical'? What Difference Does It Make?" *Evangelical Studies Bulletin* 12, no. 2 (fall 1995): 2–3.

37. "Godlessness 101," *New York Times Magazine* (December 7, 1997): 61.

38. "Church Attendance by Generation," Barna Research Group Limited (July 8, 1998).

39. Lawrence Mishel, Jared Bernstein, John Schmitt, *The State of Working America 1996–1997* (New York: M. E. Sharpe, 1997), 47.

40. Dean R. Hoge, Charles E. Zech, Patrick H. McNamara, and Michael J. Donahue, *Money Matters: Personal Giving in American Churches* (Louisville: John Knox Press, 1996), 5.

41. "Minuses: A Culture Where . . . ," *Sweet's Soul Cafe* 3, nos. 3–4 (1997): 9.

42. Hoge, *Money Matters,* 17.

43. Karen W. Arenson, "Donations to Charities Rose 11 Percent Last Year, Report Says," *New York Times,* 15 May 1996, A9.

44. John L. Ronsvalle and Sylvia Ronsvalle, *The State of Church Giving through 1995* (Champaign, Ill.: Empty Tomb, 1997), 11–12.

45. Ibid., 15.

46. Ibid., 25–27.

47. Ibid., 42–45.

Part 2 Introduction

1. J. Richard Middleton and Brian J. Walsh, *Truth Is Stranger Than It Used to Be: Biblical Faith in a Postmodern Age* (Downers Grove, Ill.: InterVarsity Press, 1995), 15.

2. Brian J. Walsh, "Homemaking in Exile: Homelessness, Postmodernity and Theological Reflection," in *Reminding: Renewing the Mind in Learning,* eds. Doug Blomberg and Ian Lambert (Sydney: Centre for the Study of Australian Christianity, 1998), 1–2.

3. Ibid., 2–3.

4. Middleton and Walsh, *Truth Is Stranger Than It Used to Be,* 145.

5. Charles E. Silberman, "High Schools That Work: Murder in the Classroom, Part III," *Atlantic Monthly* (August 1970): 226.

6. Mark Noll, *The Scandal of the Evangelical Mind* (Grand Rapids: Eerdmans, 1994), 12.

7. Os Guinness, *Fit Bodies Fat Minds: Why Evangelicals Don't Think and What to Do about It* (Grand Rapids: Baker, 1994), 14.

Chapter 7: *How Did We Get off the Tracks?*

1. Walter Brueggemann, *Hopeful Imagination: Prophetic Voices in Exile* (Philadelphia: Fortress Press, 1986), 126.

2. Ibid., 111.

3. Hendrik Berkhof, *Christ and the Powers* (Scottdale, Pa.: Herald Press, 1977), 30.

4. Lesslie Newbigin, *The Gospel in a Pluralist Society* (Grand Rapids: Eerdmans, 1989), 204.

5. Walter Wink, *Engaging the Powers: Discernment and Resistance in a World of Domination* (Minneapolis: Fortress Press, 1992), 33–104.

6. Os Guinness, *Dining with the Devil: The Megachurch Movement Flirts with Modernity* (Grand Rapids: Baker, 1993), 16.

7. Dave Tomlinson, *The Post Evangelical* (London: Triangle, 1995).

8. David F. Wells, *Losing Our Virtue: Why the Church Must Recover Its Moral Vision* (Leister, U. K.: Inter-Varsity Press, 1988), 12.

9. Rodney Clapp, *A Peculiar People: The Church As a Culture in a Post-Christian Society* (Downers Grove, Ill.: InterVarsity Press, 1996), 164–71.

10. Ibid., 164.

11. Lesslie Newbigin, "Cross Currents in Ecumenical and Evangelical Mission," *International Bulletin of Missionary Research* (October 1982): 149.

12. Tom Sine, *Cease Fire: Searching for Sanity in America's Culture War* (Grand Rapids: Eerdmans, 1995), 58–59.

13. Craig M. Gay, *The Way of the (Modern) World: Or Why It's Tempting to Live As If God Doesn't Exist* (Grand Rapids: Eerdmans, 1998).

14. Leo Tolstoy, "How Much Land Does a Man Need?" in *Introduction to Literature,* ed. Louis Locke (New York: Rinehart, 1957), 24–30.

15. David Myers, "Money and Misery," in *The Consuming Passion: Christianity, the Consumer and Culture,* ed. Rodney Clapp (Downers Grove, Ill.: InterVarsity Press, 1998), 58–59.

16. Robert Cole, "Our Self-Centered Children—Heirs of the 'Me' Decade," *U.S. News and World Report* (February 15, 1981): 80.

17. Wayne L. Boggs, *All Ye Who Labor* (Richmond: John Knox Press, 1962), 13.

18. Leland Ryken, *Redeeming the Time: A Christian Approach to Work and Leisure* (Grand Rapids: Baker, 1995), 197.

19. Clapp, *A Peculiar People,* 25–32.

20. Abraham McLaughlin, "Churches' Many New Services," *Christian Science Monitor* (September 30, 1998): 1, 5.

21. Phillip D. Kenneson and James L. Street, *Selling Out the Church: The Dangers of Church Marketing* (Nashville: Abingdon Press, 1997), 12.

22. Clapp, *A Peculiar People,* 21.

23. Francis Fukuyama, *The End of History and the Last Man* (London: Hamish Hammond, 1992), 3–18.

Chapter 8: *How Can We Find Our Way Home?*

1. Elias Chacour and David Hazard, *Blood Brothers* (Grand Rapids: Chosen, 1984), 11–12.

2. John Alexander, "Why We Must Ignore Jesus," *The Other Side* (October 1977): 8.

3. Howard Snyder, *The Radical Wesley and Patterns for Church Renewal* (Downers Grove, Ill.: InterVarsity Press, 1980).

4. Tom Sine, *The Mustard Seed Conspiracy* (Waco: Word, 1981), 11–12.

5. Walter Brueggemann, *The Prophetic Imagination* (Philadelphia: Fortress Press, 1978), 67.

6. Ibid., 45, 97.

7. J. Richard Middleton and Brian J. Walsh, *Truth Is Stranger Than It Used to Be: Biblical Faith in a Postmodern Age* (Downers Grove, Ill.: InterVarsity Press, 1995), 161.

8. N. T. Wright, *Jesus and the Victory of God* (Minneapolis: Fortress Press, 1996), 181.

9. Bernard Brandon Scott, *Hear Then the Parable: A Commentary on the Parables of Jesus* (Minneapolis: Fortress Press, 1989), 384–85.

10. Darrell Bock, *Luke, Volume 2: 9:51–24:53* (Grand Rapids: Baker, 1996), 1226.

11. J. Alec Motyer, *The Prophecy of Isaiah: An Introduction and Commentary*

(Downers Grove, Ill.: InterVarsity Press, 1993), 529.

12. Ibid., 530.

13. Ibid., 273.

14. Walter Brueggemann, *Living towards a Vision: Biblical Reflections on Shalom* (New York: United Church Press, 1984), 22.

15. Jurgen Moltmann, "Toward the Waiting God," in *The Future of Hope: Theology As Eschatology*, ed. Frederick Herzog (New York: Herder and Herder, 1970), 31–50.

16. Fred B. Craddock, *Luke: Interpretation, A Bible Commentary for Teaching and Preaching* (Louisville: John Knox Press, 1990), 63.

17. Frederick Buechner, *The Longing for Home* (San Francisco: Harper San Francisco, 1996).

Part 3 Introduction

1. Tom Sine, *Live It Up! How to Create a Life You Can Love* (Scottdale, Pa.: Herald Press, 1993), 185.

2. Emil Brunner, *Christianity and Civilization* (New York: Charles Scribner's Sons, 1948), 157.

3. Harvey Cox, *Feast of Fools: A Theological Essay on Festivity and Fantasy* (Cambridge: Harvard Univ. Press, 1969), 9–10.

Chapter 9: Reinventing Christian Life and Community for a New Millennium

1. Dietrich Bonhoeffer, *The Cost of Discipleship* (New York: Macmillan, 1959), 89.

2. Athol Gill, *The Fringes of Freedom: Following Jesus, Living Together, Working for Justice* (Homebush, Australia: Lancer, 1990), 30.

3. Joe Dominguez and Vicki Robin, *Your Money or Your Life: Transforming Your Relationship with Money and Achieving Financial Independence* (New York: Penguin, 1992).

4. Bob Buford, *Half Time: Changing Your Game Plan from Success to Significance* (Grand Rapids: Zondervan, 1994), 164.

5. Richard Foster, *Streams of Living Water: Celebrating the Great Traditions of Christian Faith* (San Francisco: Harper, 1998).

6. Donald E. Miller, *Reinventing American Protestantism: Christianity in the New Millennium* (Berkeley: Univ. of California Press, 1997), 3.

7. Sally Morgenthaler, "Out of the Box: Authentic Worship in a Postmodern Culture," *Worship Leader* (May–June 1998): 25.

8. Avery Dulles, *Models of the Church* (New York: Doubleday Books, 1991).

9. Stanley Hauerwas and William H. Willimon, *Resident Aliens: Life in the Christian Colony* (Nashville: Abingdon Press, 1990), 12.

10. George Hunsberger, "Missional Vocation: Called and Sent to Represent the Reign of God," in *Missional Church: A Vision for the Sending of the Church in North America*, ed. Darrell L. Guder (Grand Rapids: Eerdmans, 1988), 78, emphasis in original.

11. Marcus J. Borg, *Jesus: A New Vision: Spirit, Culture, and the Life of Discipleship* (San Francisco: Harper and Row, 1987), 142.

12. Quoted in Jim Wallis, *The Call to Conversion: Recovering the Gospel for These Times* (San Francisco: Harper and Row, 1981), 15.

13. Rodney Clapp, *Family at the Crossroads: Beyond Traditional and Modern Options* (Downers Grove, Ill.: InterVarsity Press, 1993), 76–77.

14. Robert Banks, *Paul's Idea of Community: The Early House Churches in Their Historical Setting* (Grand Rapids: Eerdmans, 1980), 90.

15. Sarah Boxer, "A Remedy for the Rootlessness of Modern Suburban Life?" *New York Times*, 1 August 1998, A13.

16. "Our Covenant," annotated and updated (Oakland, Calif.: Rockridge United Methodist Church), 7.7–7.8.

17. "Rockridge United Methodist Church Mission Covenant Groups: Hearing and Following the Spirit's Call, on the Inward Journey and Sanctification and the Outward Journey of Mission" (Oakland, Calif.: Rockridge United Methodist Church, 1997).

18. Brother Samuel SSF, "Mission and Community," *British Bible Society* (July 18–August 9, 1998): 14.

Chapter 10: Reinventing Christian Mission for a New Millennium

1. "A View of the City," *Tear Times* (spring 1995): 6–7.

2. Ibid.

3. Alister E. McGrath, *A Passion for Truth: The Intellectual Coherence of Evangelicalism* (Leicester, U.K.: Apolos, 1996), 63.

4. Wilbert R. Shenk, "Mission Renewal, and the Future of the Church," *International Bulletin of Missionary Research* (October 1997): 158.

5. Lesslie Newbigin, *The Gospel in a Pluralist Society* (Grand Rapids: Eerdmans, 1989), 133–34.

6. George Hunsberger, "Missional Vocations: Called and Sent to Represent the Reign of God," in *Missional Church: A Vision for Sending the Church in North America*, ed. Darrell L. Guder (Grand Rapids: Eerdmans, 1998), 77–81.

7. Jonathan J. Bonk, *Missions and Money: Affluence As a Western Missionary Problem* (Maryknoll, N.Y.: Orbis, 1992).

8. Orlando E. Costas, *The Integrity of Mission: The Inner Life and the Outreach of the Church* (San Francisco: Harper and Row, 1979), 17.

9. Of course, there were a number of conservative groups that also planted hospitals and schools as they went. But for many of these groups, this initiative was seen as being outside their theology of mission; it was often seen as a door opener for the "real" mission, which was addressing people's spiritual needs. So you still wind up with a two-track approach to the church's mission.

10. David Bosch, *Transforming Mission: Paradigm Shifts in Theology of Mission* (Maryknoll, N.Y.: Orbis, 1993), 405.

11. Ibid., 407

12. Steve Gaukroger, *Why Bother with Mission?* (Leicester, U.K.: Inter-Varsity Press, 1996), 59.

13. Bryant Myers, "Walking with the Poor: Principles and Practice of Transformational Development" (July 6, 1998), 21. At the time of this writing, this manuscript was to be published in 1999 by Orbis, under the title *Walking with the Poor.*

14. Marlin E. Miller, "The Gospel of Peace," in *Mission and Peace Witness*, ed. Robert L. Ramseyer (Scottdale, Pa.: Herald Press, 1978), 30.

15. James E. Metzler, "Shalom Is the Mission," in *Mission and Peace Witness*, 40.

16. Richard J. Foster, *Freedom of Simplicity* (San Francisco: Harper, 1981), 30–31.

17. Wendell Berry, *What Are People For?* (San Francisco: North Point Press, 1990), 131.

18. Ibid., 155, 167.

19. Wendell Berry, *Sex, Economy, Freedom and Community* (New York: Pantheon, 1992), 40.

20. Ann Scott Tyson, "Urban Farms: How Green Is My Barrio," *Christian Science Monitor* (December 4, 1996): 4.

21. Clifton Brown, "Golf Course at the Center of a Community," *New York Times,* 29 October 1998, C25–29.

22. Jerry Mitchell, *Clarion-Ledger* (Jackson, Miss.), 28 March 1998, special magazine insert.

23. Don Carrington, "Christians and the Struggle for Reconciliation," *Indigenous Leadership: A Journal for Aboriginal and Islander People,* no. 12 (August 1997): 18–19.

Tom Sine is an author, teacher, and international consultant in futures research for both Christian and secular organizations. His books include the best-selling *Mustard Seed Conspiracy*. He holds a Ph.D. in American history from the University of Washington and has served on the faculty of the University of Washington, Seattle Pacific University, and Fuller Theological Seminary. He directs Mustard Seed Associates and lives with his wife, Christine, in Seattle (tomandchrissine@compuserve.com).